T0303327

The Woman in the Window

The Woman in the Window

*Commerce, Consensual Fantasy, and the
Quest for Masculine Virtue in the Russian Novel*

Russell Scott Valentino

The Ohio State University Press • *Columbus*

Copyright © 2014 by The Ohio State University.
All rights reserved.

Library of Congress Cataloging-in-Publication Control Number
2014018801
ISBN 978-0-8142-1267-7 (cloth : alk. paper)

Cover design by Mary Ann Smith
Text design by Juliet Williams
Type set in Adobe Minion

♾ The paper used in this publication meets the minimum requirements of the American National Standard for Information Sciences—Permanence of Paper for Printed Library Materials. ANSI Z39.48–1992.

9 8 7 6 5 4 3 2 1

For Yasuko
woman in my window

And for Peter and Dante
just a little shorter

Property—the material foundation of both personality and government—has ceased to be real and has become not merely mobile but imaginary. Specialised, acquisitive and post-civic man has ceased to be virtuous, not only in the formal sense that he has become the creature of his own hopes and fears; he does not even live in the present, except as constituted by his fantasies concerning a future.

—J. G. A. Pocock, *Virtue, Commerce, and History*

There are now two great nations of the world which, starting from different points, seem to be advancing toward the same goal: the Russians and the Anglo-Americans.

—Alexis de Tocqueville, *Democracy in America*

Human beings love not so much the possibility of doing or not doing something as the possibility of talking about various things in words agreed upon among themselves. Such are the words considered to be very important among them. Such is the essence of the word *mine.*

—Leo Tolstoy, "Kholstomer: The Story of a Horse"

And what is good, Phaedrus, and what is not good? Need we ask anyone to tell us these things?

—Plato, *Phaedrus*

contents

list of illustrations

a note on the transliteration of russian

The Library of Congress standard has been used for all words and nontransliterated titles. The same system has been used for names and toponyms except for the following:

ый/ий—Bely/Dostoevsky, Yevgeny
ой—oy: Tolstoy
ь (omitted): Gorky, Gogol
я/ю—Zamyatin, Tolstaya/Yury, Tyutchev
ё—yo/e: Fyodor, Gumilyov/Kruchonykh
initial e—ye: Yefim
ье/ьё/ьи—ye/yo/yi: Leontyev/Solovyov/Ilyich
certain names with time-honored transliterations: Herzen, Tchaikovsky, Scriabin, Meyerhold, Eisenstein, Khrushchev, Gorbachev, etc.

preface and acknowledgments

This book has been slow to mature, and I have had the luxury of not rushing it. As with most things one carries around for a long time, it is hard to let it go. It somehow does not seem thick enough, though I imagine some readers will wish it were thinner. In either case, I hope long care has given it the strength to stand on its own.

My work has benefited from the comments and suggestions of many friends and colleagues, and while a mere list cannot express the depth of my gratitude, I will give their names here nonetheless: Paula Amad, Anna Barker, Shaul Bassi, Murray Baumgartner, the late Stephen Beier, the late Robert Belknap, Eliot Borenstein, Katherine Ann Bowers, Aimee Carrillo Rowe, Steve Choe, Daniel Collins, Corey Creekmur, David Depew, Douglas Dowland, Natasa Durovicova, Caryl Emerson, Jacob Emery, Ed Folsom, Gregory Freidin, Rosalind Galt, Eric Gidal, Sabine Golz, Bruce Gronbeck, Daniel Gross, Barbara Harshav, the late Michael Henry Heim, Robin Hemley, David Hingstman, Steven Hoch, Andrea Jonahs, Liza Knapp, Marcus Levitt, Christopher Livanos, the late Robert Maguire, Peter Manning, Boris Maslov, Deirdre McCloskey, Susan McReynolds Oddo, Christopher Merrill, Paula Michaels, Margaret Mills, Peter Morningsnow, Quince Mountain, John Nelson, Kathleen Newman, Seamas O'Driscoll, Irina Paperno, Ray Parrott, John Peters, Jillian Porter, John Raeburn, Oliver Ready, William Reisinger, Susan Scheckel, Jay Semel, Elizabeth Ann Skomp, Garrett Stewart, James Throgmorton, Oleg Timofeyev, William Mills Todd III, Leona Toker, Steven Ungar, Paul Valliere, Ashot Vardanyan, Sasha Waters, and Christopher Wertz. I am also thankful to anonymous readers at *Slavic Review, Poroi, Slavic and East European Journal, Partial Answers,* and *Modern Fiction Studies.* I omit here the much shorter list of people whom I do not wish to thank and the surely more entertaining reasons that make me wish not to thank them.

I was fortunate to receive an Old Gold Fellowship from the University of Iowa at the earliest stages of work on this project, in summer 1997, when I still thought it was part of a previous book. A special thanks to Irina Paperno, who suggested to me then that, faced with a 95,000-word manuscript that showed no signs of soon coming to its limit, I might actually be working on two books, not one. Two Vice President for Research Arts and Humanities Research Grants from the University of Iowa, in 2003 and 2005, helped to verify that, indeed, this was a separate book altogether by giving me time "to stand in the forest," as my partner would put it, by which she would mean to reflect and to write.

Parts of this book were published as articles. Chapter 1 contains a healthy dose of "A Catalogue of Commercialism in Gogol's *Dead Souls,*" which was published in *Slavic Review,* 57.3 (1998); chapter 2 incorporates material from "What's a Person Worth: Character and Commerce in Dostoevsky's *Double,*" which was presented at the 13th International Congress of Slavists, in Ljubljana, Slovenia, in 2003, and published in the conference proceedings by Slavica Publishers; chapter 5 includes portions of "From Virtue to Virtual: DeLillo's *Cosmopolis* and the Corruption of the Absent Body," which was published in 53.1 of *Modern Fiction Studies* in April 2007.

The annual conferences of the American Association for the Advancement of Slavic Studies (in 1999), the British Association for Slavonic and East European Studies (in 1998), the American Association of Teachers of Slavic and East European Languages (in 2011), and the Association for Slavic, East European, and Eurasian Studies (in 2013) furnished venues for discussing my ideas with colleagues. Invited presentations at Grinnell College (in 2002), the Ohio State University (in 2006), and Indiana University, Bloomington (in 2011) helped me explore portions on the character trio of double, confidence man, and woman in the window. Two rhetoric seminars in Iowa's Project on Rhetoric of Inquiry, one reading at Iowa's Eighteenth and Nineteenth Century Studies Consortium, and two presentations in Iowa's Department of Cinema and Comparative Literature helped me fine-tune both the ideas and the method of presenting them.

The four years I devoted to editing *The Iowa Review,* from 2009 to 2013, gave me a profound appreciation for writers of literary nonfiction and for ideals of clarity, expression, and entertainment that scholarly writing rarely achieves, let alone tries for. If I've succeeded at all in these pages at approximating those ideals, it is largely thanks to the examples of the numerous writers whose work I had the privilege of ushering into print. If I haven't, it is, of course, all their fault.

As with any work that takes a long time to come to fruition, this one would never have seen daylight without, first, a partner, and second, a publisher. I express my deepest thanks to the latter. The former I can never thank enough.

Bloomington, November 2013

In Search of (Russian) Virtue

Virtue Unearthed

> There is a property in the horizon which no man has but he whose eye can integrate all the parts, that is, the poet. This is the best part of these men's farms, yet to this their land-deeds give them no title.
>
> —Ralph Waldo Emerson, *Nature*

> Kiss the earth.
>
> —Fyodor Dostoevsky, *Crime and Punishment*

A colleague and friend asked, after one of the talks I gave while writing this book, what was at stake in my project. This strikes me as a healthy question, one that is not asked nearly enough in academic circles. It is a variation on the question, "So what?" which can be taken in both a sequential and a consequential manner, that is, as both "What next?" and "Who cares?" These point in two directions at once, one leading from the research at hand onward, the other looking back to premises and principles; the first following the gaze of specialists into some distant light on the horizon, the second questioning why we started off on this journey in the first place. This is why humanists often have difficulty answering the question, "What are you working on these days?" The disciplinary and the human split at the question, "So what?"

I recall a comment that Peter Manning made once about the reading pleasure of following a mind in thought. He was answering a question about the basic value of humanities scholarship, and while I certainly share that pleasure and hope that to some, at least, the trajectory I follow here will afford some similar enjoyment, it is not enough to claim a stake. I've also read books in which the erudition and expressive skill of the author seemed the main purpose. Most often I haven't finished those books. I am sensitive, too, about the superficiality of the philological web, the illumination of reference by other reference, text by other text, what Carlo Michelstaedter, in a grand neologism, once called καλλοπισματα ορφνες, or "ornaments of the darkness."[1] We word lovers will find their glitter enticing, but "so what" wonders at what might be beneath the sheen.

This is a book about the sheen of virtue, its rhetorical construction in some three hundred years of European expression, and its eventual displacement by the commercial ethic, the growth of consensual fantasy in modern life. The mind in thought is mine. The audience comprises especially those loving readers of Russian literary works who, like me, have found inspiration and deep meaning in them over some significant part of their lives. There are a few discoveries and interventions of a disciplinary nature; others are more popularly based. But there is a limit case, a conceit in the literary sense, and perhaps in a personal one, too. When asked what was at stake, this was what I recalled, the initial sense that what I was following was not merely a thought in my own mind, let alone my own mind in thought, but the answer to a question that had not yet been asked of me because it hadn't yet occurred to the questioner to ask it.

To understand the conceit is to understand the rationale and motivation behind this book.

The Very Word

Many scholars have noted that at the etymological root of the term *virtue* one finds the Latin word for man, *vir.* Few, however, have known quite what to make of this. A common and somewhat predictable strategy has been to leap backward and attempt to resurrect an image of heroism—Homeric, Roman, Stoic—as a remedy for the moral flabbiness of modern times. But such anachronistic equations of virtue with manhood or courage fail to take into account any of the associations the word has acquired since approximately Homer. These include doing good, having sex with one person only or no one at all, and establishing a republic—apparently disparate uses that are, in fact, all related. Their conceptual unity becomes especially clear when one considers the ways in which these different senses are translated across the linguistic and cultural boundaries examined in this book.

Historically the sense in which virtue—or in its Roman guise, *virtus*—related to the concept of man was physical. But it is an oversimplification to think of *virtus* in terms of mere manly strength, as the virtuous Hercules of both Classical and Renaissance representations makes clear.[2] *Virtus* was not primarily power over other bodies but mastery over one's own, especially under traumatic conditions. Thus the virtue of a soldier—which the Greeks called *arete,* and which the Latin word initially translated—lay in his ability to control the body's impulses amid the chaos of the battlefield, to hold his ground, in short, when some inner voice was screaming, "Run away!" As Alasdair MacIntyre has suggested, Plato's account of the virtues in the *Republic* was "part of his strategy to expel the Homeric inheritance from the city-state," in effect co-opting virtue for the philosopher and guiding the term away from the purview of nonreflecting, physical (as opposed to philosophical) Homeric heroes.[3] Even here, however, the root connection to marshaling the body's resources is evident: the virtues are those undisputed crystalline centers—of character, of soul—that make the wise man and teacher consistent with himself at all times, under all conditions. Whether one follows an Aristotelian understanding of the virtues, as dispositions to act in particular ways through cultivating inclination, or a Kantian view, in which acting virtuously means acting *against* inclination, the term's bodily core remains untouched. The Aristotelian thinks more of exercising, the Kantian more of exorcising, but virtue in either case is measured in relation to the body's "honesty."[4]

From here the extension of this root concept in the term *virtuoso* should be easy to grasp. The virtuoso masters the manipulation of the body's parts to achieve feats of dexterity, or at least to give the impression of achieving such feats. A virtuoso performer is one who appears to see an action with the mind's eye and be able fluidly and with ease to transform the idea into bodily movement. The achievement is all the more impressive for its lack of technological mediation, its immediate mind-to-body efficacy.

The term *virtual* derives from a functional sense that likewise may be understood through the notion of corporeal *honestas,* an inner nature that does not lie. Thus the virtue of a table is its "tableness," its capacity to function as a table; the virtue of a watch, its time-telling capacity, and so on.[5] To call someone a virtual dictator or virtual saint, then, is to make an assertion about that person's essence, which might not be recognized publicly or officially. The virtual-ness of such a dictator or saint is the manifestation of an underlying state, some real or essential being that is not immediately visible: in effect, a concealed corpus. This increasingly obsolete usage of virtue-qua-function makes the digital "virtual" of our own day possible by reducing and, in the end, releasing altogether its pressure on the physical. For if the essential being is invisible and known only through its manifestations, then you can have all the effects of a being without actually having the being: you can have a virtual being.[6] This is how we move conceptually from the virtual saint who has not been canonized, because the saintliness of his body has not been publicly declared, to the digitally generated entity staffing a virtual confessional in an online virtual church.[7] Function, effect, or force allows one to move from the merely veiled to the altogether absent body.[8]

It is understandable, with such connections in mind, how the linkage to the world of property should have become a central consideration in modern discussions of the form of virtue termed "civic," for such discussions proceeded metaphorically from individual to group health, from the virtue of the citizen to the virtue of the "body politic." The vigor of a republic, for Machiavelli and his followers over the centuries, derived from a society of independent property holders used to hard work and able to endure discomfort. That to which such natural republican agents were attached was land, especially land as property, a binding social construction that linked one person to others, giving him weight and value among his peers. Land as property was thought to extend and amplify the individual citizen's body, as it were, providing a foundation for the political body. In classical formulations, such virtuous citizens were large landed proprietors; in American reformulations of the eighteenth century and beyond, they tended to be smaller freeholders, each constituting a living stake in the republic's healthy constitution.[9]

With the European financial revolution of the late seventeenth and early eighteenth centuries, the creation of the Bank of England, public (national, governmental) debt, and the gradual replacement of landed interests by moneyed interests, the notion of a man's virtue-in-property began to give way before more liquid conceptions of the self. This was the transformation that John Pocock addressed in his writings of the 1970s and '80s, one of which appears as the first epigraph to this study.[10] While he ended his discussion in the eighteenth century, the path of thought he traced should be of interest to readers today, for in the last thirty-five years we have uncannily replayed in the digital revolution the reactions he explored in the financial. The rise and spread of forms of consensually determined values such as credit and publicly owned stock in early eighteenth-century England suggested a fantastical foundation to social interaction that some heralded as liberation, the promise of future worth, and others bemoaned as the onset of both moral and political corruption.[11] Similarly, apologists for the virtual in our own day have seen in it at least as much if not more potential for future well-being, both individual and collective, as their early modern counterparts saw in credit, while concerns about the corrosive influence of digital phenomena have tended to fall into two types, some focusing on the moral life of the individual, others on the health and sickness of the polity.[12]

The growth of credit in the eighteenth century gave rise to a counter-discourse in which virtue moralists argued for the solidity of property over the corruption of consensually determined, "fantastical" value. I used to think we had not seen an explicit virtue movement in reaction to the rise of virtuality in our own day. I suspected that the word *virtue* had become overly quaint, academic, gendered, or politically overcharged, or by contrast, that the sign might have simply lost all its freshness, become hackneyed and, for all constructive purposes, empty. Having worked on this project, however, I should say that, while not unitary, virtue theory and virtue discourse have seen a marked resurgence in the past thirty-five years, with Deirdre McCloskey's multivolume work on the "bourgeois virtues" as only one of the latest in an impressive, diverse, and still growing array.[13] By once again resurrecting this old word in these pages, I want to suggest that the conceptual thread from the bodily foundations of virtue to the absent body of virtuality are implicit in the term's usage, even when not articulated explicitly, and that the gradual decorporealization of value in modern life is largely responsible for the continued intensity of virtue talk today. In other words, people want to talk about virtue still and perhaps especially now, because they feel it questioned fundamentally in the rise and spread of the virtual. Human reactions to the increasing centrality of this "symbolic public order" range from euphoria to madness, with an aggregate of mild stimulation or anxiety in the center.[14] Thus, "consensual fantasy" may be seen as a beneficent harnessing or a malevolent unleashing of the power of human thought, and this dichotomy shares a basic similarity with the arguments about credit in early modern times.[15]

Two Visions of (American) Virtue

> The prospect is thus that the human being will gradually lose its
> grounding in the concrete life-world.
>
> —Slavoj Žižek, *The Plague of Fantasies*

The technological transformation of thought into action has long been the stuff of science fiction. In the 1956 film *The Forbidden Planet*, an ancient civi-

lization known as the Krell was supposed to have developed a means of harnessing the mental power of its citizens. While technology enabled them to
achieve astounding creative and constructive feats, it also unleashed a devastating corrosive force—identified in the popular Freudianism of the day
as "the id"—a monster of their collective unconscious that destroyed their
civilization through the dreams of its members. The scenario first envisions
consensual fantasy as a beneficent harnessing of confident mental energy that
puts the power to radically improve life at the disposal of imaginative beings.
Then it turns around to regard consensual fantasy as a malevolent unleashing
of destructive impulses, which lead to madness and the destruction of everything previously created by it.

The growing role of consensual fantasy in human life, especially in the
most affluent societies of the past several centuries, bears a marked resemblance to the Krell scenario. Most of us do not yet attach anything to our
heads, and most of our machinery remains above ground, but the transmogrifications we accomplish regularly are no less fantastical. We may see them
as mundane, indeed perhaps not as transmogrifications at all but simply as
part of daily experience, unremarkable reality. Perhaps this is because we
have grown used to the conventions of language, the conventions of money,
even the conventions of plastic money—a special compounding of consensual
fantasy in which the higher the sums involved, the more precious the metal
invoked. Remove consensual fantasy, however, and the daily experience that
seems such unremarkable reality would disappear, and most of contemporary
human life with it. I am not just referring to the kind of confidence that might
be measured by an index. I have in mind the constituents of confident modernity, the myriad promises atop which our confidence floats—the verbal, the
paper, the plastic, the digital.

The current of popular culture that recognizes such a fantastical movement in human history is strong. Far from balking at this suggestion, sci-fi
buffs will find it banal, though they will likely differ among themselves about
whether it is a good or bad thing. For their point, moreover, they will make
use of arguments that found first articulation in the conceptual history of virtue. Such arguments are of two basic kinds. The first is territorial: property,
rootedness, and propertied community are the foundations of society. This
Classical republican model was especially attractive to American thinkers
like Thomas Jefferson.[16] The second is transcendental. It holds forth the earth
(often by contrast to property), emancipation, and the liberated individual: an
Emersonian ideal. In contrast to conceiving American virtue through property and propertied social actors, the Emersonian emphasizes a divorce from
property as the means of maintaining virtue, a radical severing of the ties that

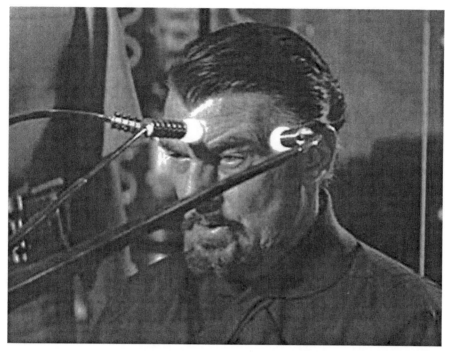

Figure 1. Consensual Fantasies. Walter Pigeon as philologist Dr. Edward Morbius. *Forbidden Planet*, dir. Wilcox, 1956.

bind—in his thinking "constrain"—individuals, thereby hindering them from becoming truly free.

These two visions have long dwelt together to make up a somewhat schizophrenic American version of the virtuous ideal—whether conceived as good or right action, or, teleologically, as the proper end of a human being. One is based in the relations of property, the other in their absence. One, as in Richard Pipes's account, predicates political freedom on the possibility of private property ownership. Societies that lack such ownership, he claims, are without the very foundation necessary for freedom, where liberty and private property are seen as practically synonyms: "Property is an indispensable ingredient of both prosperity and freedom."[17] The other suggests, with Rousseau, that property owners experience anxiety throughout their possessions, and that the extension of human beings by means of property ownership imagined by republicans actually deforms them morally if not spiritually with its weight. In this view, the only true freedom, and the only just society, may be found in liberation from such anxiety, in effect, in divorce from the constraints of real estate.

This second strain in American social thought, which parallels and in some sense does battle with the Classical republican model, makes possible the fetishization of the rootless wanderer, the frontier hero, the cowboy, and—in an elaborate and self-conscious play with consensual fantasy itself—the confidence man, who lives and prospers off of other people's hopes, dreams, and fears regarding the future, enticing them to do the same. On the one hand, then, the huge swaths of land extending westward from the seat of American government represented to republican apologists a vast repository of potential civic virtue for the new nation's citizens.[18] On the other, ironically, those same empty expanses provided the physical and social dimensions necessary for creating the quintessentially homeless, property-less American hero.[19] I'll come back to this topic below.

These extremes are evident in countless popular books, films, and television programs, especially those whose subject touches on the virtual. For instance, the 1999 film *The Matrix* and its sequels both blur and depend upon the boundaries between a technologically mediated reality, where the mind reigns supreme, and the reality of the body. The city of salvation is rooted deep in the earth, where the last "real" people live. The hero takes control of the virtual world, manipulating objects as he "uproots" himself by rising into the air and flying across the screen. Here control of the virtual represents a harnessing of the thought-power of people, for it is they—helmeted and wired to the requisite network of machinery—who power the system. The spatial relationships are consistent: When the hero is released from his initial mental captivity, his body drops down, closer to the earth below. When he reigns supreme in the virtual world, he rises up. The in-between realm of the ship, which is also the launching pad for excursions into virtuality, is a hovercraft. Still more relevant in the context of republican virtue theory are the *Star Wars* films, the first three of which portray in effect half of the modern virtue-corruption dichotomy, where the hero's origins on a farm in the middle of the deep countryside resonate with a Jeffersonian (Classical republican) ideal. Subsequent episodes fill out this picture through the image of a governing senate, the seat of ultimate corruption and the vehicle for evil, where the assembly delegates float through the air inside a structure that appears to have no floor on a planet that is one immense (farmless) urban extension.

Such examples, of which there are many more, suggest that the leap to embrace the ether and the desire to burrow into the earth are both still powerful responses to decorporealization. The fact that the fictional construct of "the civilization of the Krell" ultimately derives from Prospero's magic in Shakespeare's early modern play *The Tempest*—with its central subtexts about the power of imaginative thought, government form, and the subjugation of others and oneself—suggests once again the increased importance of consensual fantasy in modern times.

After Virtual

The virtual saint whose saintly body is not acknowledged by the church hierarchy and the virtual saint who hears confession in an online virtual confessional stand at opposite ends of a conceptual divide. One is embodied but unrecognized as such, the other is recognized but has no body. What links them is effect, force, or power. This is the sense of virtue that remains in the English phrase "by (or in) virtue of." Thus the *Oxford English Dictionary* attests to the usage of "virtual church," not as a digital entity that recognizes a-corporeal virtual saints manning virtual confessionals but as a seventeenth-century "council or similar body acting in the name of the whole church." Used in this sense, such a metaphorical body would always be "capable of producing a certain effect or result" (another of the *OED*'s definitions); it would be "effective, potent, powerful" (yet another). According to the same source, it would also be obsolete. But would it?

The question of the reality of virtual reality is not limited to popular culture. It has gained pressing importance in a variety of scholarly disciplines from psychology to political theory, from law to library science. In such contexts the effect or power of virtual phenomena is sometimes celebrated, sometimes questioned, sometimes anticipated as looming and dangerous.[20] I want to argue, however, that the central concern should not be how real virtual phenomena are but the degree to which they alter or do not alter our orientation—here I borrow an old Catholic distinction—to things and persons.[21] To the extent that the modern world has long been shaped by the power of consensual fantasy, virtual phenomena may not, after all, present much of a change. It is several centuries since we first began to be surrounded by "the exchange of forms of mobile property" and "modes of consciousness suited to a world of moving objects" whose values rise and fall with the apparent sense and order of rumor.[22] Perhaps the virtual is simply the latest stage in a history of consensual fantasy, to which we have repeatedly grown accustomed, like building up a tolerance for caffeine or alcohol, from spoken and written symbols to moving images and digital stock portfolios. The point is not how real—and therefore how liberating or dangerous—

the phenomena, but how different they are from the already a-corporeal phenomena among which we have grown used to living our lives.

Having written these words, I must take a step back, embodied as I am, and acknowledge that the virtual is not a simulacrum of a challenge. It does not seem so to me, at least. The advent of things virtual in the contemporary world—virtual documents, virtual hospitals, virtual empathy, and more—challenges us on a conceptual level as well as on moral and ethical ones. Such phenomena test the understanding and practice of life that the history of virtue concepts and representations explored here, I hope, helps to illuminate. It is not a history divorced from our current lives. Long-standing responses to the rise and spread of consensual fantasy are imbedded in the cultural artifacts explored in this book, which provide clues to our responses today and help to indicate possible paths for making our way through the challenges that we find ourselves faced with when the conceptual worlds of virtue and virtuality come into contact.

Let me put this in a different way. My nine-month-old son lifts his hand and opens and closes his fingers when prompted by the word *bye-bye*. He smiles and seems pleased without truly understanding the gesture or the word that accompanies it. If he understood, after all, he would be sad, not happy, when asked to repeat it upon his papa's departure for work. He looks at his fingers, rising and falling as if they are divorced from his body, alien entities he is only slowly learning to control. It is not yet a virtuoso performance. Nevertheless, I know that one day he will make the conceptual connections to enable him to enter the realm of consensual fantasy, to join us there and dwell among us to the end of his days. I suspect that, as a cautious boy like his father before him, he will linger on its fringes for some time, uncertain of what it means to enter, just as now he is uncertain of what it means to wave to his papa, smiling behind the glass of the kitchen door.

And I am struck by a possibility: when one day he senses the conceptual connection between virtue and virtuality and, being a thoroughly contemporary child, understands the latter word but sees the former only at the dim periphery of his life's experience, he might very well ask: "Papa, what is virtue?"

What, I wonder, will I tell him?

American Property, Russian Earth

Let me return to the distinction introduced above between land as property in civic republican guise and the Earth in neoromantic liberatory rhetoric.

The first conditions a conception of property as a repository for a person's and a people's virtue. In its most radical formulations, the second sees such property as a limitation, if not a deformation, of both. The increased commoditization of land, with the rise of commercial culture, set them in sharpest contrast, encouraging, by the beginning of the eighteenth century, a search for virtuous, uncorrupt people in virtuous, unsullied territories. This new "virtue discourse," which both rested upon and challenged long-held notions of land as a form of knightly feudal holdings, was part of the epoch's much-discussed utopianism.[23] The Swiss Alps and the "virgin" lands of the New World provided especially fecund ground for such seedlings, two very different environments that fed republican theory on the one hand and liberatory rhetoric on the other.

The most striking characteristic of this dual development lies in the attempted harnessing of consensual fantasy. Joseph Addison, then taking part in the "Court" versus "Country" debates of English political history, was one of the first to identify the explicitly republican virtues of the Swiss *montagnard*, whose simple relations to the local community contrasted sharply to both the busy complexities and the growing fantastical foundations of modern English political life. This thread was taken up by subsequent writers, most notably Rousseau, who secured its place in the popular mind-set of the day and handed it on in powerful form.[24]

The Swiss-inspired virtue ethos also inspired republican enthusiasts in the new government of the United States, who combined the repository-of-republican-virtue idea with the virgin-territory conception of the land in one and the same productive model. To early American republican advocates, "an infinite supply of land, ready for occupation by an armed and self-directing yeomanry, meant an infinite supply of virtue,"[25] and such virtue would be measured by the effectiveness of the republic to maintain itself and remain true to its uncorrupt foundation. These Americans were therefore prepared to attach themselves and their descendants to the land as a means of harnessing virtue for the republic. In contrast, the image of virtue in a work such as Thoreau's *Walden* can be understood as a reaction to classical republican attempts to encumber the human being with land-as-property. His response, like Rousseau's, is not an attempt to control and direct the forces of modernity in the manner of the republicans and their nation-building progeny. It is instead a turn to the land as buttress *against* modernity, a turn away from civilization in what Simon Schama has characterized as "a sort of blessed amnesia, a liberation of the burden of the dead in order to see what [is] truly and naturally alive."[26] For Thoreau and many a mythologizing frontiersman in his wake, the landscape of Western Europe, especially in its various propertied incarnations, was equivalent to the burden of the dead, which needed to be abandoned if one was to achieve freedom, authentic life: the virtuous ideal.[27] Land afforded such a liberating opportunity only when it could not be attached to a person in the form of property. The rootlessness of American "road" virtue, from Huck Finn to the nameless drifters of the Spaghetti Western, and the extension of republican virtue theory by early American social and political thinkers thus derive, paradoxically, from the same source. Each, moreover, is dependent on the American experience of the land—on the one hand, an infinite transcendence, on the other, a finite repository: unleashing and harnessing.

While West European thinkers provided the virtue vocabulary and laid the conceptual foundation for its subsequent elaboration, the most extreme visions of the two responses to the rise of consensual fantasy in modernity outlined here were provided not in Western Europe but in what Alexis de Tocqueville, at the end of part 1 of his *Democracy in America,* referred to as its periphery—in the United States and in the Russian Empire. In fact, the degree to which rootless and propertied virtue are dependent on the American experience of land becomes clear by comparison with contemporaneous Russia, where such notions did not develop beyond an embryonic stage among a small group.[28]

There were many factors that might have linked the two countries in the minds of contemporaries. Both were large, conceptually "empty" (to the European imagination) land masses with indigenous populations then being colonized with the help of internal myths of sovereignty. Both were thought of as new countries. Russia had entered the European scene as a "great power" only with the defeat of the Napoleonic armies in 1814; the United States had attained lasting security in their struggle against the British only after 1812. Both had experienced a subsequent euphoric moment characterized by an increased national self-consciousness and confidence in a future salvational or "redeemer" role.[29] Moreover, social thinkers in both countries long carried a chip on their shoulder in their attempts to define themselves and their work and to measure the achievements of their respective cultures against a West European standard.

Both struggled with the heritage of slavery, and noted polemical works of literature aimed at depicting the humanity of the owned person, the person as property, appeared nearly simultaneously in each, namely, Harriet Beecher Stowe's *Uncle Tom's Cabin* and Ivan Turgenev's *A Sportsman's Sketches,* both of which were published in 1852. The institution of slavery persisted in the United States until 1863, its concomitant in Russia, serfdom, until 1861. Widespread social and political unrest accompanied the respective proclamations of emancipation—the Civil War in the United States, clandestine revolutionary activity and terrorism in Russia. Two key assassinations followed, of each emancipating leader, Abraham Lincoln in 1865 and Alexander II in 1881, in the last of many attempts that began in 1866.

The development and rise to international prominence of both countries, moreover, depended fundamentally on technological innovation and massive construction projects, particularly the railroad, which brought together disparate spaces and moved people from the countryside to key cities—Moscow, Petersburg, New York, Chicago. As they grew, both countries showed similar tension and hesitation over the creation of national financial institutions, a stock market in Russia, a national bank in the United States. Both were characterized by "frontier" myths and mind-sets, to the south and east in Russia, to the south and west in the United States.

Such a list, which might be extended further, provides a sense of the multitude of considerations behind de Tocqueville's famous comparison, quoted in one of the epigraphs to this study.[30] Differences were of course easy to find as well, some of which de Tocqueville noted at the time, especially on the political front. To these I would add a fundamental conceptual divide at the base of social and political contrasts that extend before and after the two countries' rise to prominence. The importance of republican virtue in the early United States as a continuation of European thought on the subject has been well traced and thoroughly documented. This kind of thinking among Russians of the same period, however—or before or after, for that matter—had a less formative influence for the country as a whole. Perhaps Richard Pipes is correct in painting a picture in which the absence of such yeomanly property in Russian society was what most distinguished it from Western conceptions of political liberty and civic virtue.[31] But relying on an absent yeomanly property ethic to characterize Russian ideas about virtue and the state will per force only ever make Russia look inadequate by contrast to the United States, where such an ethic was thoroughly developed. This kind of reliance, moreover, fails to take into account the apparent resistance to such notions of "progress" in Russian cultural history, especially those associated with the forms of commercial self-interest and property ownership embraced by republican advocates in Europe and North America.

There is a presence rather than an absence at the heart of the approach taken in this book. It is land not as property but as something other, a hosting perhaps, something not attached to people by custom or law, but rather a thing to which people are attached by heritage, obligation, love, and faith, and perhaps especially the maternal expressions of such notions.[32] It is apparent that in both its liberatory and yeomanly modes, American virtue required that the land be motherless, an instrumental construct for republicans to which liberationists replied in their own staunchly anti-instrumental idiom. In either instance of the American vision, Robert Frost's line applies: "The land was ours before we were the land's."[33] In other words, the land existed in the minds of American social and political thinkers as something held, a tool or instrument to be wielded in the service of one or another political or moral agenda, before and apart from any sense of shared provenance, let alone responsibility, to it. The very possibility that the land might be something possessed, as conveyed in Frost's language, is a profoundly colonial thought, an American thought. And while the absence of yeomanly private property for much of Russia's history in effect precluded the kind of discussion of republican virtue that was so important to eighteenth-century American social thinkers,[34] it also meant that the reaction of a Thoreau, or a Kerouac for that matter, was unlikely to resonate in the Russian context. What one finds in its place is a different sense of rootedness, community, and landed connection—what Dostoevsky, in a distinctive response, called *pochvennichestvo* ("landedness," "grass-rootedness," "groundedness")—that is largely alien to the modern American discussion.[35]

The injunction of the Elder Zosima in *The Brothers Karamazov* to "water the earth with tears" has deep roots in Slavic premodern thought. It springs from a premodern orientation to the land, which is driven home by considering it in opposition to Thoreau's antimodern orientation to property. This is not to claim that Dostoevsky's is any less sophisticated a response to modernity than that of the American liberationist. On the contrary, in the conditions of Russian nineteenth-century society Dostoevsky's is a far more effective rhetorical strategy, for instead of eschewing the relations of property and the responsibilities of property owners to one another and to the state by a radical severing of property ties, as advocated by Thoreau, Dostoevsky's response in effect raises those responsibilities to a new level of intensity by taking them beyond civil law, beyond human law altogether, through reference to a noninstrumental, nonpropertied orientation to the earth. Land as freedom *from* in the American liberationist sense yields to earth as moral obligation *to* in the thought of the Russian writer. Here the responsibility of human beings to the earth and, by extension, to other human beings dwelling within the same community derives ultimately from their resemblance to God, not from an agreement that they are free to make or annul, not from a social contract.[36]

Conceptions of property make possible an array of startling ideas to Dostoevsky's male characters. For instance, at the start of *Crime and Punish-*

ment, in Raskolnikov's premurder nightmare of the senseless, brutal slaying of a horse, the drunken peasant Mikolka justifies himself by saying that the horse is his "goods." "Hands off," he exclaims. "It's my goods. I can do what I want." The Russian word employed, *dobro* (literally, the neuter singular noun "good"), is marked as colloquial and therefore accords with Mikolka's way of speaking. But its root associations open another path of meaning. Mikolka's brutality, his ability to beat—and enjoin others to beat—the animal to death, with sticks and a crowbar and, in the end, a great wooden beam that breaks the horse's spine, is conditioned upon a conception of property, of what Tolstoy, in a later equine exploration of the subject, would characterize as the human being's love of naming things as "mine." But it is also, through the rich and multiple associations of the word *dobro,* an implicit questioning of the reference to "goods" in a trading sense. A way of talking and thinking about goods—my property, part of me, mine to do with as I choose—is closely associated with the great evil lurking in the murderer's mind. The agreements of human beings about the nature of property and how to value it suggest a confusion and a merging of the categories of what is good and what is good *for.*[37]

An alternative might be found in the philosophical distinction between intrinsic and instrumental goods, but this would lead us down a side path. In this formulation, the earth is not worshipped for its own sake. It is not depicted as an intrinsic good. It is instead understood as the place of humanity as such, the place where human beings are human, the place, therefore, of the bodily limit, where "man strives toward an ideal that is contrary to his nature,"[38] where that nature finds expression. To embrace the earth is to embrace imperfect humanity, one's own and that of all divinely inspired but earthly dwelling humankind in general. This means human beings conceived of in a very specific way, with value that cannot be assigned by themselves. In effect, the earth is like the holy icon, a great sacrament by which human beings come together with other human beings on their path to God. A "European" conception more alien to modern property is hard to imagine.[39]

A less radical, though equally contrastive response to the onset of modernity was provided by Lev Tolstoy in his depiction of the landowner-farmer Konstantin Levin, in *Anna Karenina.*[40] Levin is associated with the peasant by means of work in common, which suggests a contact with the land that has been lost by his urban compatriots. The peasantry's connection to the land, moreover, is emphasized in Levin's claim, which he tries to support by means of a scholarly treatise, that the peasant and the land constitute an elemental relationship in the practice of farming that, like climate and soil, must be taken into consideration in any discussion of the nation's resources, the nation's wealth. Juxtaposed to this picture—which appears, in effect, to be a Russian aristocratic transformation of republican virtue theory—is the story of Anna's adulterous affair, her sexual inconstancy. This in turn is facilitated by that great demon of progress in Tolstoy's novel, the railroad, which uproots the peasantry from the land, thereby destroying the nation's moral and material foundation, and at the same time mows down the heroine in one fell artistic swoop.

The instrumentalization of property in *Anna Karenina,* as demonstrated, for instance, in the buying and selling of land, is consistently depicted as a form of corruption, practiced by the inept and irresponsible (Stiva Oblonsky, for example) or the unscrupulous and rapacious (such as the peasant Ryabinin, who purchases the Oblonsky forest). There are no circumstances in which Tolstoy imagines that such buying and selling might somehow be a good thing or might result, even in some distant eventuality, in a net gain for society. It is always net loss, always a form of corruption, social, political, and moral.

Even in what might be thought of as a more orthodox leftist work, such as Nikolai Chernyshevsky's 1863 novel *What Is To Be Done?,* which functioned as a rallying cry for numerous future revolutionaries, Vladimir Lenin among them, the author struggles with what are essentially republican categories as he depicts his hero of heroes, the mysterious, "exceptional" Rakhmetov in the guise of a landed heir of old-Russian civic-mindedness, the progeny of a family that has owned thousands of serfs. He does this apparently not in order to hold up the new man's old values to ridicule but as a badge of his revolutionary's distinctively patriotic "Russian-ness."[41]

These are examples of distinctive responses to the challenges tossed at the feet of Russian social thinkers by the rise of an increasing commercial ethic in the nineteenth century. The new conditions underlay the discussions of the clandestine philosophical circles of the 1840s, which helped to form such men as the radical anarchist Mikhail Bakunin, the moderate socialist Alexander Herzen, the Slavophiles, the Westernizers, the liberal gradualists, the monarchist reactionaries, and the militant left materialist utilitarians who would inspire two subsequent generations of revolutionary activists. What is common to all these various and sundry groups, beyond their commitment and intensity of belief, is a *nonpropertied orientation to the land,* especially the Russian land, and a simultaneous search for virtue—right action, the proper end of a human being—expressed by means of a vocabulary located largely outside the categories of character formation that were central to the modern European and, even more so, the modern American political personality.[42]

Virtue as One and as Many

The integrity of concept—by which I have in mind the play of roots and the range of connotative associations—of West European virtue vocabulary was never truly assimilated by Russian social thinkers, a fact partly evidenced by the variety of words used to translate *virtue* into Russian. The most common equivalency, *dobrodetel'*, which is formed from the roots *good* and *act*, emphasizes an ethical and religious heritage, especially in the term's medieval Latin usage.[43] The virtue of the Greek or Roman soldier is more likely translated as "force" or "power"—as in the word *sila*, whose direct connection to virtue is evident in the translation of the English phrase "by/in virtue of" as *v silu* (literally "in the force/power [of]").

This semantic split is apparent in the translation of a seventeenth-century emblem, included in Maksimovich-Amvodik's *Emvlemy i simvoly* (*Emblems and Symbols*) toward the end of the eighteenth century.[44] The infant Hercules lies in his crib, which is surrounded by snakes. The Latin caption *Hinc est labor et virtus* is rendered in English, French, German, and Russian translations, two of which split from the others over the word *virtus*. In both the French and the Russian phrases, *Dès ici le travail e la force* and *Otsiuda iavliaetsia i trud i sila*, the last words convey the sense of *virtus* as physical strength and neglect associations with moral excellence, though such excellence, as indicated previously, was part of the character's and the Latin word's associations.

A woman's virtue, in the sense of sexual constancy, is named by a different word, *vernost'*, or perhaps *tselomudrie* (chastity, as applied to women or men), but not *dobrodetel'*, which tends to designate good action in general, especially of a humane variety. Thus when Anna Karenina eschews the Christian philanthropic activities of Lydia Ivanovna's social set, she denounces those women's judgmental hypocrisy in championing virtue (*dobrodetel'*), while when she cuckolds her husband, she renounces virtue (*vernost'*) in the eyes of society. Separated still further is Konstantin Levin's brand of both chaste and virile virtue (*tselomudrie* and *sila*), which functions as a counterweight to Anna's absent *vernost'*. There does not appear to be a single Russian word that can be used to designate Levin's "centeredness" in this regard.[45]

The first Russian thinker to emphasize the inadequacy of Western virtue vocabulary and the conceptual body it governed for Russian social life was, I believe, Nikolai Gogol, who, in a famous passage from his 1842 novel *Dead Souls*, dismissed the "virtuous man" (*dobrodetel'nyi chelovek*) as a possible protagonist:

Figure 2. Hinc est Labor et Virtus. The infant Hercules strangling the serpents. Maksimovich-Amvodik, *Emvlemy i sivoly*. Hippisley, ed., 1989.

> A virtuous man has not been chosen as a hero. And we can even say why. Because it's time at last to give the poor virtuous man a rest; because the word "virtuous man" flutters emptily across one's lips; because the virtuous man has been turned into a workhorse, and there doesn't exist a writer who wouldn't go out riding on him, urging him on with a whip and whatever else might turn up; because the virtuous man has been so worn down that not a shadow of virtue is in him anymore, and all that's left is ribs and skin in place of a body; because the virtuous man is not respected.[46]

I shall return to this key passage more than once in the pages of this book. Here let me note simply that the rationale given for not choosing the virtuous man as hero suggests that it is, indeed, in the interest of virtue that Gogol's narrator avoids the well-worn character type. In other words, he opts against depicting the virtuous man because such a character is all worn out and, as such, would not be an effective choice—for conveying virtue. Over the course of the next decade, in two projected subsequent volumes to his great national epic poem, Gogol would try to reform his hero and make the self-interested commercial "scoundrel" of the first part of his book into a fresh and effective "virtuous man" for Russians to emulate in all his splendor.

Many have speculated on the reasons for Gogol's failure to finish his work, and I do not wish to add still more speculation to this well-worn topic.[47] It is clear, nevertheless, that Gogol had run up against a major cultural impediment in the conflicting representations of virtue and commerce, and that his failed attempt subsequently to transform his hero introduced in effect an open question into Russian nineteenth-century social thought: How could the notion of self-interest—so important to the development of modern society in Western Europe and North America—be appropriated by Russian society without what was seen as its socially corrosive concomitants? In other words, how might a self-interested commercial agent be depicted in the Russian social context as a nonfragmented masculine character, socially valuable in a manner that redirected, or directed appropriately, the very impulses that motivated him in the first place, those impulses that Gogol was in fact satirizing with such devastating force?

This search was continued in the twentieth century, always in antipropertied forms that upheld the values of virtuous action without having recourse to the underlying vocabulary and conceptual tools that West European and, especially, North American social thinkers had assumed were fundamental. Other scholars have seen the key to such Russian attempts in a basic absence amid the country's social, economic, and political development, an empty center or groundlessness at the heart of what would become Soviet attempts to create a "new man." This study suggests another path of thought, another ground altogether.

Three Modern Characters

The Double, the Con Man, and the Woman in the Window

> I preferred to excuse myself and blame this unknown thing that
> was in me but was not part of me. The truth, of course, was that I
> was a complete whole, and my own impiety had divided me against
> myself.
>
> —Augustine, *Confessions* V, x, 18

> For what is trade? It is the constant adjustment of the claims of dif-
> ferent parties, a man's self being one of the parties.
>
> —Orville Dewey, "The Moral End of Business"

The Speaker's Ethos

I resist claims, various and sundry, of a multiplicitous self. Is that because
they describe me too nearly? Perhaps I'm just another fox who really wants to
be a hedgehog. Or is it because such claims tend to be held most tenaciously
by the most one-dimensional of people, those who surprise by having just
about any hobby other than, say, reading mysteries? The regularity of the
mystery, after all, is like a soothing balm to the decentered self. Or maybe this
is everyone's problem, and I've merely found a different way of describing the
modern condition. No way, no rule, no law, in the sense suggested by Yosef
Yerushalmi, only facts and figures, all of which are memorable, but none of
which is key. "Our real problem," he writes, "is that we are without a halakhah," by which he means not a religious law in the usual sense of that term
but "the complex of rites and beliefs that gives a people its sense of identity
and purpose," a "commonality of values" that might help to show what can be

discarded. We lack, he says, a principle of forgetting.[1] Perhaps the problem I have is not with the multiplicity of self but with the regulation of such multiplicity in the absence of a Path, a Tao that knows what to keep and what to leave behind.

Postmodernists may want to quote Keats on living in uncertainty here: "I mean Negative Capability, that is when a man is capable of being in uncertainties, Mysteries, doubts without any irritable reaching after fact and reason."[2] This would be an ironic move: the Romantic is probably the most unitary of the modern characters still available to us, up to a certain age, at least. Beyond—let us call it—midlife, the response starts to ring hollow. There is almost nothing as out of place as an old Romantic. More to the point, how would one begin to decide, savoring the uncertainty all the while, of course, what a right course of action might be amid inner pluralism? Would not the shrillness of contemporary moral disagreement, the storms of hurled assertions and counterassertions, increase tenfold once the debate turned inward? Even worse, might not the banality of evil lurk most suspiciously behind the multiplicitous self, with some character or other always in reserve to make even the most despicable little slur seem acceptable? An absent *halakhah*, I fear, combines poorly with a many-sided self.

I am behind the times, of course, a half-century at least. Not only are several selves no longer disturbing, they have become a collective model of psychological and social health. Identity—of individuals and groups—is now routinely approached as multiform by scholars in disciplines as diverse in their approaches as political science, anthropology, education, literature, psychology, and law. The stated assumptions behind these myriad contemporary studies are variations on a theme: the unified subject has been discredited, identity is flexible and changing, the self is socially constructed in discursive practices, we are the performances of who we are, and so on. There are far too many examples to cite. The following illustration should suffice.

In her 1997 book *Life on the Screen*, psychologist Sherry Turkle encourages us "to think of ourselves as fluid, emergent, multiplicitous, flexible, and ever in process."[3] She refers to a time "when identity was defined as unitary and solid" and suggests that "a more fluid sense of self allows a greater capacity for acknowledging diversity. It makes it easier to accept the array of our (and others') inconsistent personae—perhaps with humor, perhaps with irony, [without feeling the need] to rank or judge the elements of our multiplicity."[4] This is Keats and more. The picture suggests Erving Goffman's role-playing "self presentation" as a manner of living our lives on a daily basis, or the performance of self advocated by social therapists. Indeed, the thought Turkle outlines might be considered one of many strands that continue Goffman's, only updated for the digital age. As such, it suffers from the same shortcomings that critics of Goffman's views have pointed out.[5] I do not wish to repeat them here, partly because I don't doubt that such approaches have proven salutary in many therapy situations (which, it should be noted, is Turkle's point of departure), and partly because the critiques themselves lie outside my focus.

Nevertheless, the suggestion that we might somehow be more accepting of diversity if we think of our individual selves as multiple rests upon a naïve supposition: there is no necessary connection between accepting multiplicity in oneself and being accepting of racial, ethnic, or any other kind of diversity in a community. Such a notion could just as easily lend itself to other kinds of intolerance. Nor would it preclude the possibility of someone performing one tolerant self that just happened to get voted down more often than not. I am, moreover, suspicious of my own multiplicity and the uncanny manner in which it can slide into duplicity. Could it be that a self in reserve might step in to provide just the right rationale for giving nothing to the homeless man I see on my way to work, for uttering cruel words to a neighbor, eating too much at dinner, cutting down all my trees? Augustine's sense of guilt whispers distinctly in my ear, and if I am not a complete whole, at least I would like to be. These are personal biases, of course, not an argument, not yet. For now they merely sketch an important background picture for the problems I want to clarify and for the subject position I want to hold.

Characters

> You will be on the road to knowing and using your professional persona as a leader.
>
> —C. K. Gunsalus, *The College Administrator's Survival Guide*[6]

For this argument I must change terms slightly. Where multiplicity is concerned, *character* is a better word than *self.* It is endowed with a far richer store of referents. In fact, "multiplicitous self" has an oxymoronic ring, as if the many were being somehow herded into the one, creating an image almost grotesquely out of proportion with that championed by social therapists: philology clashing with psychology. By contrast, *character* has long had a multiplicity of selves. A character can be a symbol, like a letter or a pictograph. It can also be a defining trait, as in the phrase "the character of modern society." It can be a literary constituent, like plot or theme; in this sense it is akin to the Latin *persona,* or speaking role, in a dramatic performance. This extends to what people mean when they say someone is "such a character," an intensification of persona that makes it stand out from the chorus. Character can also be associated more closely with a moral self, or rather, *the* moral self, for used in this manner it invariably has the kind of singular aura that, as Turkle says, is associated with "traditional" notions of identity. The old and new self she describes can be understood, then, as the difference between having a character and playing a character, between an intrinsic and an instrumental good, being one and using one. I'll come back to this.

Character retains this moral dimension while *self* seems to have lost it, probably because of the latter's long association with the discourse of the social sciences, which, as Lawrence Becker has argued, long ago bought the fact-value distinction peddled to them by philosophy.[7] Character suggests representation and modeling at the same time. In this it retains something of the nineteenth-century German notion of the cultural type, which doubles as genus and genius, fixing the prosaic, perhaps unremarkable but nevertheless distinctive traits of a culture in figures that overflow the boundaries of their immediate contexts, the limited frames in which they are pictured. Characters retain this double sense in our own day, too, a fact noted by Alasdair MacIntyre when he singled out what he called the central characters of modern society: the aesthete, the therapist, and the manager.[8] He failed to note the distinctiveness of English in this regard, which uses one word where other languages typically use two. Thus the distinction between playing and being is made in French (*personnage* and *caractère*), Italian (*personaggio* and *carattere*), German (*Rolle* and *Charakter*), and Japanese (*doujoujimbutsu* and *seikaku*), as well as in Chinese, Russian, Uzbek, Swedish, and other languages, too. These languages frequently make a further distinction between the two senses above and a character as a written symbol. English, by contrast, appears to fudge boundaries, perhaps even mixing categories, and in the end, it exposes a bridge between represented and lived experience in the word's singularity.[9]

Multiplicity is just one of the two main features of the MUD, or "multiple-user-domain" sort of character Turkle has described. The other is its lack of fixity, its liquidity. Of course, she is not referring to the quality of the character as such, at least not at the start, but this is the implication of contrasting a fixed, solid, old-fashioned identity with a youthful capacity to maintain open lines of communication among a variety of diverse voices, performed selves, personae. Fixity of character is thus imagined as an osteoporotic coating, rigid and unyielding. Fluidity among the parts is seen as supple, healthy in its malleability and accepting of difference within and outside itself. This is a rhetoric of old age and youth.

It is no historical accident that liquidity of character, like liquidity of assets, depends on a socially determined context: on a cross between

Foucauldian discursive practices and Derridean deferred communicative objects, yes, but also, and more importantly for this discussion, on the whims of one's fellows. The worth attributed to such a character turns out to be equal to what one can get for it in a social market, its rate of exchange, according to a floating standard of evaluations, usually performed in words, applied to one by others—"she's a whiz," "in over her head," "a good person," "a tough cookie," "a know-it-all," and so on. Liquid characters are contextualized within, and therefore subject to, the fluctuations of other people's opinions, desires, and fantasies. The claim for this kind of characterological liquidity is easily discerned beneath a phrase such as "humans are social animals," which concentrates within it an array of undigested social philosophical propositions about the manner in which the self is formed through the social process of communication by means of signs, through play, games, and other conventionally organized phenomena.[10]

This may or may not be a valid way of conceiving the self's constitution and development. I don't know. Perhaps it has always been the case that people's conceptions of themselves have been formed exclusively through social interaction and the alternate donning and shedding of sets of outward behavioral conventions. But it is only recently that this way of behaving and this way of conceiving the self have come to seem a social good, not something to condemn or rebel against. In the service of such a good, in fact, we have witnessed the creation of a healthy modern character that accords with a polymorphous self to such an extent that it has become difficult to know what might be out of the modern character's character. We moderns "have access," as Deirdre McCloskey has put it, to any number of characters in a kind of smorgasbord, presumably for taking up and discarding as they seem useful or not.[11] Playing in a blues band in your spare time from dentistry? Watching porn and smoking pot after putting the toddlers to bed? Reading the Qur'an after a hectic day of sharp elbows on the stock exchange floor? These can be complementary rather than contrasting behaviors. The healthy contemporary character is fluid and multiple.

I should repeat that I am not arguing that one way of conceiving the self—as unitary or polymorphous—is somehow more empirically true. The fact that the oracular "know thyself" is grammatically singular and masculine in its original Greek form indicates the phrase's complex *Sitz im Leben* as much as does the multiplicity we now see hailed on all sides. The same, or something very close to it, is implied in the Polonial "to thine own self be true," which echoes the Greek phrase's gendered and heroic tones. Both are conditioned, situated, and reflective of particular historical conditions. That's not the point. The point is that neither statement has a plural referent; both assume an integrated, singular kernel, and historically speaking, they are not at all unusual in doing so. Nor were they for several thousand years.

I asserted the unitary nature of the Romantic character earlier and need to return to this, for it is likely to be disputed. The conflicted, brow-furrowed Romantic unitary? Is he not the quintessential divided identity, a man at odds with himself, fighting against a dark past, destiny, tragic obligation, and so forth? The mad woman in the attic unitary? Is she not the expression of society's most pressing ills, perpetually out of step with her own desired and desiring self? Yes to all of the above. But no one would think to describe them as *healthy* in their divisions. They remain appealing options throughout the Romantic era and beyond because they are acknowledged, explicitly or not, as aberrations from a norm, because behind each lies an unarticulated image of the healthy unitary individual, a sincere self—not one character among others but an authentic Character—neither fragmented nor performing anything other than what it is, certainly not doubled, tripled, or more.

The Amazing Mr. Golyadkin (Junior)

This firm normative character stands behind the nineteenth- and twentieth-century fascination with literary madness, giving shape to its various incarnations from the dancing doppelganger of E. T. A. Hoffman's "Princess Brambilla" to the "madwoman in the attic," Doctor Jekyll, Humbert Humbert, and a host of others. The healthy unitary character informs all such depictions as what Charles Taylor has called a framework, an assumption about the normal that makes the particular forms taken by the abnormal conceivable, even likely.[12] Such figures often appeal to a frightening, unknown, and perhaps unknowable aspect of human psychology, contrasting the smug certainty of scientistic pronouncements. The dark flip sides of these exceptional personae are driven by elicit, often violent passions, gripped by self-destructive impulses, and surrounded by a tragic mode that is inevitably tense and irony-free.

This is why the rather benign double of Dostoevsky's 1846 eponymous novel is so unusual. Mr. Golyadkin Junior does not murder, violate, or otherwise mistreat anyone after all. He's no monster. On the contrary, he appears to be more socially adept than his senior counterpart, as well as friendlier, more successful, and more popular. He is officious in the performance of his duties at the office, has a boisterous if not endearing sense of humor, and an impeccable feeling for decorum. "How does he do it?" wonders Golyadkin Senior, green with envy. Why is this at all frightening, we may ask?

That the replacement of one middling persona by another exactly like him in external appearance might have been a scary prospect to Dostoevsky's 1840s readers is implied by the gothic mode in which the double makes his first appearance.

> Suddenly . . . suddenly [Mr. Golyadkin's] whole body trembled, and he lurched away involuntarily a few steps to one side. He began to look around him with inexplicable anxiety; but no one was there and nothing in particular had happened, though . . . though it seemed to him that someone just now, that very minute, had been standing there, close by, next to him, leaning on his elbows like him against the parapet and—the strangest thing!—had even said something to him, said something hurried and abrupt, not altogether clear, but about something very close to him, something concerning him.[13]

The spirit sinks, the wind lashes its poor victim in four directions at once, and phantasmal St. Petersburg is on the verge of being inundated, while Golyadkin rushes wildly home, slipping in through a crack in his door just behind his shadowy sputnik. The scene ends in darkness and silence, gothic chords clanging. But this is not the story's only mode. Why it should be both gothic and mock heroic—an incongruous mix at first glance—will, I hope, become clear below.

Let me dispel the mistaken interpretation of *The Double* as a nearly clinical treatment of the onset of psychological disorder, whether conceived of as nineteenth-century madness or the schizophrenia of subsequent ages. In this line of thinking, all Golyadkin needs is some meds to make everything fine. Such a reading depends on an assumption of realism that the book itself calls into question. It is and is not realism simultaneously. There is no firm ground on which to make an ultimate decision about whether or not Golyadkin has a "real" psychological problem, for Dostoevsky has peppered his book with equal evidence to support opposing conclusions, in effect inviting his readers through the smoke and mirrors into an interpretive impasse. No, what looms at the margins of Golyadkin's troubled character is not the threat of a psychological disorder, it's the threat of a social one, of a society that accepts the multiplicitous self as normal, in which one pretends to be what one isn't in order to become what one wants to be, in which one creates a public self, a mask, to use as one's own, in the service of one's own—here's the dirty word—*ambition*. From Dostoevsky to Erving Goffman the notion of a "front" or mask as employed by social actors on the stage of everyday life shifts from diagnosing the moral illness of a society to prognosticating its members' psychological health. In the latter world, the double is not frightening anymore. He may even be rather quaint.

There is a difference between duality and multiplicity, of course, especially in the conception of nineteenth-century character. The first often borders on madness, while the second tends to be balanced and prudent. Nevertheless, these two characters—the double and the *parfait négoçiant*—are related, I shall argue, precisely in their *Sitz im Leben,* the conditions in which they are born and their contrasting receptions, which lament the rise of "the miserable details of commerce," all while celebrating the advent of "confidence" as a driving force for progress and human well-being.[14]

Gogol's Man of Confidence

The historic vehicle on which Golyadkin is traveling, which takes him from unitary to multiform character-hood—or, put the way McCloskey has suggested, which gives him access to multiple characters—is commercial culture, "refined" (*doux*) avarice, the civilizing spread of trade. Golyadkin, in effect, learns what Orville Dewey, quoted in the second epigraph to this chapter, claimed was central to the business life: how to treat oneself as an instrument of trade, adjusting it as needed for commercial intercourse. Thus when, at the beginning of Dostoevsky's book, Golyadkin rushes from one merchant to another to arrange purchases for some future time, or changes his larger bills into smaller ones so as to have a fatter wallet, he manipulates the details of commerce in order to give himself the appearance, and perhaps the inner sense, of affluence. The same may be said of his hiring a carriage, renting livery for his servant, driving around town, and paying a call on his doctor. These are the trappings of a station higher than the one he occupies, and his eventual exit from the scene may be understood, as Dostoevsky himself indicated, as the result of an urge for upward social mobility, in short, ambition.[15]

This, like all Dostoevsky's early works, has often been contextualized by literary historians in relation to the oeuvre of his great predecessor, Nikolai Gogol, particularly the latter's Petersburg stories, where downtrodden petty clerks attempt to make their way amid the crushing bureaucracy of a monolithic state, with invariably tragicomic consequences. But Golyadkin's depiction links *The Double* less to the world of the petty clerk, that is, to such 1830s stories as "Diary of a Madman" and "The Overcoat," than it does to Gogol's *Dead Souls.* In fact, this latter relation appears to have been most prominent in Dostoevsky's mind at the time of *The Double*'s initial creation but has tended to be neglected because of the author's subsequent revisions, which removed most of the direct references for the book's 1866 revised edition.[16] Their connection remains fundamental to understanding both works and to following the thesis of this book.

To see how Dostoevsky responded to *Dead Souls,* one must call to mind the reactionary vision the earlier book deployed before an encroaching progressive commercial ethic in the upper echelons of Russian society. That progressive vision, in turn, is bound up with my second "modern character." I shall explore the details of reading Gogol's work as a reaction to commercial progress in chapter 2. Here it is enough to state that what have often been understood as Chichikov's nonsensical wanderings actually proceed along a continuum of possible Russian worlds, each corresponding to a different landowner's response to the business proposition put before him or her. The principle of development that moves the narrative from the a-commercial, sentimental state of the first encounter (with Manilov) to the inflationary final encounter (with Plyushkin) is the gradual acceptance of *commerce in human souls* by the middle terms: Korobochka, who is fearful but acquiescent, Nozdryov, who is trade incarnate—along with deceit, cheating, and gambling in a kind of wild west of nascent Russian business—and Sobakevich, whose knowing subjection of questions of human worth to questions of price leads directly to the degradation of worldly value at Plyushkin's estate. Gogol's depiction thus links commerce among the landowners with fraud, depravity, corruption, and ultimately, slavery,[17] and Gogol's hero comes off as both a Russian Satan, gathering up deceased serfs still alive on paper, and a Russian confidence man, out to defraud the government by acquiring loans against the collateral of his apparently still-living "souls." The satanic and the commercial thus travel hand in hand through the heart of Russia.

There is, however, a fundamental ambiguity in *Dead Souls* with regard to the commercial processes the work implicitly critiques. It is the equivalent of what Joseph Frank refers to as the "puzzling ambiguity of attitude" in *The Double,* where "a character is shown simultaneously as socially oppressed and yet as reprehensible and morally unsavory because he has surrendered too abjectly to the pressure of his environment."[18] All while suggesting the morally inflationary effects produced by the action of trading in human souls, Gogol provides a hero, the explicitly unvirtuous Chichikov, who is both the commercial agent par excellence and the work's only catalyst for social change. This dual role reveals Chichikov's most important connection to *The Double.*

As a social catalyst, he represents a revolutionary force, which explains the rumor among the town's inhabitants that he is "Napoleon in disguise," not the heroic general or the liberating emperor but the upstart who, by obtaining power and wealth, will cease to be who he was and become someone new, in a move of consensually fantastical social, political, and economic advance-

ment. The reference to Chichikov as Napoleon thus symbolizes the emergence of the modern social actor. The ambiguity at the heart of Dostoevsky's
Double may be understood in much the same way: in order to rise from one's
place, one must break with oneself, perhaps take on a disguise or deceive and
manipulate others. One must create an image of oneself in the eyes of others,
which may or may not correspond to one's own "true" character (as understood in this nineteenth-century idiom). Indeed, truth of character takes on
an uncertain, dubious quality in these new conditions, where any middling
proactive persona might manipulate the icons of consensual fantasy, including the very image of character he has fashioned, in a thirty-year-mortgage-
style attempt to translate his imagined character, his consensually fantastical
character, into something "real," "solid," "propertied," in the future.

While his actions are not usually understood in these terms, this pseudo-
magical manipulation is precisely what Chichikov attempts: a self-directed
association of his image with the collective fantasy of the dead serfs' value,
by means of which he will acquire real estate and transform himself into a
landed nobleman. The power he tries to harness is suggested by the wildly
fluctuating results of his actions: he becomes a millionaire, then a worthless
kidnapper, then Napoleon in disguise, all in consequence of the collective
fantasy of the town's inhabitants, whose speculations raise, lower, and altogether reform his social image, his social and political value, with the fluidity
of rumor, or stocks floating in a market. In his relation to Golyadkin, the fact
that Chichikov does not suffer psychologically from these shifts of "identity"
has prompted critics to look elsewhere in Gogol's oeuvre for a suitable model,
but this leads to side paths. The petty clerk atmosphere of such works as "The
Overcoat" and "Diary of a Madman" furnishes only a superficial resemblance
to that of *The Double*. The best way to understand *The Double's* relation to
Dead Souls is to look deeper into the origins of Chichikov's character, which
takes us further back than the scope of this chapter comfortably allows—for
all but dogged literary sleuths.[19]

The manner by which value is to be generated and maintained in the modern world is indicated from the very start of Golyadkin's adventure. The government bank notes (*assignatsii*) over which he begins to gloat after springing
out of bed are objects of beauty and sensual pleasure. He must wipe his hands
before touching them. He counts them for the hundredth time in the course
of two days, caressing each in his fingers. Even in their numeric specificity,
they represent a rather indeterminately splendid sum of money. In a similar fashion, the office document, another kind of valued paper (*bumaga*),
must be beautified before it is turned in. It is under the pretext of scratch-
ing out a blot that Golyadkin Junior is able to wrestle the crucial paper away
from his twin in order to begin worming his way into the good books of their

superiors. The government-issued money and the government office document are thus powerful in an equivalent manner: through their appeal to desire and imagination.[20] As such, they may be filled, on the one hand, with all Golyadkin's hopes of success and, on the other, with his fears of conspiracy and betrayal.[21] But they are more than mere personal symbols. These are public phenomena that have undergirded modern European society since the early eighteenth century. As such, they are filled with the hopes and fears of the public as a whole, and they are powerful only to the extent that humans agree among themselves to value them and, most importantly, make good on their promises.

Here Dostoevsky broaches a theme that echoes throughout his creative work: the centrality of promises, especially monetary promises, in modern life. A quick glance at two of Dostoevsky's postexile novels illustrates what I have in mind. Raskolnikov is brought to the attention of the investigating authorities because he faints at the police station, where he has been summoned because of a stale IOU he gave to his landlady. The entire subsequent story hinges on the fainting spell, which the broken promise to pay has brought to the surface.[22] Dmitri Karamazov is led to his fateful encounter with Grushenka because his father has threatened to sell her Dmitri's promissory note. For the same reason, he pulls Snegiryov by the beard, which so humiliates the latter's son that the little boy takes on his whole class in a fight that leads to his death.[23] The note thus links the three characters in the novel's main conflict, the murder of the father and the court trial of the son, and also prepares the death of little Ilyusha in what provides its greatest resolution, Alyosha's oration by the stone. In neither work is the piece of paper the central problem. In both it serves as a catalyst, a container for potential inside the stories, which mirrors the actual role of promissory notes, and indeed, all forms of credit. The power of such phenomena lies in the kind of imagination—consensual fantasy—that underpins modernity, especially in its commercial and digital modes.

The Woman in the Window

> Look, all orderly citizens—look from the windows, women!
>
> —Walt Whitman, "A Boston Ballad"

In *The Double* Dostoevsky has effectively concentrated the fantastical potential of modern commercial culture in the mind of a single individual. Golyadkin begins his journey by fantasizing about his paper bank notes. He toys with the trappings of wealth to create an image of himself as prosperous in the eyes of others. He sinks himself in the symbols of the bureaucracy that serve to verify the greatness of the Russian state, its power and "benevolence," and by extension, the power of each of its human cogs. The split that takes place in him as a result of this wholehearted acceptance of 1840s modernity is merely a coming to terms with the trade-off his complicity necessitates. The double and the confidence man merge through the creation and subsequent acceptance of the mask, the public self, as a substitute for the real thing. In this interpretation Dostoevsky's story may be seen as yet another history of the moral or spiritual decay that accompanies the rise of modern commercial culture, evident in such works as Ivan Goncharov's *An Ordinary Story* (1847) and Honoré de Balzac's *Illusions perdues* (1837–43), as the growth of social dependence in the forms of salaried office, personal and professional patron-age, "the exchange of forms of mobile property," and "modes of consciousness suited to a world of moving objects" with fluctuating values point to a funda-mental transformation in the social and political life of the individual.[24] The forms of property embraced by Golyadkin, moreover, are precisely those most opposed to the agrarian ideal: "salaried office, reliance on private or political patronage . . . public credit." From a landed standpoint, the masculine charac-ter that Golyadkin is in the process of constructing is founded upon "fantasti-cal," "imaginary" forms of property and a vision of the self as fundamentally alterable according to one's circumstances.[25] I shall return to this shortly.

To the dual questions of what one might forego, beyond psychological integrity, by coming to terms with such a commerce-inflected world, and what might constitute an appropriate rebellion against it, this early work of Dostoevsky's furnishes intriguing responses. The first dovetails with what Albert Hirschman has called the "Romantic critique of the bourgeois order," which, from Fourier and Marx to Freud and Weber, portrays the triumph of the ideology of self-interest as an impoverishment of the "full human per-sonality." In this line of thinking, we moderns long ago lost the Schilleresque beauty of soul that made our predecessors capable of appreciating life in all its fullness. The irony of such a critique stems from its historical forgetful-ness, since, as Hirschman explains, "capitalism was precisely expected and supposed [by its eighteenth-century apologists] to repress certain human drives and proclivities and to fashion a less multifaceted, less unpredictable, and more 'one-dimensional' human personality."[26] For Dostoevsky, particu-larly in his pre-exile, humanist phase, this irony would have weighed little in comparison with the very real conditions of early nineteenth-century Russian society, with its entrenched serfdom and dehumanizing bureaucracy. Golyadkin's complicity in the modern world, his desire to raise himself in it through the manipulation of his public persona, may be seen therefore as an impoverishment of his humanity, depicted as a fundamental division.

More centrally for this discussion, the sense of humanity's moral diminution has long been related in European thought to a perceived loss of heroism, particularly as a chivalric, aristocratic ideal, in modern times, when striving for honor and glory comes to seem anachronistic, if not ridiculous, in any but a historical or military context. Dostoevsky gestures toward the lost chivalric mode many times, most prominently by having his hero look up to the window behind which Klara Olsufyevna supposedly awaits him, thereby invoking the gaze of the devoted knight toward his inspiration. What looks back from the window, however, is not his beloved, or at least not the beloved woman Golyadkin expects. It is, instead, a purely public gaze:

> Suddenly, in all the windows at once, a strange commotion took place, figures appeared, curtains opened, entire groups of people gathered at Olsufy Ivanovich's windows, everyone looking for something and examining something in the courtyard. Sheltered by his pile of firewood, our hero, too, began in turn following the general commotion, stretching his head from right to left with curiosity, at least as far as the little shadow from the woodpile concealing him would allow. All at once he froze, trembled, and all but sat down on the ground from fright. It occurred to him—in a word, he guessed it with all his being—that they weren't looking for something or someone: they were looking for him, Mr. Golyadkin. Everyone is looking now, pointing in his direction. . . . Suddenly they have all seen him, all seen him at once, and are waving at him, nodding toward him, saying his name.[27]

This substitution of public evaluation for the approval of an exalted, untouchable woman is a masterstroke of literary transfiguration, by means of which all the "tainted" ambitious motives of the hero are stripped of their idealist veneer. The utterly confused Golyadkin Senior does not have the conceptual wherewithal to comprehend that what emerges from the ball to meet him in the next moment is not an alien enemy-twin but the public self his own desires and fantasies have unleashed, the same desires and fantasies contained in the bank notes of the opening pages.

The story's mock heroic narration alluded to above, the subject of much critical speculation,[28] is also best understood within the context of the demise of heroic glory in the modern world.[29] Here again Dostoevsky's text appears to take its cue from Gogol's *poema,* which functions as a lament on the disappearance of the hero, "the virtuous man" dismissed from service. Gogol develops an opposition between the virtuous man and the confidence man, the trading man engaged in commercial transactions conceived of as shady by their very nature, a long-lived attitude toward self-interested endeavor in Russian culture.[30] Dostoevsky's social critique, however, does not limit itself to showing the morally inflationary consequences of allowing commerce to infiltrate culture. Instead, he directs his attention inward, to modernity's fantastical foundations, to the fashioning of public personae, the donning of masks, the acquisition of status, and the effects of such progress on the inner life of one "not handsome, but also not bad looking, neither too fat nor too thin" individual.[31] His story is not that of the petty clerk crushed by the monolithic bureaucracy but of the ambitious everyman who tries to be successful in it. The monumental struggle between the two Golyadkins, then, is mock heroic in a truly historical sense, that is, when placed alongside what Bakhtin has called the "externalized" heroes of the past, particularly those of ancient Greek epic.[32] For the modern individual, by contrast, Golyadkin's inner struggle is, more often than not, the only kind of heroism there is. In effect, this modern glory-free heroism has yielded a split—or, to use the Greek-derived word, a crisis—in masculine character, which the woman in the window, or rather her absence and substitution by the public gaze, serves to locate more precisely.

The woman in the window is not a character like the other two I have described above, for she is devoid of her own content, let alone her own agency. She is also rather static both temporally and spatially. These marked absences are partly what transform the trope, which is of course quite old, into a modern literary and, I would claim, social construction. She is first of all a face value, a floating currency, a printed character on a page, filled with the "fansy and agreement" of those who trade in her. In this she exemplifies an older set of reading practices, "flatter" and less pregnant.[33] Her inaccessible distance is essential, her desire not so much. She can want the hero or not; it is not that important. She anchors him by her emptiness, her ample readiness to accommodate his fantasy and ours, to take it in and safeguard it, preferably in rigid confines. A convent cell does nicely, or an attic room in the home of a tyrannical parent or guardian.

Her appearance in *The Double* is as uncertain as everything else in the story. She may or may not have been there at all, as Golyadkin reads her letter once but cannot find it afterward. Pushkin's usage of the trope in his "Queen of Spades" is likewise slippery but from another side: Hermann only pretends to be in love with Liza, staring at her window for three days running before making his assault on the house. But Chichikov is truly thrown off course by the vision of the governor's daughter, pictured through her carriage window, which yields one of the book's most straightforward lyrical moments.

> And meanwhile the ladies drove off, the pretty little head with its slender features and slender waist disappeared, like something resembling a vision [*videnie*], and what was left again was the road, the brichka, the troika of horses familiar to the reader, Selifan, Chichikov, the flatness, and the emptiness of the surrounding fields. Wherever in life it may be, whether among its tough, coarsely poor, and untidily moldering mean ranks, or its monotonously cold and boringly tidy upper classes, somewhere a man will at least once upon his road meet with a phenomenon unlike anything he has happened to see until then, which that once at least will awaken in him a feeling unlike those he was fated to feel all his life. Wherever it is, across whatever sorrows our life is woven of, a resplendent joy will gaily race by, just as a splendid carriage with golden harness, picture-book horses, and a shining brilliance of glass sometimes suddenly and unexpectedly races speeding by some poor, forsaken hamlet that has never seen anything but a country cart, and for a long time the muzhiks will gape open-mouthed, their hats in their hands, though the wondrous carriage has long since sped away and vanished from sight. So, too, did the blonde girl suddenly, in a completely unexpected manner, appear in our story and also disappear. (87–88)

With the subtle slowing of the passage's first sentence, the blonde vision (*videnie*) carries Gogol's narrator into a moment of reverie, first for "a man," then for all "our life." It is important that she be pictured here in an only temporarily immobilized carriage and that the encounter come about through chance, but there is much more in this meeting than a question of her perceived agency as mobility or of the juxtaposition of planned and unplanned encounters by the protagonist.[34] The clash of the confidence man and the woman in the window is a clash of two epochs, two visions of masculine and feminine character, one modern and commercial, the other medieval and heroic. The mode in which their encounter unfolds, and the relatively clear indication that he will come out the loser in it, is marked by the lyrical reverie that her entrance motivates. Gogol's narrator points to two ways that a "man on his road" might react to such a vision.

> If, instead of Chichikov, some twenty-year-old youth had happened to be standing there, a hussar, or a student, or simply someone just starting out on his path—then, God! What would not have awakened, stirred, spoken

Figure 3. Vassily Tropinin, "Woman at the Window," 1841.

up in him! For a long time he would have stood insensibly on that spot, gazing senselessly into the distance, forgetting the road, and all the reprimands ahead of him, and the rebukes of the delay, forgetting himself, and the office, and the world, and all there is in the world. (88)

But Chichikov is not that man. "Nice wench!" he says, and begins to speculate on how much she might be worth, concluding that with the right kind of dowry she would make "a very tasty little morsel" (*lakomyi kusochek*, 89). On this first encounter he transforms her, in other words, into a consumable, and kicks himself for not having found out who she was. But the effects of the vision have their way in the end and lead to his fall and flight.[35] That the confident Chichikov should lose his poise, even if momentarily, in coming into contact with the woman in the window is not surprising at all. That he should regain it is an indication of his progress along the path of commercial culture, the Tao of regulating all social life to a set of exchange relations. As we have seen, doubt sticks more securely to the dubious Golyadkin.

For an exalted figure, she is surprisingly common in the nineteenth century, but then, that is the nature of currency.[36] She appears as Lucie Manette at the end of Dickens's *A Tale of Two Cities*, invisible behind the window that Sydney Carton gazes at before sacrificing himself for her happiness. In Turgenev's *A Nest of the Gentry* she is Liza, whose handheld candle Lavretsky spies from the garden on their one enchanted evening together. In *War and Peace*, she is Natasha, unseen again but overheard from the window above his room by Prince Andrey on a night that changes their lives forever. In Henry James's *The American*, she is Madame de Cintré, locked behind the walls of the Carmelite Convent, which Christopher Newman looks up to longingly, or in his best imitation of such an emotion. Dreiser's Caroline Meeber is in her window when a destitute and aged Hurstwood glances up from the street below in one of the final scenes of *Sister Carrie*. Levin is lost in *Anna Karenina* when he sees her through Kitty's carriage window in a clear echo of the Gogol scene from thirty years before. The trope is so expected that it might even be created in retrospect, as in Nikita Mikhalkov's 1979 film adaptation of Goncharov's *Oblomov*, which contains a magical scene of the hero gazing up to Olga's window that is not in the novel. Then there are the variations and reversals—a reborn Raskolnikov glimpsed in the infirmary window by Sonya Marmeladov as she stands in the prison yard in a moment of nearly divine revelation for her; a woman looking out on the soldiers looking up at her in Whitman's *Leaves of Grass*.[37] Nor is she limited to literary depictions, nor does she disappear with the nineteenth century's end, as Zhivago, *Cinema Paradiso, Olivier, Olivier, Lolita,* and myriad other examples make clear. Looking for her incarnations and finding her shadows is likely to be an entertaining parlor game. Understanding what she is doing so prominently displayed in such a variety of centrally important works of the century and a half of science and revolutions is a more serious undertaking.

Let me suggest that she is an evocation: of the masculine heroic ethos, and of that ethos in opposition to an image of compromised and searching masculinity. She gets a modern facelift in the early nineteenth century and

Figure 4. At Her Window. *Cinema Paradiso,* dir. Tornatore, 1988.

multiple makeovers from then on. Exactly where she begins is hard to know, for this is not simply a case of first attestations: the trope is far too old for that. I have in mind a rebirth or transformation, an old trope for a new age. For this reason, as a modern phenomenon, she needs to be understood in relation to the other two figures discussed in this chapter. She is part of their story, and they are part of hers: three stalwart traveling companions. She materializes somewhere between the unspoiled potential that Gogol's confident hero imagines in the governor's daughter and the ambitious fantasy (or fantastical ambition) that Dostoevsky's Golyadkin imagines in Klara Olsufevena.

In its most robust formulation, a knight looks up to her window. That Dostoevsky knows as much is suggested by the genealogical key Golyadkin provides, as his thoughts wander on that stormy Petersburg night when he contemplates meeting *her:*

> Come, she says, jump for joy! Be in a carriage, she says, under my windows at a certain time, and sing a touching serenade in Spanish. I await you, and I know you adore me, and I'll run away with you, and we'll live in a little hut. But really, it simply can't be done, it can't, my dear madam . . . it's impos-

sible, it's forbidden by law . . . . And in our day and age, I tell you, madam, nobody lives in a little hut. No indeed! And in our industrial age, my dear madam, you won't get anywhere without moral principles—a fact of which you now furnish a terrible example. . . . Fiancés, madam, will come along in their own good time—yes indeed! Of course, it is doubtless necessary to have acquired some accomplishments, such as playing on the piano some-times, speaking French, history, geography, divine law, and arithmetic—yes indeed!—and nothing more. In addition to cooking; doubtless cooking must enter into the comportment of any moral young woman! But what is going on here? In the first place, my charmer, my fine young lady, you won't be allowed out, and if you are, there'll be a hue and a cry after you, and you'll be put away in a convent. Then what, my dear young lady? What would you have me do then? Would you have me behave like somebody in a stupid novel, come to some near-by hill-slope, dissolve in tears at the sight of the icy indifferent walls of your imprisonment, and in the end fol-low the example of certain awful German poets and novelists, and die, is that it, madam?[38]

Layers of fantasy multiply and divide, as Golyadkin Senior polemicizes with his projected idea of her in her window, filtered in the end through the poetry of Friedrich Schiller's, and Vassily Zhukovsky's, *Knight of Toggenburg.*[39] He thus upbraids his self-projection for having a literary conception of the rela-tions of people "nowadays" (*v nash vek*), "in our industrial age" (*v nash pro-myshlennyi vek*),[40] playing on the cliché of the corruption of feminine morals through excessive novel reading.[41] She holds his fantasies multiple times over, his desires for a point of security amid modern flux, someone to fix his unwavering gaze upon, his unacknowledged hopes to raise himself through marriage to the daughter of a superior, and his fears of the social corruption brought on by the spread of fantasy itself.

On some level, he appears to know, too, that what could save him from the simultaneous fickleness of the natural world and the unleashed fancies of modern society is precisely the strength of character he lacks. It's the kind of deep realization that makes him blush in his sleep and try to suppress his blushes at one and the same time. Rankled by the little public rebuffs of his enemies, Golyadkin

mumbled something like here, for example, it might be possible to dis-play firmness of character [*tverdost' kharaktera*], in this instance one could display considerable firmness of character, and then concluded, "But why firmness of character!? Why bring that up now?" What most angered and irritated Mr. Golyadkin, however, was the way in which, summoned or not, a certain personage renowned for his disgracefulness [*bezobrazie*] and his satirical propensities made his appearance, at that very moment, and also— in spite of everything being crystal clear already, one would think—also began mumbling with an ill-natured grin, "But why firmness of character!? What sort of firmness of character do you and I have to show, Yakov Petrovich?"[42]

This self-reflection on the main character's character, or rather on his absence of character, surfacing as it does during the only dream of what some readers will see as one long nightmare, returns us to the virtuous man dismissed by Gogol.

The retiring, conscientious Golyadkin Senior wants firmness of character but does not see that the reason for such a desire is its concomitance with the woman in the window. The ingratiating, polymorphous Golyadkin Junior sees such firmness as irrelevant because it clashes with the malleability, dependency, and "false consciousness" that make his own existence possible. His observation, moreover, that neither of them has it anyway suggests that the fall of heroism and its rejection amount to nearly the same thing. Losing oneself in the new world and making oneself anew in it are equally unsavory. One leads to impotence, the other to "disgracefulness," "ugliness" (*bezobrazie*), a word that combines aesthetic and moral categories in a manner Dostoevsky would exploit extensively in his future works.[43]

The absence to Gogol's and the young Dostoevsky's contemporaries was palpable in either case. It was anchored amid the vicissitudes of the natural world, counterweighted against the insatiable fancies of modern social life, with firmness of character, "frank and open character" (*primoi i otkrytyi kharakter*),[44] strength of character—in short, Character, one, not two or more, not fragmented, divided, or deferred: the virtuous man.

The Commercial Ethic in Gogol's *Dead Souls*

> In the comparatively peaceful, tranquil and business-minded
> Europe of the period after the Congress of Vienna, the world sud-
> denly appeared empty, petty, and boring and the stage was set for
> the Romantic critique of the bourgeois order as incredibly impov-
> erished in relation to earlier ages—the new world seemed to lack
> nobility, grandeur, mystery, and, above all, passion.
>
> —Albert O. Hirschman, *The Passions and the Interests*

Order in the Gallery

Toward the end of part 1 of Nikolai Gogol's 1842 novel *Dead Souls,* the town
of N's officials debate the identity of the "hero," Pavel Ivanych Chichikov,
lately arrived among them. While the possibility that he might be Napoleon
in disguise is roundly dismissed, says the narrator, it was true that "when
they thought about it, each examining the thing for himself, they found Chichikov's face, if he were to turn and stand in profile, was very similar to the
portrait of Napoleon."[1] This noted resemblance harkens back to Alexander
Pushkin's portrayal of Hermann in his 1834 story "Queen of Spades." Hermann's similarity to Napoleon is noted, appropriately, thrice.[2] First, Tomsky
comments to Liza, "He has the profile of Napoleon and the soul of Mephis-
topheles." Then the narrator, indirectly through Liza's eyes: "He was sitting
on the window sill, frowning fiercely, his arms folded. In this attitude he
bore a striking resemblance to the portrait of Napoleon." Finally, for apparent
emphasis: "This resemblance struck even Lizaveta Ivanovna."[3]

Such references suggest an implied similarity of theme and tone: Hermann is the "Napoleonic hero, the man of will, obsession and dream,"[4] the
man of Fate, whose ambitious aims accord with cosmic forces, raising him

and those who follow him to glorious exploits and power. In a slightly more ambiguous vein, Hermann resembles Napoleon the manipulator, who reduces others to the means of achieving his own ends. Pushkin's use of this comparison in the story, as Iurii Lotman has shown, plays on the distinction between partner and instrument. Hermann offers the old countess a partnership in several social "games": he appeals to her "feelings as wife, lover, mother," all while attempting to use her as an instrument for making his fortune. Lotman has called this notion—that we may each be the instrument of another's ends—"the essence of Bonapartism."[5] In this version of his story, Napoleon assumes the place of both historical marker and generational inspiration, as Pushkin's narrator laments in *Eugene Onegin:*

> But even friendships like our heroes'
> Exist no more; for we've outgrown
> All sentiments and deem men zeroes—
> Except of course ourselves alone.
> We all take on Napoleon's features,
> And millions of our fellow creatures
> Are nothing more to us than tools . . .
> Since feelings are for freaks and fools.[6]

Here I want to build upon this latter aspect of Bonapartism by adding to its mix of attributes the entrepreneurial: this is Napoleon as a self-made man who ceases to be who he was and becomes someone new, even if only—or perhaps especially—in the eyes of society. Such sociopolitical and socioeconomic advancement amounts to an overthrow of the old aristocratic system of landed wealth and title, passed on from generation to generation, which fixed the future position of a man in society as rigidly as did fate.[7] In this new Bonaparte-inflected world, the means by which one advances oneself include deceit, magic, gambling, albeit with the near certainty of outcome provided by magic and, of course, money. Pushkin's Hermann, like Napoleon, will transform himself into a new man through will and wealth.

Gogol's allusion to "The Queen of Spades" via the suggested resemblance of Chichikov to Napoleon is strengthened by numerous parallel themes: deceit or false representation (Hermann pretends to be in love with Liza), social and economic climbing achieved by criminal means, and the subjection of questions of value to the measure of money. *Dead Souls,* moreover, carries on where Pushkin left off, presenting a complex, politically conservative reaction to a perceived loss of social value as the result of the rise of commercial culture among the post-Napoleonic gentry. This loss of value, which is represented as a gradual and complete disintegration, appears most clearly in the sequence of landowners encountered by Chichikov as depicted in chapters 2 through 6.[8] Each landowner exhibits a varied, historically specific, and morally significant reaction to Chichikov's commercial proposal, while the sequence as a whole represents the progress of commercialism and its—for Gogol—spiritually inflationary consequences.[9] Behind this progression lurks the concept of the soul: the great soul, the meager soul, the living soul, and the dead.[10]

My argument is not for reading the landowners sequence in *Dead Souls* as an economic allegory, which would follow the trends of contemporary "disciplinolatry" and separate economic from broadly moral, ethical, and historical issues.[11] Such a separation was rarely if ever performed by Europeans, let alone European Russians, of the early nineteenth century. It would be shortsighted of us to do so in reading their works. It is worth recalling that in Eugene Onegin's knowledge of the world political economy figures importantly,[12] and financial factors were certainly among the most pressing facing the Russian state of the late eighteenth and early nineteenth centuries.[13]

Gogol's depiction is more broadly significant. That he thought about credit in the form of moneylending is evident from its treatment in his 1835 short story "The Portrait." There, moreover, he invokes the commercial ethic by focusing on the auction as a space for the transmission of art, culture, and hence, in a Romantic understanding, spirit. The commercial engagement of *Dead Souls* may be read as a raising of the stakes—from trading in the product of the spirit to trading in the spirit itself.[14] Or, in the conceptual frame developed in this study: from virtue to virtuality.

A Commercial Catalogue

The enterprise begins amid the mannered atmosphere of Manilov's estate, with its discussion of solitude, "spiritual bliss" (29), true friendship, and the beauties of nature in the countryside—a checklist, in short, for moralizing Sentimentalist fiction. On approaching the manor, Chichikov's carriage passes a summerhouse with the sign, "Temple of Solitary Reflection" (23). Manilov's children have vaguely foreign-sounding names—Alkid and Femistoklius—further suggesting, and parodying, names such as Erast and Aris in works of Russian Sentimentalist fiction.[15] The language in which the encounter takes place is peppered with turn-of-the-century words and phrases like *delicates* (28), *mikstura* (29), and *v nature* (32). Chichikov refuses additional food with the formulaic, "Thank you kindly, I am satisfied. A pleasant conversation is

better than any dish" (31). Both the sense and the style of speech are characteristic of precious gentry etiquette.

Chichikov's proposal has every chance of succeeding here, for where the
notion of commerce is concerned, Manilov lives in a state of ignorance, perhaps, denial. He appears to belong, by manner, language, and understanding
of the world, to a pre-Napoleonic era, in which commercial transactions are
given little attention by the truly refined. Such dealings are not suitable for
gentlemen, being subordinate to the greater concerns of friendship, love, and
heartfelt intercourse. All this, of course, is treated ironically. Even if Gogol
believed that such a past existed, his portrayal of Manilov's association with
it could hardly be called laudatory. But as Manilov's concern for feelings and
propriety clearly eclipses his business sense, Chichikov does not appear to be
overly troubled about the form of his proposition. He presents what he wants
bluntly, assuming, it seems, that his interlocutor will agree out of pure good
form or embarrassment.

> "It's not really quite that I'd like peasants," said Chichikov. "I want to have
> the dead . . ."
>
> "Pardon? Excuse me, but . . . I'm a little hard of hearing. I heard quite a
> strange word."
>
> "I propose to obtain dead ones," said Chichikov, "which, by the way,
> according the census would be marked as living." (34)

When Manilov hesitates, Chichikov asks him directly: "It seems to me you're
troubled?" and "Do you perhaps have some doubts?" (35), an approach in
sharp contrast to his later dealings with Sobakevich. Manilov is at last utterly
reassured by Chichikov when the latter states simply, "I believe it will be good
[for the state]" (35), though he does not quite explain why.[16]

This first landowner's generosity in giving the serfs to Chichikov free
of charge indicates the chasm that separates the two characters. Chichikov
approaches the encounter in the manner of a businessman, finding what
Manilov cares about and connecting to those cares by adopting an outward
attitude that appears to match that of his interlocutor. As Orville Dewey
might put it, his "self" is one of the parties to the exchange, and he adjusts
it to the needs of the moment.[17] In the slightly more contemporary idiom of
Dale Carnegie, he is a good listener, talks in terms of the other person's interests, makes the other person feel important, and appears to do so sincerely.[18]
Manilov, for his part, understands very well that the serfs are dead, a thought
he expresses as their having "in some manner completed their existence" (36).
He does not, however, appear to comprehend their use *as a commercial object.*

The association of Manilov with a previous age and his inability to comprehend the commercial transaction to which he has just been a party are brought into sharp relief in the chapter's final lines. Chichikov's carriage has disappeared, and Manilov, having settled in his study, begins to ruminate.

> He thought about the well-being of a life of friendship . . . then he started to build his bridge across the river, then an enormous house with a belvedere so tall you could see Moscow from it, and you would drink tea there in the evening . . . . Then he imagined how he and Chichikov would be going into society somewhere, in a good carriage . . . . Chichikov's strange proposal suddenly cut short his musings. *The idea of it couldn't quite get through to his head: no matter how he turned it over, he couldn't explain it to himself.* (38; emphasis added)

The sequence of Manilov's thoughts repeats the events of the previous few scenes: the pleasantries of the Sentimentalist encounter are cut short by the "strange proposal" Manilov cannot quite fathom. Into the fantastical realm where Manilov erects bridges and is made into a general by the tsar comes Chichikov, both in the flesh and in Manilov's musings. Viewed in this manner, Chichikov's entrance into Manilovian, Sentimentalist space is equivalent to Napoleon's crossing of the Niemen as it serves to shock the Russian gentry into the modern age, the age, that is, of universal commerce. If it is true that the word *commerce* long denoted a kind of polite social intercourse,[19] then in this first encounter commerce of souls can be said to meet commerce *in* souls.

Korobochka's main concern is that Chichikov, this "merchant [who's] come from God only knows where and at night to boot" (50), might try to trick her. She's ready to grant that there is no value in the dead serfs themselves and admits she has never had occasion to sell anything of the like before, but she still fears being taken in, suggesting, in one of the many classic statements of the work, "They might somehow be worth more" (51). If Manilov gives the impression of belonging to a pre-Napoleonic a-commercial state, Korobochka must be seen as a later development. The sensibilities of her generation are hinted at in the portraits Chichikov observes hanging in his room: Kutuzov, the hero of Russia's war against Napoleon, and "some old man with red shirt cuffs, the kind they used to wear *under Pavel Petrovich*" (46, emphasis added). As Korobochka's description makes clear, in her Chichikov has to do with a representative of the Russian provincial nobility reared in a previous age, perhaps, as the latter portrait suggests, that of Tsar Paul I, who died in 1801, but which arrived in present-day Russia, as the former portrait hints, with the Age of Napoleon.

Her physical age and status as widow further serve to locate her in a transitional moment. This moment is highlighted by her use of language, which contrasts sharply with Manilov's Gallic idiom. For instance, such words and phrases as *chai* (perhaps), *otets moi* (sir; literally, "father mine"), *neshto* (something), *manen'ko* (a little), and *avos'* (in case) are all stylistically marked as rustic and archaic. The tendency toward rusticity extends to what she talks about, too. She asks Chichikov whether he wouldn't be interested in buying her chicken feathers and hog fat, and whether he wouldn't like his feet scratched before bed.

Why, however, with her archaic speech patterns and her Old Russian ways, does Korobochka come *after* Manilov in the sequence of landowners? Why might she not be associated with a period of Russian life before Manilov, before the onset of French-inspired gentry preciousness in Russia? The best answer, it seems to me, lies in her acceptance and acknowledgment of the serf as an object of commerce. "Goodness me," she says, "the merchandise [*tovar'*] is so strange, so unheard of!" (52). Where Manilov could not fathom the notion of the serf as a commodity, Korobochka accepts the idea, albeit with uncertainty and suspicion. And in later venturing out to discover whether she might not have been cheated, she makes clear her definitive complicity in what Gogol represents as both the temporal and spiritual transition to the commercial age in Russia.

Korobochka's transitional status is further indicated in her tendency to waver between addressing Chichikov familiarly (*na ty*) and formally (*na vy*). She begins with *ty*; adjusts to *vy* as she asks who he is; changes over to *ty* as she wishes him good-night and offers to scratch his feet; goes back to *vy* the next morning; changes over to *ty* again in the midst of Chichikov's famous proposal; returns to *vy* during their negotiations, when proposing to sell Chichikov her hemp instead of her deceased serfs, then immediately reverts to *ty* after Chichikov invokes the devil's name; goes once again to *vy* in asking Chichikov why he must hurry off and wouldn't he like to buy her hog fat; and at last reverts once more to *ty* in announcing to Chichikov that his carriage is not yet ready (42–56). While the specific twists and turns of their dialogue might yield a separate sociolinguistic study, what is worth emphasizing here is the degree to which Korobochka's manner of address places her squarely between the world of fashionable, self-effacing *politesse* of Manilov's estate, where *vy* is the exclusive rule, and the social free-for-all that is the estate of Nozdryov, who always and only addresses Chichikov with *na ty*.

With the visit to Nozdryov's estate, Chichikov's travels, and the commercial ethic that motivates them, reach a crucial turning point. Scruples, doubts, or suspicions about the appropriateness of the object of exchange have been

utterly obliterated, as have, in general, all scruples or doubts about the appropriateness of any object of exchange, not to mention any means of exchang-
ing it. The idea that anything might be traded has been accepted in principle
and with enthusiasm. Nozdryov enacts it with blind abandon. "A gun, a dog,
a horse—everything was an object of exchange [for him], but not at all so
he could come out ahead; it just happened out of some implacable briskness
and liveliness of character" (69). Nozdryov's compulsive commerce extends
to everything; he engages in trade for its own sake, it appears, unconsciously.
His passion for acquisition is equaled only by the ease with which he loses
what he has just acquired.

> If he was fortunate enough to come upon some simpleton at a market and
> fleece him, he would build up a pile of stuff that had previously flashed
> before his eyes in the stalls: horse collars, tapers, kerchiefs for the nurse, a
> stallion, raisins . . . as long as his money held out. Still, it was rare that all
> this would make it home; almost that very day everything would be lost to
> another, more fortunate gambler, sometimes along with Nozdryov's own
> pipe and his tobacco pouch and holder. (69)

Just as Nozdryov is a compulsive trader, so is he a compulsive gambler, liar,
and cheat.[20] All these are treated in equivalent terms, and so Nozdryov's commerce is linked to his gambling and his dishonesty. One quality is never iso-
lated from the others, and Nozdryov is equally impulsive and spontaneous in
the practice of each. He buys goods because he has money, which he has won
or stolen; he then trades his acquisitions or gambles them away. There is never
any net gain involved, only the activity of exchange.

Such, then, is the face of emerging Russian commerce: energetic, impulsive, inexperienced but simultaneously unstable, treacherous, and potentially
violent. (I am referring to the 1840s.) All of the exchange activity at Nozdryov's is, moreover, arbitrary. Just as he has no reason to buy the goods he finds
at market, he has no reason to suggest to Chichikov any of the items in his
various counterproposals. It is significant that in refusing them, Chichikov
indicates professions or activities in which the objects in question might be
used: he does not want the stallion because he has no stud farm (76); he does
not want a dog because he is not a hunter (77); he does not want the barrel organ because he is not a German "to go dragging it along the roads and
asking for money" (77). For Chichikov, these objects are connected to well-
defined social roles, just as his acquisition of the dead serfs is linked with his
desire to attain a certain socioeconomic and class status.[21] For Nozdryov, on
the other hand, the objects are socially neutral, free-floating, as it were, in a

helter-skelter trading world in which it is essential merely that things change hands, one way or another.

Chichikov's final refusal, in which he says simply, "What am I, some kind of idiot? See here, why should I acquire something I have absolutely no use for?" (78) puts an end to Nozdryov's commercial propositions and spurs a seemingly effortless transition to gambling. "Well, then," says Nozdryov, "please don't say that. Now I know you very well indeed. Such a rascal! Listen, if you want, we'll make a little wager. I'll put all the dead on a card, the barrel organ too" (78). In Nozdryov the shift from trade to gambling (and rigged gambling at that) is made explicit and effortless. His statement, "I'll put all the dead on a card," represents in shorthand form a new stage in the advancement of commercial intercourse: Russian commerce in its purest, most uninhibited Nozdryovian form is equated with gambling, lying, and cheating, while notions of personal dignity and propriety, let alone any moral or ethical considerations, are set aside. The wholehearted acceptance of the commercial ethic, as shown in Nozdryov, points toward social corruption. As such, his depiction harkens back to the long-standing European contrast between trade's morally corrosive core and the moral and social health embodied in the virtuous ideal. I shall return to this thread below.

While Nozdryov's brand of trade might be seen as an impulsive and, in some measure, unconscious phenomenon, Sobakevich's is all too deliberate. It is true that Nozdryov is guilty of complicity in the commerce of serfs/souls: he is first willing to sell them, provided Chichikov will pay well; then he wishes to trade them; and finally he proposes gambling them away. But the spontaneity of his character is a mitigating circumstance. After all, as the narrator emphasizes several times, he can't help it. Even Chichikov remarks to himself, "Oh my, some indefatigable demon's taken hold of him!" (77). With Sobakevich, however, no such mitigating circumstance can be found. He is the first—and this is his most essential role in the sequence—to understand fully the nature of the transaction he engages in with Chichikov. Just as at Korobochka's, Chichikov notes the portraits on Sobakevich's walls.

The pictures were all of heroes, engravings of Greek military leaders in all their stature: Mavrokordato in red trousers and a uniform dress coat, glasses on his nose, Kolokotronis, Miaoulis, Kanaris.[22] All these heroes had such thick thighs and unheard of mustaches that a shiver ran down one's spine. In the midst of the strong Greeks, who knows how or why, Bagration was situated, gaunt, skinny, with little banners and cannon balls in the foreground and in the tiniest of frames. Then followed the Greek heroine

> Bouboulina,[23] just one of whose legs seemed bigger than the entire torso
> of any of the dandies that fill the hotels of today. (90)

The ostensible reason for the narrator's surprise at finding the Russian amid the Greeks is that he is not large and does not appear to be physically strong. Yet the oppositions Gogol has set up fall together along other, more suggestive, lines as well. By placing the Russian hero in the ranks of the Greeks and implying that he somehow does not belong, Gogol invites skepticism as to his legitimacy as a great leader of a great people in a great cause. The Greeks, after all, represent a noble struggle for liberation from the Turkish yoke, which conjures images of the glories of their ancient heritage as a great European nation. They are solid and substantial, with their thick thighs and the enormous leg of Bouboulina to support them. What, by contrast, do the Russians have to stand on? The bodies of today's hotel dandies are puny in comparison. Bagration is skinny and sickly. The "small flags and cannon balls in the foreground" of his portrait suggest empty symbols of military pretense.[24] Read in this way, the scene suggests Sobakevich's girth may, like the small flags and cannonballs before the Russian general, have little or nothing behind it.

But there is another, more startling line of thought suggested by Bagration's unusual placement in the panoply. The suggestion of his weakness contrasts sharply with the traditional *strength* of the Russian military, at least since the time of Peter the Great, a strength made possible, as mentioned above, by the soul tax around which Chichikov's exploits circulate. Indeed, it was that strength Napoleon wished to subdue, as it was in the cause of maintaining it that Bagration achieved both fame and martyrdom.[25] On the one hand, then, the placement of Bagration in the role of Russian exemplary hero, defender of the Russian land, indeed, martyr to the cause of its defense, makes him a particularly poignant witness to the deal that is about to be done. On the other, Chichikov's supposed resemblance to Napoleon suggests the continued encroachment of "foreign" ways—in this case a progressive commercial ethic—into Russian life. The weakness of the Russian military to prevent such an encroachment even while defeating Napoleon himself is no surprise, for it was in the decline of the centuries-old aristocratic ideal of glory that commerce is thought to have gained its great foothold in the modern world.[26] This is the reason that, through Gogol's ironic lens, Chichikov wears "armor" (46); this is why "in these days, even in Rus', giants have begun to make themselves scarce" (18); and this is why great generals look on as Chichikov and Sobakevich haggle over humans.

Of all Chichikov's clients, Sobakevich is by far the best businessman. He is the best bargainer and the biggest stickler for the details of their transaction. He is also the most aware of what it's all about. At the end of Chichikov's dog-

and-pony-show introduction of his theme, which touches, as the narrator puts it, "on the entire Russian state," and during which it is not always clear Sobakevich is awake, let alone listening, Chichikov forms the least direct of his propositions with the words "And so . . . ?" Sobakevich's reply, "You need dead souls?" uttered "without the slightest surprise, as if they had been talking about bread" makes not only his attention but his understanding quite clear (96). Manilov does not understand the concept of the serf as a commodity; Korobochka accepts it, though with trepidation; Nozdryov is willing not only to sell serfs but also to trade them and gamble them away—but all, seemingly, without any conscious understanding of such transactions. Sobakevich, however, cuts immediately through Chichikov's obfuscation and circumlocution to the essence of the matter. His sole concern becomes getting the best deal he can.

The degree to which Sobakevich is consciously engaged in a commercial transaction, the object of which is the human being, is underlined by his careful enumeration of the serfs to be sold. He knows them all by name, elaborates on their personalities, strengths, and skills (97–98). Yet it is only with Sobakevich that the issue of price becomes central. His interaction with Chichikov may be reduced essentially to the process of dickering over the price—read: value—of the dead serfs. The questioning of price, the attempt by each party to raise or lower it to his advantage, rests upon a more fundamental questioning of value beneath it.[27] Gogol toys with the play of price upon value through the characters' use of words. Chichikov asks for a "little list" (*spisochek*, 100); Sobakevich requests a "small-ish advance" (*zadotochek*, 101); Chichikov asks for a "small-ish receipt" (*raspisochka*, 101); and Sobakevich comments that the money is "oldish" (*bumazhka-to staren'kaia*, 102). The diminutives, particularly striking in the mouth of the bearish Sobakevich, play up the question of worth—of things and persons—at the heart of their conversation, which prepares the sharp contrast that will emerge in Gogol's panegyric to the Russian word in the immediately following passage.

During their business, all considerations are subordinated to the deal. It is no accident that only here is the connection between the *dusha* as serf and the *dusha* as soul made explicit. "Truly," says Sobakevich, "to you the human soul is worth no more than a stewed turnip" (100).[28] But coming from Sobakevich in this context, the phrase, with all its potential depth of meaning, is only a bargaining tool. This is why it is Sobakevich who, among all the landowners, is described as soul-less or with a misplaced soul. "In that body there seemed to be no soul at all, or else there was one, only not where it ought to have been but rather, as with Koshchei the Immortal, somewhere beyond the mountains and concealed by such a thick shell that whatever might happen in its depths produced not the slightest tremor on its surface" (96). In Sobakevich the sequence of landowners peaks and begins its descent. Here the distinction between serf and soul rises to the narrative's surface, pointing to the questionable status of Russia's own soul beneath it. This qualitative shift indicates a modulation in the narrative as a whole.

Metaphors and symbols of emptiness, a Gogolian trademark, are associated with each landowner. Where Manilov is described as having no object of zeal or fervor (*zador*) and indeed "nothing at all" (25), the intimation of emptiness or lack is indicated by the names of both Korobochka (literally, "little box") and Nozdryov (from *nozdria,* "nostril").[29] In Sobakevich it is his head, shaped like a Moldavian pumpkin, the kind out of which balalaikas are made, thus suggesting a pumpkin emptied of its contents. All alone, however, such details of depiction do not make clear the notion of progression inherent in Gogol's meticulous sequence. Just as Korobochka's acceptance of the serf as commodity represents a developmental advance over the previous, Manilovian, state, Sobakevich's relegation of all considerations to that of the commercial represents an advance over Nozdryov, in whom various and sundry forms of "trade" can be said to be vying for supremacy. Sobakevich has become a "man-*kulak*" (100).

The qualitative shift in the depiction of landowners may also be discerned in Sobakevich's insistence on the real, living value of his dead serfs. Manilov admits the serfs have "in some manner completed their existence" and gives them away. Sobakevich, however, while attempting to get as much for them as he can, appears to think of the serfs as still in some manner alive. He reacts strongly to Chichikov's proposal that they are, in being dead, but a dream.

> "Well, no, not a dream! I'll prove to you what kind [of a man] Mikheyev was, you won't find such people anywhere: such an enormous machine that he couldn't get inside this room—no, no, that's no dream! And in his great shoulders there was more strength than in a horse. You just tell me where you could find that kind of a dream anywhere!" He pronounced these last words after turning to the portraits of Bagration and Kolokotronis hanging on the wall, as usually happens with people in a conversation when one of them suddenly, for some reason, turns away from the person to whom his words are being addressed toward some other, even completely unknown, person who happened to appear, from whom he knows he will hear neither a response, nor an opinion, nor a corroboration, but at whom he directs such a significant glance that he seems to be asking for mediation. (98)

Despite, or perhaps thanks to, his treating the serfs as still living, Sobakevich's central aim is to translate their value into monetary terms. This speech, like his invocation of the immortal soul noted previously, serves to increase the market value of his wares. Such a function is clearly indicated in Chichikov's response, when, after Sobakevich's long outburst, he says simply, "No, I can't give you more than two rubles [each]" (98). Sobakevich's inclusion of Kolokotronis and Bagration in the conversation, which Gogol suggests as accidental or arbitrary, is not that. They are called to witness, as it were, the accuracy of Sobakevich's assertion, his claims that the dead serfs are something more than a dream, and their presence, as silent observers to the transaction, highlights both its outlandishness in their eyes and its essential pusillanimity. The projected point of view implied by the inclusion of the two leaders is crucial to the scene's thematic development.

At the climactic moment of their haggling, Chichikov and Sobakevich break off, each firm in maintaining his price, and for the last time the wall paintings enter the scene: "Sobakevich grew silent. Chichikov also grew silent. A few minutes passed in silence. From the wall Bagration with his aquiline nose looked extremely attentively *on this purchase*" (*na etu pokupku*, 100; emphasis added). Where the scene begins with all the Greek heroes along with Bagration and Bouboulina in attendance, the focus then narrows to Kolokotronis and Bagration, and finally leaves Bagration all alone, thus suggesting that, in fact, he has been the most important witness all along. As a martyr for the cause of defending Holy Russia against Western invasion, Bagration watches the progress of Bonaparte's advance into Russian culture still, now in the form of "Bonapartism." The new order, the upstart, Europe and Russia, the confidence man, the post-Napoleonic bourgeois, commercial age—all these themes come together in this description, as Bagration looks on. And the center of them all is the purchase.

The encounter with Sobakevich is the narrative's center point, both spatially—the middle of the fifth chapter out of eleven—and thematically. The marked decay of Plyushkin's estate is shown as the immediate consequence of Sobakevich's conscious commercial ethic and the resulting loss of soul. The worth of things has been thrown into disarray, a notion symbolized in Plyushkin's enormous collection of odds and ends on his bureau and the great heap in the corner of his living room (108).[30]

The modulation is gradual but unmistakable. At the conclusion of his business with Sobakevich, Chichikov departs for Plyushkin's estate and is brought, en route, into contact with "the pure Russian word," in the form of the peasant's obscene sobriquet for Plyushkin. The word is rich and fresh, uncontaminated by outside influences. Gogol describes its uniqueness in the most lush and expressive of terms.

Just as the countless multitudes of churches and monasteries with cupolas,
domes, and crosses strewn throughout holy pious Rus', so also the countless
multitude of tribes, generations, and peoples crowd, color, and race across
the face of the earth. And every people, bearing the pledge of its own powers within, filled with the creative potentials of the soul, its own brilliant
particularity, and other gifts of God, has each differed uniquely according
to its own word, which, in depicting any object whatsoever, reflects in such
expression a part of its own character. . . . But there is no word so sweeping and lively, no word that tears itself so from the heart, that so boils and
pulsates, as the aptly spoken Russian word. (103)

The thought is Romantic: the word is a national phenomenon and expresses
the soul of a people.[31] The tone is lofty, nearly oratorical, and irony has disappeared. Moreover, the transition to the subsequent chapter (chapter 6) is
achieved by continuing the stylistic distinctness of this panegyric, thereby
maintaining the elevated, devotional tone, while thematically juxtaposing
the uniqueness and freshness of the Russian word with the loss of such freshness in the narrator's vision of the world: "Before, long ago, in the years
of my youth, in the years of my childhood that irretrievably flashed by, it
gave me joy to come upon an unknown place . . . . Now I approach with
indifference every strange village and gaze with indifference on its vulgar
exterior" (104). The dilapidation of the narrator's *vision* of the world corresponds to the subsequently described dilapidation of Plyushkin's estate,
onto which Chichikov wanders while still thinking and laughing about the
rich sobriquet applied by the peasant to Plyushkin.[32] The re-entry of Chichikov's thoughts thus allows a reprise of the passage's central antithesis.
In other words, Chichikov serves initially as the perceiver of the sobriquet,
giving occasion to the narrator's panegyric; the panegyric then contrasts to
the narrator's disillusionment, his loss of "youth" and "freshness," which is
then interrupted by Chichikov's continued musings on the (fresh, pure, etc.)
sobriquet and his simultaneous arrival at Plyushkin's dilapidated estate. The
combined points of view of Chichikov and the narrator work together, therefore, to achieve the transition from Sobakevich's loss of soul to the utter degradation of Plyushkin.[33]

From Plyushkin Chichikov obtains not only dead but also runaway serfs.
As at Manilov's, he pays nothing for them, but the reason has now been
reversed. Manilov is willing to give Chichikov his dead serfs out of friendship
and because he does not see them as an object of commerce; they are worthless because they are dead. Nor does he see them as a liability. They are simply
outside the system or "algorithm" according to which he lives and thinks.[34]

Their value as commodity grows in the course of Chichikov's travels, reaching its height at Sobakevich's, where, consequently, Chichikov pays his greatest price. After this there is a break, a qualitative shift. Their market price falls, as it were, and Chichikov obtains both dead serfs and runaways at Plyushkin's without paying a kopeck.[35] The commodity has suddenly and dramatically lost all value.

The continuously dubious (dead souls/dead serfs) basis of the narrative provides more than one explanation for this development. On a primary level, the laws of supply and demand suggest a glut; Sobakevich confirms this by his assertion that at Plyushkin's peasants die "like flies" (94). The names of dead serfs that clog Plyushkin's account books are thus a financial liability, and he is glad to be rid of them. Their value, which was nil at Manilov's, questionable at Korobockhka's and Nozdryov's, and firmly equated with price at Sobakevich's, has now sunk to a point below zero, that is, a negative value, a liability or debt. On another level, that on which the pun of the book's title relies, the serfs have been rendered worthless by the effective equation of human value and price, by reducing persons to both the most materialist of terms and, simultaneously, the most secular and consensual—an agreement among men. This is not the first instance of such an operation in the novel. Chichikov's initial chance encounter with the governor's daughter on his way to Sobakevich's prompts him to wonder who her father might be and whether he is rich. "Really," he thinks, "if, say, the girl had some two hundred thousand worth of dowry, she would make a very tasty morsel" (89). Chichikov thus translates the "vision" that "anywhere a man might encounter but once on his road" into a price. Her value is *how much* she is worth.[36] And then he translates her into a piece of food, taking the almost inevitable step from commodification to consumption.

The progressive order in which the landowners are arranged is punctuated by the inclusion of Plyushkin's biography. Plyushkin's life history stands out conspicuously as the only history given. Coming last, it functions as an echo of the whole transformation that Gogol's sequence implies. The technique is similar to the synopsis of the encounter between Chichikov and Manilov that is contained in Manilov's musings after Chichikov's departure. There as well, no explicit reason is given for the qualitative change at the sequence's center, when Manilov mentally runs up against the riddle of Chichikov's proposition. In the case of Plyushkin, all we know is that "the good housewife died; the share of the keys, and with them, of the small cares, passed to him" (112).[37] Plyushkin's biography hints at a notion of sequence and summary in the process by which his attention turned from the "main shares of the household" to "the little papers and features he collected in his bedroom" (113), making the suggestion of gradual change explicit, but without answering the riddle of what lies behind it.

Finally, the purchase at Plyushkin's marks a shift in the transformation of the serfs' value from past-based—at Sobakevich's, where they are, in Chichikov's words, "but a dream"—to future-based, in Chichikov's wild musings of the subsequent chapter, where he fantasizes to such a degree as even to create dialogue for his imaginary purchases. The implication is clear: value in the commercial world is both contingent and conventional. It is as much a product of men's agreements with one another as their speculations concerning the future. It is, in this sense, as rootless and wandering as the runaway serf himself—a promise of worldly value to a state and its army supported only by millions upon millions of other such promises existing in the minds of men.[38]

In the end, Chichikov's speculation in the value of dead serfs is based on the same sort of fantasy as the state's speculation in the value of living ones. They are both a form of borrowing: Chichikov's from the earthly city, the state's from the divine.[39]

The Advent of Refined Avarice

> It is practically a general rule that wherever there is commerce there are refined manners, and wherever there are refined manners there is commerce.[40]
>
> —Montesquieu, *De l'esprit des lois*

To recap the argument thus far, with the notion of the serf as commercial object functioning as a measure, the sequence of landowners appears as a progression. The effect resembles the rhetorical figure of asyndeton so often employed by Gogol elsewhere, reinforcing the impression of a tonal movement across part 1, a gradual rise in intensity as each new key is introduced and explored, until the narrative changes qualitatively.[41] At its center—the encounter with Sobakevich—the novel turns: before that point Chichikov's identity is unnecessary and virtually unmentioned; after it, the question of who he is gradually becomes so essential that it must be answered. This need motivates the penultimate scene's biographical account of his life and adventures up to the moment of the book's opening.

Gogol's male protagonist is the epitome of *le parfait négoçiant*. The overemphasized detail of his refined and agreeable nature may be explained as a natural corollary of his commercial impetus. He is the model self-interested agent, and his activities remain balanced nearly throughout. Indeed, balance might be his defining trait, while the narrator's initial description of him as "neither too fat nor too thin, neither this nor that" can be understood as a grotesque overapplication of the principle of moderation that underlies his protagonist's actions. Chichikov is not carried away; his passions are in accord with, and under the careful control of, calculation. Gogol thus provides the context for invoking a long-lived European debate that has often been overlooked in discussing his work. By revisiting the major points of the debate here, I hope to place Gogol's choice of a "non-virtuous" hero in sharper relief. Chichikov in fact turns out to represent a set of progressive values for his time, though in Gogol's hands whether this is good or bad is not easy to say.[42] To understand how acquisitive behavior, or in medieval terms, avarice, came to be upheld by the middle of the eighteenth century as a primary and in essence positive motivation in the governing both of individuals and society, we must briefly review the concept's history, especially within the context of the now largely forgotten contrast of the *interests* to the *passions*.[43]

This dichotomy, which was formulated in the political discourse of the seventeenth century, finding its way subsequently into the thought of numerous eighteenth-century writers on ethics, moral psychology, and political economy, had its ultimate origins in Machiavelli's search for alternative principles to the traditional moral and religious precepts by which princes were supposed to govern, for a scientific, positive approach that would correspond more completely to the advances in knowledge of his day. His prescription of a characteristic behavior for rulers of states inspired the initially synonymous concepts of *interesse* (interests) and *ragione di stato* (reasons of state).[44]

The notion of interest, therefore, arose as a contrast to the unbridled whims of a sovereign but also to religious and moral constraints, which had been judged as failures by thinkers of the Renaissance. Interest came to be understood as a constraint on the passions of the prince, and in the same period, the notion of princely interest came to be applied more generally to the interests of various groups among the ruled and, eventually, to nonruling individuals. It was likewise in this period that interest came to be discussed more frequently in terms of economic aspirations. The ultimate reasons for such a shift in usage—from associations of honor and glory, as part of an aristocratic ideal, to those of wealth—are a matter of speculation. "Perhaps," writes Hirschman,

> it was due to the old association of interest and money-lending . . . . Possibly, too, the special affinity of rational calculation implicit in the concept of interest with the nature of economic activities accounts for these activities

eventually monopolizing the contents of the concept. . . . Perhaps no other explanation is needed for the narrowing of the meaning of the term "interests" once the beginnings of economic growth made the "augmentation of fortune" a real possibility for an increasing number of people.[45]

Regardless of the precise causes, economic well-being and the accumulation of wealth became the term's primary connotation. With this development, a curious turn in the history of ideas took place. When interest, as a centrally economic consideration, was now set beside the notion of constraint, it rendered a startling thought possible, namely,

> that one set of passions, hitherto known variously as greed, avarice, or love of lucre, could be usefully employed to oppose and bridle such other passions as ambition, lust for power, or sexual lust.[46]

Thus did avarice become a respected counterweight to a variety of passions considered by prominent thinkers of the seventeenth and eighteenth centuries as the most dangerous to the well-being of society.

The interest counterweight had a number of strengths. First, the emphasis of the French *encyclopédistes* on "rehabilitating" self-love was in part a reaction to medieval Christianity. Stephen Holmes cites in particular the thought of Augustine, in which self-love was equated with hatred of God while love of God was identified with contempt for oneself. The neo-Machiavellian suggestions of *interesse* and *ragione di stato* were clear alternatives to such a tradition. Indeed, the gradual acceptance of worldly pursuits by Enlightenment political and moral theorists, particularly seeking after personal advantage, was due in part to the continued reaction against this tradition of "Augustinian misanthropy."[47] The old approach to human morality was roundly critiqued by eighteenth-century thinkers like Hume and Voltaire, both of whom, according to Holmes,

> by removing the pejorative connotations of personal advantage seeking . . . hoped to make man appear worthy in his own eyes. At the very least, their hostility to religious self-abnegation helped reinforce their relatively welcoming attitude toward the principle of rational self-interest.[48]

It was, therefore, as the result of a strange confluence of associations and arising circumstances—interest opposed to religious precepts, interest opposed to passion, interest in the lending of money, and the growth of economic well-being—that seeking after personal advantage, which is to say, moneymaking and the acquisition of worldly goods, came to carry, in Hirschman's words, "a *positive* and *curative* connotation."[49]

An additional advantage of a world ruled by self-interest was its constancy. "In the pursuit of their interests men were expected or assumed to be steadfast, single-minded, and methodical, in total contrast to the stereotyped behavior of men who are buffeted and blinded by their passions."[50] Interest made the world a safer place because it made men predictable. "Avarice," wrote Samuel Johnson in *Rasselas,*

> is a uniform and tractable vice. Other intellectual distempers are different in different constitutions of mind; that which soothes the pride of one will offend the pride of another; but to the favor of the covetous there is a ready way: bring money and nothing is denied.[51]

Hume echoes the thought. "Avarice," he writes, "or the desire of gain, is a universal passion which operates at all times, in all places, and upon all persons."[52] Holmes summarizes the effect of such an evaluation in the realm of eighteenth-century moral psychology in the following terms:

> The self-interested agent is "cool and deliberate." . . . It is much easier to defend oneself against enemies fretting about their interests than against opponents reeling from selfless emotions and bursting with inspiring ideals. The most difficult adversaries to outwit or buy off are probably those seized by envy.[53]

It must strike the contemporary, post-Marxian reader as a curious fact that commerce should have once been considered not only a "harmless" but also a socially mollifying and, indeed, civilizing force. Nevertheless, such a mind-set appears to have been widespread in the thinking of Europeans of the seventeenth and eighteenth centuries. Samuel Johnson's famous aphorism, "There are few ways in which a man can be more innocently employed than in getting money," only scratches the surface: self-interested commerce would be the agent of both the world's enrichment and its civilization.[54]

Hirschman identifies the first instance of designating commerce as an especially beneficial, "gentle," or "refined" (*doux*) occupation in Jacques Savary's seventeenth-century textbook for businessmen, *Le parfait négoçiant.*

> [Divine Providence] has not willed for everything that is needed for life to be found in the same spot. It has dispersed its gifts so that men would trade together and so that the mutual need which they have to help one another

would establish ties of friendship among them. *This continuous exchange of all the comforts of life constitutes commerce and this commerce makes for all the gentleness* (douceur) *of life.*[55]

Beside its use in the domain of trade, the word *commerce* had long designated a polite interchange between educated speakers, often between two individuals of the opposite sex, and it was likely in such a context that it first acquired the epithet *doux.*[56]

The staunchest and most influential advocate of *le doux commerce* was Montesquieu. "Wherever manners are refined [*moeurs douces*]," he states in *De l'esprit des lois*, "there is commerce; and wherever there is commerce, manners are refined. . . . Commerce . . . softens [*adoucit*] barbarian ways."[57] Such notions were widely held throughout Europe by the middle of the eighteenth century, giving rise to the distinction, commonly made in England and Scotland in the second half of the century, between the "polished" and the "rude and barbarous nations" of the world, that is, between the countries of Western Europe, where increasing wealth was perceived in combination with the expanded role of commerce, and the as yet underdeveloped, "a-commercial" remainder. The phrase *le doux commerce,* thanks primarily to Montesquieu, had become a commonplace by the eve of the nineteenth century; it served as a point of ridicule for Marx in *Das Kapital* and was apparently a private joke between Marx and Engels as well.[58]

My aim in this brief history is not to trace any direct connections between individual political or moral theorists and the work of Gogol. The issue of what specific works Gogol may have read, long a point of contention, not to mention considerable speculation, is not relevant for my argument.[59] Essential here is the degree to which certain key notions, widespread to the point of being cultural commonplaces by the early nineteenth century, condition Gogol's novel, furnishing an intellectual context that was largely implicit to his contemporary readers and that greatly expands the work's meaningful potential today.

Le doux Chichikov and the Worth of a Man

The manner in which Gogol introduces the Enlightenment pairing of the passions and the interests into *Dead Souls* implicitly places the self-interested agent in contrast to the virtuous man, commercial undertaking in contrast to virtue. In the process it simultaneously draws a parallel to the evaluation of human beings generally—not just dead serfs—in Gogol's fiction. I would argue that it also indicates the same fundamental anxiety over what Jean-Joseph Goux calls the "unlocatable standard" or "uncertain reserve value" of contemporary financial representation.[60] In Gogol's case the anxiety is generalized not around money but around property—both the land that is the supposed goal of his hero's elaborate scheme and the "property of the person" upon which conceptions of modern liberty were founded in the late eighteenth century.[61]

We can now turn to the essential, and thus far omitted, question that lurks behind the sequence of landowners treated above, that of the nonvirtuous Chichikov's place in it. He is, of course, not a landowner per se, or rather, he is one only potentially, for as a serf-owner in name, he is something of a *pomeshchik* already, even if his serfs are only graphemes on a paper. But what role does he play in Gogol's depiction of the progress of the commercial ethic in Russia? I have two initial responses.

First, he is a catalyst.[62] It is Chichikov who introduces into the world and nurses into maturity the concept of the serf as commodity; in a sense, he and it travel together, bringing self-interested commercial enterprise inside Russian gentry culture. Thus, it is not so much that "social interest" is absent from the book, which Pyotr Pletnev long ago suggested, as that such social interest is framed in commercial terms.[63]

Second, Chichikov's actions, which are entirely self-motivated, are also the only evidence of social change the book has to offer. In other words, without Chichikov's undertaking, the world is stagnant; it is he who provides the motivation for all the action, suggesting an ambiguity of attitude in Gogol's representation of commercial behavior: it is not necessarily the excessive or *passionate* expression of blind avarice, and thus degradation, of a Plyushkin.

But these provide just part of an answer. The crucial discussion of Chichikov's nature in *Dead Souls* takes place within the frame of the hero's biography. Let us read the passage again with this larger context in mind. "It is very doubtful," says the narrator, in prefacing that discussion,

> that our chosen hero will be pleasing to readers. The ladies will not like him, that can be stated positively, for the ladies demand that a hero be an absolute perfection, and if he's got some little bodily or spiritual blemish, then there's trouble! However deeply the author might look into his soul, even were he to reflect his image more purely than a mirror, they won't value him at all [*ne dadut nikakoi tseny*]. . . . All the same a virtuous man has not been selected as a hero. And we can even say why. Because it's time at last to give the poor virtuous man a rest; because the word "virtuous man" flits emptily across one's lips; because the virtuous man has been

turned into a workhorse, and there isn't any writer who wouldn't go out riding on him, urging him on with a whip and whatever else might turn up; because the virtuous man has been so worn down that there isn't even a shadow of virtue in him anymore, and all that's left is ribs and skin in place of a body; because the virtuous man is invoked hypocritically; because the virtuous man is not respected. (210)

The conceit is masterfully developed to the point that the quality of virtue becomes the occasion for lack of respect, expressed in the final line. "No," concludes the narrator, preparing the biography of the next nineteen pages, "it's time to hitch up a scoundrel. So let's hitch up a scoundrel!" (211). The subsequent life history may be read, then, as an exposition on the hero's status as scoundrel, on his absence of virtue.

The conclusion, "Acquisition was the cause of everything" (*Priobretenie—vina vsego,* 227), not only makes clear the central antithesis of the entire biography—virtue to self-interested acquisition—but introduces the work's only explicit discussion of the passions that, in the context of contemporaneous West European social theory, served to contextualize interest, particularly commercial self-interest.

Everything transforms quickly in a man; you don't have time to look around before a horrible worm has grown up inside, despotically drawing all the living juices to itself. And many a time has not only a great passion but a worthless passionette for some insignificant thing dispersed in someone born for better deeds, forcing him to forget his great and holy obligations and to see the great and holy in paltry trinkets. Numberless as grains of ocean sand are the human passions, and none resembles another, and all, the base and the beautiful, are at first obedient to man but then become his frightening masters. Blessed is he who has chosen for himself the most beautiful of passions; his measureless bliss grows tenfold with every hour and minute, and he enters ever deeper into the boundless paradise of his own soul. But there are passions whose selection does not issue from man. They were born with him at the moment of his entry into the world, and he is not given the strength to turn from them. They are guided by designs from above, and there is something in them that is eternally calling, implacable throughout life. They are destined to accomplish a great earthly deed: it matters not whether as a dark image or as a bright vision that flashes by, making the world rejoice, equally are they called upon for a blessing [*blago*] unknown to man. And perhaps in this very Chichikov the passion leading him forth is not from him [*ne ot nego*] and in his cold existence is contained that which will later throw man onto his knees in the dust before the wisdom of the heavens. And it is still a mystery why such an image has come forth in this *poema* now appearing in the world. (227–28)

Perhaps the most initially striking feature of the passage is the image of various and sundry human passions, "as numberless as grains of ocean sand," in search of a principle of constraint. In Chichikov, it would seem that acquisition, "the cause of everything," has become the passion that is his "frightening master." Why it is not as devastating in Chichikov as it is in Plyushkin, I think, can best be answered by reference to the genealogy of self-interest in West European social discourse. In effect, Chichikov is driven by modern self-interest, Plyushkin by medieval avarice: we find ourselves thus at a crucial turning point in Russian social development, the turn from the medieval world to the modern. The fact that Gogol chooses to contextualize his hero's guiding motivation as part of the eighteenth-century passions-versus-interests debate indicates at the very least a familiarity with the fundamental claim of early capitalist apologists: namely, that self-interest was a tractable vice that could function as a positive and curative constraint on lust, envy, pride, and all the other socially detrimental passions—or, in other words, that one passion could be a counterweight to all the rest, for the benefit of society. But here too we have only breached the surface.

The passage marks the end of the biographical oasis in which Chichikov's background is divulged. The frame is evident in the sentence immediately following that quoted above, in which the narrator returns to the subject of the readers' displeasure with his choice of a hero, returning, in essence, to the subject that gave rise to the biography in the first place—the fact of the hero's absence of virtue. The shape of the oasis can be imagined in the following manner.

First, Gogol's narrator invokes his readers' displeasure with Chichikov's lack of virtue, throws out the virtuous man as a possible hero, and "hitches up" the scoundrel. Second, the scoundrel's biography is recounted, at the conclusion of which the subject of his absence of virtue is implicitly renewed by suggesting "acquisition," from among the "numberless passions," as "the cause of everything." And third, the narrator returns to his readers' displeasure: "But the fact that readers will be displeased with the hero is not what's difficult" (228), echoing, in the very next sentence, the same construction he used at the beginning of the biography. The Russian is explicit. The first phrase, from before the biography, reads, "*Kak gluboko ni zagliani avtor emu v dushu*" ("No matter how deeply the author might look into his soul"; 210); the second reads, "*Ne zagliani avtor poglubzhe emu v dushu*" ("Should the author look still deeper into his soul"; 228). The discussion of Chichikov's essential character flaw thus continues, as if in mid-sentence, across the hero's entire nineteen pages of inserted biography. It is not unusual, therefore, that readers might not at first see the continuation of the discussion as organically connected to its introduction.

Such a connected view, however, provides a means of responding to the riddle—the form of interpretive challenge—that Gogol's final sentence in the passage quoted above thrusts into the face of his readers: Why is the admittedly dark "image" of a man ruled by the passion of self-interested acquisition appearing in the present *poema*? The best answer, it seems to me, appeals not to what Gogol wanted to do in the future, how he might have wished to develop his hero further, but to the discursive consequences of Gogol's invocation of the passions-interests theme. Within that tradition of thought, as noted above, the acquisitive impulse was rationalized as a positive, indeed, socially progressive trait, both in the cultivation of personal manners and in the development of social and even national well-being. That Gogol was likely ambivalent to such an ideal need not be strenuously argued. Indeed, the designation of his hero's passion as perhaps "not from him" (*ne ot nego*) and the suggestion that that very passion may perhaps "throw man onto his knees and into dust before the wisdom of the heavens" make clear the implicit cosmic dimension of the Gogolian version of the passions-interests debate, which could never be a purely civic humanist affair in this writer's hands.

Chichikov's is an attempt to construct, or rather reconstruct, a stable social self from the remains of a picaresque life, which will raise him in the process from obscurity and social marginality to prominent or at least respectable personhood. In other words, from the variety of personae he has played in his past, he is attempting to constitute himself as a singular character, which will also be a legal persona, as he makes of himself a *pomeshchik*. The principles by which he is to do this include the manipulation of an embryonic system of commercial credit and the manipulation of others through cool and deliberate calculation. In these dual manipulations, following the suggestion first made by Pushkin in *Eugene Onegin* and, more obliquely, in "The Queen of Spades," he is associated with Napoleon. The resemblance, which is made to look absurd by an insistence on the character's physical features, comes to seem rather sensible when one thinks instead of the character's character, particularly vis-à-vis a commercial ethic that would be nothing less than revolutionary in its social and cultural impact over the next two hundred years of Russian life. Gogol's special irony is on display when he explores the *merchants'* fear at the specter of Napoleon.

The merchants were really scared [about Napoleon's release], for they believed completely the prognostications of a certain prophet, locked up some three years before; the prophet had come from who knows where, in bast sandals and a hoodless sheepskin coat, which smelled terribly of rotten fish, and proclaimed that Napoleon was antichrist and was being held by a stone chain beyond six walls and seven seas, but afterward he would break the chain and take over the world. The prophet, as is proper, had fallen into prison for his prognostications, but nevertheless he had already done his deed, completely stirring up the merchants. For a long time after, even amid the most profitable transactions, merchants, going off to the tavern to take their tea, would talk about antichrist. (194–95)

The passage's apocalyptic overtones should not distract anyone from the implied overthrow of the medieval system of trade at its heart. Nor is this the first instance in *Dead Souls* where a moment of commercial intercourse has been situated within a larger, religious or spiritual context. As noted above, Bagration, hero of the Napoleonic War and martyr to the cause of defending the country, is said to look with particular attention on the "purchase" (*pokupka*) being transacted by Chichikov and Sobakevich. This framing of the commercial transaction suggests a standard that is in fact locatable, only not in the conditions of trade themselves, and perhaps not in earthly conditions at all. Chichikov's brand of self-interested commercial entrepreneurship would overthrow the entire system of landed wealth were it to succeed. In effect, a different kind of revolutionary invasion is underway, with Chichikov at its head. Gogol's fusion of the commercial and the Napoleonic here acquires a further depth of associations: there is now both a national stake, in the struggle with Napoleon, and an eschatological one, in the struggle with antichrist.

More important still, the excerpt demonstrates one of the many instances of the word as rumor breaking free from its immediate boundaries—the closed-door speculations about Chichikov's identity among the town's administrators—and running free in some inexplicable (or at least unexplained) manner among the population at large. Here it is not Chichikov's identity but Napoleon's rumored release that jumps, in an apparent digression, from the private discussion into the populace.

Many from among the government administration and well-born nobility had also involuntarily started thinking about [Napoleon and antichrist], and, infected by mysticism, which, as everyone knows, was all the fashion then, saw in every letter of which the word Napoleon was made some special significance; many even found apocalyptic numbers in it. So there's nothing surprising in the fact that the administrators involuntarily started thinking about it. (195)

Words here, even the letters of which they are made, have taken on a strange and magical significance, suggesting an eternal otherworldly standard, even in the midst of the ephemeral, everyday, apparent nonsense of this world.

The degree to which such linguistic transformation—the life of words on their own—is integral to the image of Chichikov as a character may be found in the dramatic rise of his worth, the symbolic value with which he is equated, through the words of those he meets. From merely "well-intentioned," "sensible," "learned," "respected," "kind," and "pleasant" (the adjectives applied to him at the end of chapter 1—none of which, it should be noted, touches on economic status), Gogol's protagonist becomes, overnight, immensely rich.

> Rumors passed all around that he was neither more nor less than a millionaire. Even without that, as we saw in the first chapter, the inhabitants of the town loved Chichikov with all their soul [*dushevno poliubili Chichikova*], but now, after such rumors, they loved him with even more of it [*eshche dushevnee*]. (147)

Resorting to the same narrow pun on which the entire plot teeters, the *dusha* is further subordinated to a question of the monetary worth or price—the same Russian word either way—of Chichikov himself. His worth, moreover, is divorced from the notion of physical property: much to his chagrin, Chichikov owns no land, just as he owns no living peasants, not yet. This worth of his is an imaginary, *consensual fantasy* of the town's populace, without rooting in earth or heaven. It gestures toward the dangers of social corruption that thinkers of the late eighteenth and early nineteenth centuries, in opposition to Montesquieu and his compatriots, often associated with the spread of commercial relations. Pocock summarizes the issue in this way:

> Once property was seen to have a symbolic value, expressed in coin or in credit, the foundations of personality themselves appeared imaginary or at best consensual: the individual could exist, even in his own sight, only at the fluctuating value imposed upon him by his fellows, and these evaluations . . . were too irrationally performed to be seen as acts of political decision or virtue.[64]

Here we come full circle to the question of Gogol's dismissal of the virtuous man. What generates the enormous value in question, Chichikov's worth among the town's inhabitants, and what destroys it in the next breath is also what gives value to any form of symbolic currency, whether coin, paper, or credit: consensual fantasy, determined in part by rumor, people talking. And in a system where an individual's worth is subject to the irrationally performed, rumor-based evaluations of his fellows, the "virtuous man" is not a cliché, it is an anachronism.

When we consider the context of the eighteenth-century notion of *le doux commerce,* Chichikov's practice of a balanced, "refined," and pleasant form of commercial intercourse appears rather humorous. His being neither too fat nor too thin, neither this nor that, makes him seem an excellent exemplar, if not a caricature, of the *parfait négoçiant,* engaged in the commerce that makes for life's "refinement" and "softens barbarian ways." That is a funny idea. But if it were a proper understanding of Chichikov's business, then one would expect him to be interested in Korobochka's chicken feathers and hog fat. Of course he is not, and this makes the implication of *le doux commerce* quite devastating. To invoke once again that other realm within which exchange relations are situated in Gogol's work, the objects of Chichikov's trade—dead souls—do not exist in this world. The worth of the serfs he has purchased is no longer dependent on the consensual fantasies of men, a realization that makes all too clear the fact that it once was.

t h r e e

In Search of the Virtuous Man

Minor Readings

> The worst thing a reader can do is identify with the characters in a book.
>
> —Vladimir Nabokov

The question I am following is how the advent of the virtual man inflects the notion of the virtuous one. Positing this as a question might seem merely clever. Portraying it as a quest might seem anachronistic. But with consensual fantasy as a middle term, especially as it developed with the rise and spread of symbolic value and modes of commercial consciousness through commercial development, the two other terms take on a different kind of weight, and the virtuous man, the man whose propertied corporeality was once thought to substantiate the health and rationality of a polity, that man's character is called into question. The quest, then, conflates with the question: What sort of character steps forward when the virtuous man has passed out of sight? This chapter explores two responses.

Divided Man

> To draw interest to itself, science must speak primarily about the questions that have most importance for the country. If 'The Economic Indicator' follows this rule, it will bring great benefit to its activity—the activity of spreading economic concepts among us.
>
> —Nikolai Chernyshevskii, *The Economic Indicator*

Symbolic value and its effect on the depiction of the modern masculine character pervade Dostoevsky's first post-exile novel. Amid the consensually fantastical world of his surroundings, Raskolnikov struggles to come to terms with a stable image of personhood and personal action. Indeed, the first concrete emotional assessment of the hero conveyed in the novel, the "somewhat sickly and cowardly sensation" we are told he feels in passing his landlady's door, is explained as the simple result of debt: "[Raskolnikov] was in debt up to his ears to his landlady and was afraid of meeting her."[1] Raskolnikov is himself struck by "the fear of meeting his creditor" (6) and of all the "trifles" (*pustiaki*, 7) associated with her, especially when compared with the "thing" (*delo*, 7) he has been considering. How can he be afraid of her and what she represents and still be capable of *that*? The idea of the murder is thus introduced by its combination in Raskolnikov's mind with the fear, cowardice, and simultaneous shame of debt, a lack of credit: "I want to attempt such a business and at the same time fear such trifles!" "Why," he asks himself, concluding the same paragraph, "am I going [there]? Am I really capable of *that*? Is *that* really serious? Not serious at all. So it's just out of fantasy that I'm amusing myself; games!" (*igrushki*, 6). Raskolnikov dismisses his own resolve as pure fantasy; he lacks trust, faith, credit—the tendency to treat these equivalently is suggested by his equation of fear before meeting his creditor and anxiety before his planned action. The "fantasy" to which he attributes his fear and anxiety applies equally to each: they are both imaginary, both promises about the future, real only to the extent that the imagining agent can be trusted to carry them out.

Raskolnikov's desire for a kind of integration, his "thirst for people" (11), is contrasted to the malignancy of his alienation. He is divorced from family, friends, and the society around him, alone, a free-floating agent in the urban Petersburg sea. He has "sunk into himself and distanced himself from everyone else" (5). On the street he lapses into a kind of forgetfulness, "not noticing his surroundings and not wanting to notice" (6). The most dramatic and poignant moment of such alienation comes just after the murder, when, having wandered onto Nikolaevsky Bridge, he is mistaken for a beggar, beaten with a whip by a coachman, laughed at, and given alms. At that moment he looks across the Neva to St. Isaac's Cathedral and finds his previous ideas and interests unthinkable.

> All that recent past seemed to him covered over somehow, down below, somewhere barely visible beneath his feet, the ideas of before, the tasks of before, the themes, the impressions, all that panorama [around him], and he himself, and everything, everything . . . He seemed to have flown

away somewhere above and everything had disappeared from his view. At an involuntary motion of his hand he suddenly felt the two-given coin clutched in his fist. He opened his hand wide, looked intently at the coin, and threw it in a wide arc into the water; then he turned and went home. It seemed to him he had cut himself off from everyone and everything at that moment as with a pair of scissors. (90)

The symbolism of the passage is carefully controlled. The value of coin—conventional, changeable, consensually fantastical—has served as the pretext for Raskolnikov's departure from the earth, the ostensible motivation for murder. He looks down, senses the earth's solid presence somewhere below the bridge, the water, and the consensually fantastical world in which he has immersed himself, but he cannot connect to it; indeed, in the elation of uprooting, he no longer wants to connect. Like the dream he has realized in his actions, he has entered the realm of human-made consensual value completely. But in doing so alone, he no longer has any use for the supposed value that initially invited him in; the consensual fantasy of valued coin means nothing to the man who has opted out of the consensual.

The degree to which such alienation can be understood as a correlate of commercial endeavor is underlined by Raskolnikov's premurder ruminations on the crime he is about to commit, that which will supposedly propel him into the midst of civic activity and a life of virtuous (*dobrodetel'nyi*) devotion to society, the "service to all human kind and to the common cause" (54) that the old lady's money will make possible.[2] For the fact that Raskolnikov uses the word *delo*, which may equally well signify a thing as a business deal, is no mere fluke of language. Indeed, he appears to think of the projected murder and theft as a kind of entrepreneurial venture.

> He had already begun to look [at it] differently, and despite all the teasing monologues concerning his own powerlessness and indecision, he had somehow even against his will got used to considering the "hideous" [*bezobraznaia*] dream as an enterprise [*predpriiatie*], even though he didn't believe himself yet. He was even going right then to make a *test* of his enterprise [*predpriiatie*], and with each step his anxiety grew stronger and stronger. (7)

The translation of the unreal dream or fantasy into a real event is accomplished through the vehicle of the enterprise, endeavor, undertaking, venture, or *predpriiatie*, a concept laden with modern commercial overtones. Moreover, Dostoevsky's qualification of the dream as "hideous," "ugly," or *bezobraznaia*, emphasizes both its present formlessness (*bez* means "without," *obraz* means "shape" or "form") and its juxtaposition to the divine or heavenly, where the notion of the icon, divine form, or *obraz* is latent.[3]

Just as in Gogol's usage, and Pushkin's before him, here the medium of commercial enterprise, the subjection of questions of social and ethical good to consensually fantastical human agreements, coalesces in a single monumental *business deal*—the result of the hero's long speculations on an "unreal" dream of future value. Furthermore, the hero's dream is linked, as in Gogol's and Pushkin's earlier depictions, to the Napoleonic, though this time Napoleon's image contains another dimension: his exemplary role as an upstart and grandiose manipulator is less important than his place on Raskolnikov's list of "extraordinary individuals" who have transgressed moral boundaries to give their "new word" to the world.[4]

Here again, as with Hermann and Chichikov, the most elementary explanation of the hero's behavior begins with a desire to gain riches and thereby raise himself from his current circumstances. On the surface, Raskolnikov's motivation appears to be calculated rational self-interest, the most straightforward, albeit rather simplistic, argument for which is furnished by Luzhin.

> Until now when I was told to love my neighbor . . . what happened except that I tore my coat in half, shared with my neighbor, and both of us were left half naked. . . . Science tells us, love yourself before all, for all the world is based on personal interest. If you love only yourself, then you'll take care of your affairs as is proper, and your coat will remain in one piece. Economic truth adds that the more private affairs there are in society and the more, so to speak, whole coats there are, then the firmer its foundations will be and the better served will be its common cause. (116)

One might prefer to dismiss this theory of econo-ethical activity, especially as it comes from the supercilious and repugnant Luzhin. And Luzhin is, in fact, criticized by the good Razumikhin in the same scene for cynically appropriating and distorting these ideas merely to justify his own exploitative actions. It should be recalled that Raskolnikov draws the conclusion that one may murder from this theory: "Take what you were just saying to its logical consequences, and it follows that people's throats can be cut" (118). There is no explicit response to the "logical consequence" of self-interest offered in the novel. Raskolnikov's remark is greeted by his interlocutors with indignation and Luzhin's response, "There's a limit [*mera*, which is also "measure" or "balance"] to everything," and the subject is dropped.

The seemingly unconnected transition, in Raskolnikov's subsequent question, to the subject of Luzhin's apparent approval of Dunya's poverty, is of course not unconnected in the mind of the male protagonist, nor, as we shall

see below, in the novel's moral schematic. Luzhin's planned financial subjugation of Raskolnikov's sister is part of the same problem that generates the
permissibility of murder.[5] Having entered the system of consensually fantastical value, humans determine the measure (*mera*) themselves. The organic
connection to Raskolnikov's theory of the great individual should be evident:
symbolic value depends on human agreements, which are all "formless" and
contingent, only as real as any plan or promise can be acted upon. As part of
the same system, any limit someone might choose to apply to them would
require an external standard.

Luzhin, Svidrigailov, and Raskolnikov all attempt to instrumentalize peo-
ple in the realization of their particular dreams, and in this they resemble
Pushkin's Hermann, Gogol's Chichikov, and Dostoevsky's Golyadkin Senior.
The secret of the cards sought by Hermann functions equivalently to the ruse
Chichikov attempts to pull off and the social gambit employed by Golyadkin
Senior, all of which turn back on them as they lose control of the forces they
have set in motion. These treatments make it very clear that such forces issue
from people themselves. Moreover, the "magic" that the hero counts on to
advance his interests actually serves to undermine them. The same is true of
the relation between Raskolnikov's dream and the medium by which it comes
to be "real." For the event that sets in motion Raskolnikov's downfall and his
eventual confession is, as noted previously, the calling in of a loan, a failed
promise.

Just as, at an earlier point in the book, Raskolnikov mentally connects
his debt to the murder he is about to commit, so, immediately after the murder, is the same connection made via the story's narrative pattern. The same
shameful debt from the novel's opening pages, for which he has apparently
given his landlady an IOU (77), serves as the pretext for getting him to the
police station, where he is undone. All he can think of is the murder during
his time there, so that when he discovers that he is not a suspect, he is filled
with "a minute of complete, unmediated, purely animal joy" (78). His relationship to the police officers, his conception of self in relation to others, shifts
momentarily from murderer to merely debtor, and, contrary to his previous
debtor's sensation, he reexperiences the postmurder elation of leaving behind
all worldly attachments. And he faints.

The journey to the police station is what brings him to the attention of
the authorities and, more importantly, transforms him in his mind back to
being a suspect in theirs. Following his fainting spell, and the apparently
greater attention the officers pay to his whereabouts of the previous evening
as a result of it, his final thought on leaving the station is, "They suspect!" In
much the same manner that the hero's magic doubles back on him in Push-

kin's, Gogol's, and Dostoevsky's previous treatments of commercial, entrepreneurial, "Napoleonic" enterprise, so Raskolnikov's promise to pay serves as the pretext for introducing the idea of his guilt in the minds of the authorities, an idea on which the novel's entire subsequent development pivots.

Afloat in the sea of consensually fantastical valuations, modern man needs an anchor or a raft, and Raskolnikov's various theories and rational attempts to explain his actions and the motivations for them are chock-full of holes. Even after his confession, trial, and internment in a Siberian prison, he suffers from the same absence, the same dull grasping at rational understanding. In the end, the support he finds is mediated, like his transformation as a whole, by Sonya Marmeladov. And Dostoevsky, never one to shy away from a literary allusion, constructs the crucial scene on the shoulders of his predecessors, even perhaps on those of his own previous self:

> It was the second week after Holy Week; warm, clear, spring days had arrived; the windows had been opened in the prisoners' ward (barred windows beneath which a guard patrolled). Sonya had only been to see him in the ward twice during the course of his illness; she'd had to acquire permission each time, and that was difficult. But she had often come into the hospital courtyard, beneath the windows, especially toward evening, sometimes just in order to stand for a minute in the courtyard and look from a distance at the windows of the ward. Once, toward evening, Raskolnikov, then almost fully recovered, fell asleep; when he awoke, he happened to go up to the window and suddenly saw Sonya in the distance, at the hospital gates. She stood there and seemed to be waiting for something. Something seemed to pierce his heart just then; he started and drew back from the window. (420)

The craftsmanship of Dostoevsky's final sentences here is apparent: the "something" (*chego-to*) that Sonya is "somehow" (*kak by*) waiting for appears to be the same "something" (*chto-to*) that "somehow" (*kak by*) pierces Raskolnikov's heart in the next sentence. Nor can there be much doubt that she sees him framed by the window and understands, as does he, that "something" transformative has taken place between them. But why invoke the well-worn trope and why reverse the usual roles for the man and the woman in it? Why put Raskolnikov in the place of the maiden in the tower and Sonya in the place of her devoted knight?

An easy answer would see a transcendent ideal replacing an earthly one, where Raskolnikov's resurrection, an embodiment of Christ's suffering and rebirth, comes to occupy the center of meaning for a loving believer in him and what he stands for. Such an interpretation finds ample support on the page following that just quoted: "But he was risen [*voskres*], and he knew it, felt it fully in all his renewed being, while she—she lived only through his life alone!" (421). And so, in the traditional woman-in-the-window trope, a man would look up to her casement and find all the meaning of his life there. The confinement suggested by the added parenthetical details of the bars across the windows and the guard patrolling below them in Dostoevsky's scenic depiction accord perfectly with the trope's historical use—she is in a convent or her parents' house or a castle keep, thus unattainable, inspirational, and anchoring. The gender reversal is necessary, in this interpretation, for readers might otherwise mistake the inspiration for a purely Romantic one (like that for an inspired poet) or a purely romantic one (like that for a lover). These would be wrong, for he is up there because of his greater sin, his greater suffering, and she is down here looking up because he more closely embodies an ideal of Savior. This treatment of the trope could be understood with or without irony. He is a murderer, after all.

There is more, however, to the gender switch than a simple replacement of a figurative representation by a sacramental one, important as this may be.[6] Previous instances of the trope in Dostoevsky's works suggest that the question of masculine character, particularly the degree of the hero's heroism, is integral to the author's use of it. Makar Devushkin, who repeatedly looks up to the heroine's window from the opening scene of *Poor Folk* onward, is shown as emasculated by a variety of means, from the potency of his rival to his family name (*devushka* means "young woman"). And, as shown previously, Golyadkin Senior's climactic downfall is mediated by his loss of control over the trope's suggestive power, as it is wrested away from him by a more powerful public gaze.[7] Moreover, the German Romantic origins of the reinvigorated trope, of which Dostoevsky appears to have been aware,[8] place it in the discursive domain of Schiller's beautiful soul and the republicanism of the early nineteenth century. Such talk permeates *Crime and Punishment*, making a hero of the lover of life, the lover of humanity with his rational, civic vision, a vision that Dostoevsky's novel questions from start to finish.

That he was not alone in employing the trope to explore the zeal of republican-inspired enthusiasts can be deduced by comparison with Dickens's use of it in the climactic scene of his 1859 *A Tale of Two Cities*.

"Remember these words to-morrow: change the course, or delay in it—for any reason—and no life can possibly be saved, and many lives must inevitably be sacrificed."

"I will remember them. I hope to do my part faithfully."

"And I hope to do mine. Now, good-bye!"

Though he said it with a grave smile of earnestness, and though he even put the old man's hand to his lips, he did not part from him then. He helped him so far to arouse the rocking figure before the dying embers, as to get a cloak and hat put upon it, and to tempt it forth to find where the bench and work were hidden that it still moaningly besought to have. He walked on the other side of it and protected it to the court-yard of the house where the afflicted heart—so happy in the memorable time when he had revealed his own desolate heart to it—outwatched the awful night. He entered the court-yard and remained there for a few moments alone, looking up at the light in the window of her room. Before he went away, he breathed a blessing towards it, and a Farewell.[9]

Sydney Carton here has just prepared the ground for his swindle of the French republican government by impersonating the imprisoned Darnay and going to the guillotine in his place. As a dead ringer for Darnay, he doubles him; the con of the French authorities, and the devoted glance upward to Lucie Manette's window (Darnay's wife and the love of Carton's life), complete the character trio—double, con-man, and woman in window—whose union serves to deepen Dickens's already profound tone and increase the sense of closure in the scene, a group photo as it were, with familiars who, we realize only in the end, have been in this story all along.

The invocation of a precommercial heroic ideal, inspired by the inaccessible, inspirational woman, contrasts the republican ethic of the revolution, especially in its formless, "hideous" early excess. The contrast also anachronistically deploys a Romantic devotion to an idealized feminine form. But where Dickens's depiction sticks to a rather conventional usage of the woman-in-the-window trope, Dostoevsky's strikes out in a radically different direction, in effect standing the precommercial heroic image on its head by advancing an alternative notion of heroic masculine character. This is not the championing of trade noted by de Tocqueville, who "[could] not express [his] thoughts better than by saying that the Americans put something heroic into their way of trading."[10] Nor is it the absorption and transformation of virtue by the bourgeois ethic suggested by Dierdre McCloskey in *The Bourgeois Virtues*.[11]

That it is an alternative to both the heroic and the commercial masculine character becomes evident when one considers the role of the double, Svidrigailov, in this work, particularly the manner in which his life comes to an end. Svidrigailov's suicide in a dirty side street is witnessed by an "official" of the state, a Jewish fireman, which impressively combines heroic and commercial ethics in one and the same image.

A milky thick fog lay upon the city. Svidrigailov walked along the slippery, dirty, wooden sidewalk in the direction of the Little Neva. [. . .] Then the wooden sidewalk came to an end. He was in front of a big stone building. A dirty, shivering mutt, its tail between its legs, cut across his path. Some-one dead drunk, in an overcoat, was lying face down on the sidewalk. He glanced at him and kept going. A tall watchtower off to the left caught his eye. "Hah!" he thought, "this is the place. Why go to Petrovsky? At least in front of an official witness . . . " He almost smirked at his new thought and turned down N— Street. [. . .] By the big locked gates of the building, lean-ing with his shoulder against them, stood a little man wrapped in a gray soldier's coat and wearing a brass Achilles helmet. With drowsy eyes, he cast a cold sideways glance at the approaching Svidrigailov. His face bore that eternal, grumbling sorrow that is so sourly imprinted upon all faces of the Jewish tribe without exception. The two of them, Svidrigailov and Achilles, studied each other for a while in silence. Achilles finally thought it out of order that the man was not drunk but was standing there three steps in front of him, staring at him point-blank and saying nothing. (394)

There follows an oft-quoted conversation between Svidrigailov and the Jew-ish fireman, which caps both their encounter and Svidrigailov's existence, and which seems to have baffled several generations of critics.[12] Achilles main-tains his prominent metonymic presence throughout, reappearing in mock-heroic phrases such as "Achilles raised his brows" (*Akhilles pripodnial brovi*, 394) and "Achilles roused himself" (*vstrepenulsia Akhilles*, 395). The effect is darkly comedic, as others have pointed out, but it is far from uncanny or inexplicable.

The figurative invocation of the heroic ethos combines here with the tacit association of the Jew to the trading, commercial world, the world of every-day commerce. Dostoevsky's emphasis on the cosmic dimensions of this par-ticular Jew, the "eternal (*vekovechnaia*) grumbling sorrow" in his face, and the reference to the Jewish tribe (*evreskoe plemia*), appear to serve the same purpose as the metonymic reference to the fireman through his helmet: they raise the representational stakes, as it were, and make the contrast between lowly "Hebrew" and heroic Greek that much more palpable. Dostoevsky has managed the combination with such efficiency that, without unraveling the expressive resources tapped in its construction, the image has tended to strike some readers as mere comic relief and others as a clear indication of the author's anti-Semitism. Both these readings fall short.

The notion of a Jewish Achilles contains within it a stark contrast, one that was widely accepted in Dostoevsky's time and has seen various versions both before and after. Matthew Arnold's variation, which he termed Hebraism versus Hellenism, emphasized Hellenic honest realism as opposed to the proper conduct of the Hebraic. "The uppermost idea with Hellenism is to see things as they really are," he wrote; "the uppermost idea with Hebraism is conduct and obedience,"[13] a distinction that applied to the interconnected history of Renaissance humanism and medieval Christianity. In the twentieth century, Hannah Arendt characterized the Greeks as preoccupied with greatness and contrasted this with the Hebrew appreciation of human life in all its aspects, not just the heroic ones.[14] One might cast a glance further back to Heinrich Heine or again forward from Dostoevsky to Nietzsche, Heidegger, or Harold Bloom, but the details of these or other takes on the Greek versus Hebrew models of character and the representation thereof are not the point: the point is that the two categories Dostoevsky has crystallized in his Jewish Achilles—or, translated more correctly given this analysis, his Hebraic Achilles—combine aspects of European thought of his day that are far more profound than anyone has seemed to notice. Their combination may have very little to do with any sort of personal anti-Semitism on Dostoevsky's part.[15] The effect of the mixture is something like Chichikov wearing armor (*dospekhi*), or the rise of Chichikovian self-interest in a heroic Rus' being abandoned by its heroes.[16]

Alternative modes of masculine character—the commercial and the heroic—are thus set to one side in a rather humorous if not offensive gesture, like the portraits in Sobakevich's drawing room watching the purchase go down, and the dual modes of libertine and ascetic are highlighted for a brief moment before the aesthete blows his brains out, leaving just one masculine character standing in the end. As Raskolnikov's double, Svidrigailov in death implicitly contrasts Raskolnikov in rebirth, and the mediation of Svidrigailov's death by means of a Hebraic Achilles can be seen in its proper perspective, namely, by contrast to the new image of masculine heroism that Raskolnikov's placement in the window has foregrounded. Rather than simply rehashing the woman-in-the-window trope and offering it up to his lost hero as an anchor or a raft, Dostoevsky creates a new vehicle altogether, a new image of novelistic heroism, self-made in a sense and thus "American" in its spirit.

Raskolnikov rushes away from the debt that had hounded him toward a variety of liberatory modes—the confident, the criminal, the entrepreneurial, the Napoleonic—but in apparently raising himself ever upward, his crime sinks him further into a primordial indebtedness that he struggles to explain. While the aesthete aristocrat Svidrigailov thus heads off to America with his ironic announcement to an impotent Hebraic Achilles, Raskolnikov sets off for a different New World, accompanied by Sonya, through a recognition of his own sin and suffering, and the recognition by another of his sin and suffering as great and all too human.

Whole Man

For men are bad in countless ways but good in only one.

—Aristotle, *Nichomachean Ethics*[17]

When, in the midst of a discussion with his brother, Konstantin Levin claims that the motor (*dvigatel'*) of all our actions is self-interest (*lichnyi interes*) and that no activity can be lasting unless it is based on such interest, Koznyshev offers the following response: "The main task of philosophy through the ages has been comprised of finding that necessary connection between self-interest and public interest."[18] Thus does Tolstoy explicitly take up the theme addressed in these pages.[19]

The form in which the brothers have expressed their idea points to a more specific episode in the history of Western social thought than Koznyshev's response might suggest. While questions of the public and private good may be found in the history of ideas from the Ancient Greeks onward, the contrast of self-interest to public or social interest grew into the form in which we recognize it today only with the early moderns, and in fact, as explored in chapter 2, it is there that one finds the term *interest* coming into use in much the way it would continue to be used to our own day.[20] Self-interest was considered as a "motor" for social benefit in the writings of Montesquieu, James Stewart, Adam Smith, and a host of others. Aspects of commercial endeavor, especially in the realm of credit and national debt, the stock and bond market, were debated in the publications of Joseph Addison and Richard Steele and Daniel Defoe and discussed widely by such figures as the Earl of Shaftsbury and David Hume. In Russia the views of Nikolai Novikov, Mikhail Speransky, Nikolai Mordvinov, the Decembrists Pyotr Pestel', Nikolai Turgenev, and Mikhail Orlov, as well as Alexander Herzen and Nikolai Ogarev, show an implicit familiarity with the ideas of their West European contemporaries.[21]

One of the most powerful opposing standpoints, later to be upheld variously by Thomas Carlyle, Alexis de Tocqueville, and John Stuart Mill, pointed to the detrimental effects of such cultural commoditization and contrasted commercial self-interest to an agrarian ideal, especially that of an idealized landed citizen, often a Roman one. In the writings of the eighteenth century, one finds two extremes of conceptualizing postfeudal propertied individualism, one agrarian and the other commercial.[22] In opposition to the commercial, writes Pocock, there is "a conception of property which stresses possession and civic virtue."[23] According to this view, "moral personality is possible only upon a foundation of real property, since the possession of land brings with it unspecialised leisure and the opportunity of virtue."[24]

Such a conceptual history of apologies for self-interest makes it at least counterintuitive if not deeply ironic that Konstantin Levin should uphold it as the foundation for human well-being, the motor for social progress. Given his staunch defense of aristocratic values and heritage,[25] one would expect him to be at least skeptical of the theory that once functioned as the main rationale for the expansion of commercial enterprise throughout Europe. Even more striking in this context is the fact that the very same notion of self-interest has in the course of the century's development now passed into the arguments of a new set of progressives, Nikolai Chernyshevsky and his followers,[26] all while continuing to be used by the emerging bourgeoisie. The question is, why would Levin, or Tolstoy for that matter, wish to promote the notion of self-interest as the motor and foundation of human well-being when, with its close associations to both commercial ideology and left radical politics, its usage contradicts the gentry agrarian principles for which he stands?[27]

On the one hand, this may be deliberate Tolstoyan iconoclasm, a desire to debunk or contradict established ideas simply because they are established. The contradictory character created by such a means would be no less engaging, and indeed, there is some evidence for seeing Levin's portrayal as deliberately complex in such a manner. He shows a consistent willingness to allow inconsistencies to enter his arguments, a trait that drives his brother batty. One might also look to the specific circumstances in which the idea is expressed: perhaps Levin is merely trying it on for size, perhaps he is simply appeasing his vacationing brother, or perhaps he is trying to end an argument that he has little taste for. He is impatient about getting back to the mowing, after all.

Here I explore a third explanation, one that resonates more fully through the work and its larger literary-historical context, namely, that Tolstoy, through his somewhat contradictory character, and in a somewhat iconoclastic manner, has offered up the concept of self-interest for scrutiny, especially in the face of the other usages just noted, that of capitalist apologists and the new radical ethics. This is where the concept of virtue in its historical context becomes important. The principle of self-interest espoused by Levin dovetails with certain other of his traits and ideas in the virtuous ideal dismissed by Gogol some thirty years before, the landowning nobleman whose unspecialized leisure enables him to cultivate virtue in his person, his family, and his political life. That Tolstoy does not present these traits in an immediately recognizable form has partly to do with the cultural history of the concept of virtue in Russia.

As noted earlier, the semantic whole once contained within *virtus,* especially in its civic humanist sense—as obedience to a moral standard, devotion to the public good, the establishment of conditions of equity between the governed and the governing, and the active civic life of the citizen[28]—was only poorly if at all rendered by the Russian word *dobrodetel',* which increasingly in the nineteenth century intimated a precious gentry etiquette that was less and less in step with contemporary society: it grew archaic and womanish at one and the same time. In contrast, the Roman and later Renaissance concept of *virtus,* like several of its senses in the English word *virtue,* emphasized the aspect of steadfastness, moral and physical, that could combat the world's changeability.

> The *baraka, mana,* or *charisma* (to use terms from other cultures) of the successful actor . . . consisted both in the quality of personality that commanded good fortune and in the quality that dealt effectively and nobly with whatever fortune might send; and the Roman term for this complex characteristic was *virtus.* Virtue and fortune—to Anglicize them—were regularly paired as opposites, and the heroic fortitude that withstood ill fortune passed into the active capacity that remolded circumstances to the actor's advantage and thence into the charismatic *felicitas* that mysteriously commanded good fortune. This opposition was frequently expressed in the image of a sexual relation: a masculine active intelligence was seeking to dominate a feminine passive unpredictability which would submissively reward him for his strength or vindictively betray him for his weakness. *Virtus* could therefore carry many of the connotations of virility, with which it is etymologically linked; *vir* means man.[29]

Precisely these "connotations of virility" are lacking in the Russian *dobrodetel',* which, ironically, in its overt associations with the erudition and gentility of aristocratic culture, came over time to suggest effeminacy. By contrast, the virtuous man is, like the Hercules of the Renaissance, an exemplum of moral fortitude and soulful steadfastness in the face of *fortuna.*

Tolstoy's usage in *Anna Karenina* is consistent with this historical picture. *Dobrodetel',* even when it is not explicitly associated with women (the majority of cases), connotes superficial gentility, absence of "heart," and lack of authenticity, as in Lydia Ivanovna's and Madame Stahl's philanthropic activities.[30] Moreover, the process of learning to be virtuous in this self-conscious and, for Tolstoy, inauthentic manner begins early: when little Tanya Oblonskaya gives up her dessert for Grisha, "the consciousness of her virtuous [*dobrodetel'nyi*] act" brings tears to her eyes (310). Here as elsewhere in Tolstoy's oeuvre, self-consciousness suggests falseness, even and perhaps especially in children as they are learning to act in social settings, as they come to terms with the routine phenomena of everyday life.

Kitty's association with Madame Stahl and Varenka introduces an extended treatment linking the questions of life's worth and worthiness that permeate the novel. What Kitty hopes to find in Varenka are the "interests of life, the dignity of life" (*interesov zhizni, dostoinstva zhizni*, 254). If the commercial overtones of such words seem dubious, Tolstoy's elaboration brings them into focus: Kitty wants those interests and values that are "outside of the social relations of men and women, which now seemed disgusting to [her], a shameful display of *goods before a buyer*" (254; emphasis added). The opposition is clear: Kitty's fascination with the authentically virtuous Varenka is motivated by a desire for independence from the exchange relations that have come to dominate social interaction, particularly in the commoditization of women.

The more Kitty observes her, the more convinced she is that Varenka is "that most whole being" (*samoe sovershennoe sushchestvo*, 254) she seems to be. Kitty wants to know where such "independent calm" (260) comes from and is especially impressed that Varenka was "utterly indifferent to praise" (260).[31] The reduction of an individual to a commodity with a price, as Kitty perceives the relations of men and women, is placed in direct opposition to the completed, integral, and independent being she sees in Varenka. The whole person is thus removed from an exchange relation represented as part of the new social environment; she is spared the subjection of humans to commodity speculation, to their treatment as acquisitions for the satisfaction of self-interested ambitions.

The opposition of completeness or wholeness (*sovershenstvo*) to a commercial partiality and dependency is not limited to the novel's treatment of the "woman question." It is interwoven, often metaphorically, with fundamental aspects of human worth amid changing social mores. With all of his morally fragmented nature, Oblonsky is perhaps the most astute judge of Levin's character in this regard: "You are yourself an integral character (*tsel'nyi kharakter*) and you want all of life to be composed of integral phenomena, but it isn't" (55). Just such integration lies at the heart of the virtuous ideal, which is ultimately a Socratic notion of living fullness, commitment, and purity—but also, and perhaps most importantly—independence, particularly from the growing norm of salaried bureaucratic functionalism.

The opposition of such living excellence to the moral corrosiveness that results from the application of exchange relations to human relations is clear in a number of the novel's key scenes. For instance, the crucial opening conversation between Oblonsky and Vronsky on the station platform puts men and women into commercial intercourse in none too subtle a sense. With the frame of the train's approach, the two men discuss Levin's supposed proposal to Kitty of the evening before, and Vronsky, his chest swelling from the knowledge that she has turned Levin down on his account, shifts the conversation in a telling direction, translating the entire affair into a hypothetical encounter with a prostitute:

> I think she can count on a better match [*rasschityvat' na luchshuiu partiiu*] . . . Yes, it's a difficult position. Instead of that sort of thing most prefer women of the demi-monde [*znat'sia s Klarami*]. Failure there simply means one doesn't have enough money, but here—one's dignity is on the line [*dostoinstvo na vesakh*]. But here's the train. (75)

Vronsky's sense of personal self-worth shines through here by means of a contrast to the buying and selling of sex. Moreover, he does not limit calculation, which amounts to a cost-benefit analysis, to himself and Levin; Kitty does likewise, he intimates, when she "counts on" a better match. The crudeness of the exchange—replete with risk, gain, and worthiness (dignity, *dostoinstvo*) being weighed on a scale—comes across when one considers that an alternative to the kind of human interaction that Vronsky believes he, Levin, and Kitty have just been a party to would be sex for money.

This suggestion of marriage, or at least the relations of men and women in preparation for marriage, as a form of legalized buying and selling of sex, is an early form of the radical stance Tolstoy would take in the 1880s and of a later narrative treatment like that of "Kreutzer Sonata." In *Anna Karenina*, however, there still appears a contrast to be drawn between inauthentic interaction as a form of exchange relations, on the one hand, and non-exchange-oriented intimacy, authentic feeling, "the real thing," on the other. Thus we find the crude equivalence of marriage and a commoditized relationship suggested in the letter Karenin sends to Anna demanding her return to their St. Petersburg home after she has confessed her love of Vronsky. In effect, the letter's contents demonstrate the falseness of the Karenins' intimacy by highlighting its basis in exchange relations.

The letter arrives in the hands of a courier as the household is in a flum-mox over preparations for a sudden departure for Moscow, announced by Anna that morning to her servants. "'Very well,' she said, and as soon as the man went out, she tore open the letter with trembling fingers. *A wad of unfolded bank notes in a sealed wrapper fell out of it*" (343; emphasis added). This is the fourth time to which this particular money "for her expenses" has been referred, and the second time Tolstoy has managed to arrange for Karenin to humiliate Anna by rubbing her nose in it. It is on the day of the races (the fifteenth of the month) and in Karenin's thoughts that it makes its first appearance, an apparent excuse amid Karenin's apparent clarity of mind (239). Next he announces to Anna, in Betsy's presence, "I also came to bring you money, since nightingales aren't fed on fables. . . . You need it, I suppose." She initially says no, but then acknowledges that in fact she does, "blushing to the roots of her hair" (243). Then comes Karenin's point of pride, the strategically nonchalant postscript to his letter: "Enclosed is the money you may need for your expenses" (334)—the same money nearly eighty pages after its previous appearance, which finally falls from the letter she reads as a crass wad of unfolded notes another half dozen pages later. In between, she blushes once again in reflecting on her position, and "a hot flush of shame [pours] over her face," while it occurs to her that "the accountant would now come to turn her out of the house" (338), the accountant being apparently the lowliest individual she can imagine who might be entrusted with such a duty.

An equally if not more striking dramatization of intimacy as mediated by exchange relations is enacted by Anna and Vronsky, in their immediately postclimactic encounter, the notorious lover-as-murderer simile.

> There was something horrible and repulsive in the memory of *what had been paid for with this terrible price of shame [za chto bylo zaplacheno etoiu strashnoiu tsenoi styda]*. Shame in the face of her spiritual nakedness pressed down on her and communicated itself to him. But, despite all of the murderer's horror before the body of his victim, he must cut it into pieces, hide it, use that which he has gained by murdering.
>
> And with bitterness, as if in a passion, he throws himself on the body, drags it, and hacks it; so Vronsky covered her face and shoulders with kisses. She held his hand and didn't move. Yes, those kisses—that was *what had been purchased with shame*. (*to, chto kupleno etim stydom*, 178; empha-sis added)

Here Tolstoy has framed the more striking comparison within one that may seem unconscious or accidental by contrast, especially to modern readers.

We are so used to living in a world so thoroughly permeated by commercial concepts that it is easy to dismiss such language. Given the degree to which issues of modernization function thematically in Tolstoy's book, this would be a shallow reading.

The most important statement of the fortune theme, however, its linkage to the fate of the country and global notions of value and change, is contained in the railroad. The symbolic, consensually fantastical values of the commercial world are preparing, largely with the promises of foreign finance capital, to lay tracks at Levin's doorstep, suggesting that his desire for "integral phenomena," as Oblonsky terms it, springs ultimately from the same source as Kitty's for "completeness." The specific forms of Levin's search are, however, quite different. Two stand out.

First is Levin's proposed study of the agricultural laborer, whose character, he claims, should be "taken as an absolute given, like climate and soil," so that to climate and soil data would be added the "certain, unchanging character (*izvestnyi neizmennyi kharakter*) of the laborer" (181). The notion of a worker's character as an absolute given, like climate or soil, contrasts the fluidity of contemporary bureaucratic, financial, social, and moral affairs as depicted up to this point in the book—for instance, in Stiva's paper officialdom at the office, Stiva and Dolly's marital life, the choosing of a suitor for Kitty, the uncertainties of medicine and doctors, and the depiction of Karenin's and Anna's loss of footing in the immediately preceding scenes. Levin, of course, does not have in mind a particular laborer but an abstraction. Such is the only manner—without the kind of ignorant simplification of the peasantry for which Koznyshev is implicitly criticized—by which one might arrive at the notion of the laborer's character as certain and unchanging. The supposition of the worker's unchanging nature, moreover, in a society rapidly transforming, largely under the influence of Western-oriented modernizing trends, is in no way a given aspect of 1870s Russia, a fact that Tolstoy's treatment makes evident elsewhere, particularly through Anna and Vronsky's dream of the French-speaking peasant. This, then, I would suggest, is yet another of the many "linkages" that Tolstoy suggested run throughout his text:[32] the notion of changing social mores—from Princess Shcherbatsky's troubles in negotiating the newfangled practice of nonarranged marriages to the use of birth control techniques and the railroad-facilitated uprooting and dislocation of the peasantry—is associated with the growing role of fortune, especially with its large-scale commercial associations, in the contemporary world.

The second occurs in the course of the same conversation between Levin and Koznyshev with which I began. The ability to act in the service of the public good, Levin thinks, "may not be a quality but actually a lack of something—not of good, honest, noble desires and tastes—but of force of life [*sila zhizni*], that which they call heart, the yearning [*stremlenie*] that makes a man choose one road out of all the possible ones and desire only that" (282).[33] Somewhat like his notion of the unchanging character of the laborer, though in a more heroic manner, Levin appears to have in mind a kind of constancy and purity of action, perhaps under difficult conditions in the face of the world's changing circumstances. He appears to associate it with personal over public interest, and he suggests that its connection to elemental force, power, and desire for life make it a positive character trait. This has all the markings of the Ancient Greek concept of *thumos*,[34] or "spiritedness," and Levin's attempt to zero in on a character trait whose absence might account for a tendency toward devoting oneself to the service of others suggests, on the one hand, a remarkable psychological self-characterization, but also, on the other, a response to the question of how self-interest might be considered in a positive light.

In terms of the representation of the character's thoughts and emotional life, his suggestion is consistent with a tendency to see himself as slightly unworthy, yet to be overly sensitive about this at the same time. Overbalanced toward emotion rather than intellect or erotic love, Levin appears to be identifying his own tendency toward thumotic anger and physicality as a positive trait, especially compared to his brother's logocentrism and Stiva Oblonsky's eroticism. On the social side, a self-interested, thumotic impulse is suggested here as that thing which centers a man and gives him purpose. To revert to a previous formulation, it tosses him an anchor or a raft amid the sea of life. To make it the sea of *modern* life, we need our woman in her window once more.

He came out of the meadow and headed down the main road toward the village. A slight breeze rose up, and it became gray, cloudy. There was a gloomy moment, the kind that usually precedes the dawn, the victory of light over darkness.

Hunching up from the cold, Levin walked quickly, his eyes on the ground. "What's that? Someone's coming," he thought, at the sound of bells, and raised his head. Forty paces away, headed toward him on the same wide, grassy road down which he was walking came a carriage-and-four with leather trunks on top. The shaft horses were pressing away from the ruts, toward the shafts, but the skillful coachman, sitting crossways on the box, guided the shafts along the ruts so the wheels would run on the flat ground.

Levin noticed only that much and, without wondering who might be traveling, glanced absentmindedly inside the carriage.

An old woman dozed in the corner, and, at the window, apparently just having woken up, sat a young woman, the ribbons of her white bonnet gripped with both hands. Bright and thoughtful, filled completely with a delicate and complex inner life to which Levin was a stranger, she looked past him toward the glowing sunrise.

At the very moment when that vision was about to disappear, the honest eyes glanced at him. She recognized him, and her face lit up with joyful surprise.

He could not have been mistaken. Those were the only eyes in the world like that. That was the only being in the world capable of concentrating for him all the light and meaning of life. It was she. It was Kitty. He realized she was on her way to Yergushovo from the train station. And all that had been troubling Levin during that sleepless night, all the decisions he had made, all that was suddenly gone. He recalled with disgust his dreams of marrying a peasant woman. Only there, in that carriage moving quickly away and crossing to the other side of the road, only there was the possibility of resolving the riddles of his life that had so painfully afflicted him of late.

She did not look out again. The sound of the springs could no longer be heard, the bells grew nearly inaudible. The barking of dogs indicated that the carriage had passed off through the village—and all around there remained the empty fields, the village ahead, and he himself, alone and distant from it all, making his way alone down the wide, deserted road. (325–326)

The passage has a lyrical arc with a marked orchestral punctuation at the dual phrases, "It was she. It was Kitty." The scene resonates, moreover, with the earlier-invoked man-on-his-road passage from Gogol's *Dead Souls*, where a man's vision (the same word, *videnie*) of a woman appears suddenly and just as suddenly vanishes, leaving the hero stunned amid the empty fields. In Gogol's work it is the narrator who takes the next step to wonder about the vision's meaning; in Tolstoy's the experience is filtered through the hero's point of view. In either case, the vision serves as an impetus to a certain kind of action and is channeled into the hero's "force of life."

In Tolstoy's works, however, getting the girl is never an appropriate end for such a driving impulse. Levin continues to struggle with the proper end of his own life energy even—and perhaps especially—*after* his marriage and the apparent filling out of his domestic life. This problem, faced at a later stage in life by Levin, is faced at an earlier one by Andrey Bolkonsky in

War and Peace, who appears in the early pages of the novel bored out of his wits by domesticity and primed for a leap into a life of heroic, Napoleonic, warrior-based glory. Levin, as Bolkonsky before him, is in effect faced with the problem of bourgeois happiness, which of course is only a problem when the driving impulse of the male protagonist is essentially heroic in nature. Such a character is faced with the question, "Is this all that I am good for?" We in turn can understand this clearly now as, "Is this all that the virtuous, manly ideal amounts to?" The domestic sphere casts its dark shadow over the hero, who is threatened with the mundane details of an essentially procreative and therefore "un-heroic" household.

Levin and Vronsky are threatened with the power of the domestic sphere both at once, and their responses, as the diagram below demonstrates, are systematically contrasted. Tolstoy's treatment of the problem follows historical precedent, as the depiction of the dual male protagonists, Vronsky and Levin, suggests a turn to either politics or sports as a way of exercising the heroic ethos that the domestic sphere would turn to flab. And, as in the case of the inauthentic in love, a healthy marriage remains distinctly possible at this point in Tolstoy's imaginative life: it is indicated through the appropriate reactions of Kitty to her husband's absence, by contrast to the imbalanced and manipulative behavior of Anna. Squarely between the two, indeed, the medium that connects them in this part of the novel, if not the work as a whole,[35] is Dolly Oblonsky and her household, arguably the center of unheroic, mundane, procreative family existence. The ideal of Dolly—for she is idealized, by Levin, and by Tolstoy as well—is remarkable for its dependency. By contrast to what Kitty admires in Varenka, Dolly's way of life, perhaps because it is that of her sister, appears all too familiar. It can certainly function as a truth hidden "in plain view," as Gary Saul Morson has argued, but it does not turn out to be productive for any character in the novel other than Kitty. Anna has seen that life, lived it to some extent, but left it behind. Levin sees it only from the outside and can never truly adopt it. He is a manly man.

Tolstoy's woman-in-the-window scene is thus developed for his main male character: it can motivate him, give meaning to his existence, at least for the moment, and direct his "force of life." Its framing, moreover, suggests a deeper interrogation of the trope than this single instance might otherwise suggest. Having made his decision to marry a peasant woman and start a new life, Levin looks up to the sky and finds his thoughts reflected in a beautiful mother-of-pearl cloud formation that has appeared when he was not looking; just after his vision of Kitty, he looks again to the sky and finds that the shell that seemed to agree with him is gone.

Part V

First 50 pages   (Moscow)
(True family)

**Levin & Kitty
family life**   Kitty's
pregnancy

"Shcherbatsky element"
Koznyshev
Varenka

Arrival of Oblonsky,
Veslovsky
(Society)

Veslovsky introduces impurity
into Levin home, with it the topic
of Anna. Attempted flirtation
with Kitty. Jealousy of L.

Veslovsky relocates

Levin departs for "natural," "manly"
hunting expedition

Dolly's visit serves as a transition

and as a representation of genuine
family happiness from Levin household

Levin away from
home

Levin's departure marked
by his obvious reluctance
to leave his wife

Levin's act of generosity in giving
Dolly the carriage and horses

but she suggests that
he go, knowing he was
bored at home

Oblonsky advises Levin to
assert his independence

Levin receives note from Kitty telling
him everything's fine and that he
may stay another day if he likes.

Levin ———— meets —
is baffled by elections
and is inept at them

Figure 5. Sports versus Politics.

Second 50 pages

(St. Petersburg)
(Society—convention)

Anna & Vronsky family life

purposeful absence
of pregnancy

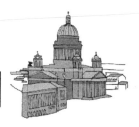

Princess Barbara
Tushkevich (Sviazhsky)

Veslovsky is completely
accepted; begins
flirtation with Anna

↓

Veslovsky

Absense of jealousy
on V's part.

Vronsky departs
for elections

Vronsky away from
home

The reported stinginess of
Vronsky in feeding Levin's
horses before Dolly's return

Vronsky's departure marked
by Anna's obvious wish for
him not to leave and by clear
conflict between them.

Vronsky reasons to himself
that he must demonstrate his
independence.

Vronsky receives note from
Anna with reproach for his
being one day late.

——————— Vronsky
finds himself perfectly at ease
and is skilled at them

There, in the unattainable height, a mysterious change had taken place. No trace of the shell was left, but spread over half the sky was an even carpet of fleecy clouds growing smaller and smaller. The sky turned blue and shining, and with the same tenderness, yet also with the same unattainability, it returned his questioning look.

"No," he said to himself, "no matter how good that simple life of labor may be, I can't go back to it. I love *her*." (326)

Careful readers of Tolstoy's fiction will recall an equally magical and dubious encounter between one of his main heroic exemplars and the natural world—Prince Andrey and the oak in *War and Peace*.[36] A detailed comparison is not necessary. I merely wish to point out the similarity of pattern, where the hero's encounter with the woman in the window is framed by an attempt by him to find corroboration for the general course of his life in some aspect of nature, which is obviously in flux. In both cases, the initial appearance of corroboration and the resulting certainty yields to a sense of dubious excitement about the potential ahead, and in both cases the core of the shift in the character's thinking is found in the trope in question. The only sure thing for him is her image.

The invocation of the woman in the window at this moment of *Anna Karenina*—a mere twenty pages after Levin's conversation with Koznyshev regarding self-interest as the basis for human well-being—makes clear the suggestion of masculine centering and the redirection of the masculine heroic tradition to which the trope is connected. Viewed from a different perspective, the scene provides an answer to Kitty's search for a nonexchange relationship, one based on something other than the "newfangled" wares-on-sale approach to fostering intimacy among marriage-aged young people that she and her family have found so difficult to adopt.

Tolstoy's novel resists schematic summaries, especially through the depth and richness of its characters.[37] But the opposition of a thumos-inspired virtue to the contemporary world's fickleness brings many of its stark dichotomies into focus. On one side lies a wholeness of character that renders one independent, capable of coping with the world's uncertainties. On the other lies changeability as such and the various dependencies on which people build facades of security to support themselves until "real life" causes a collapse. The shift from landed (virtuous) to symbolic (virtual) conceptions of property afforded a wealth of such flimsy certainties to Tolstoy's readers. It would continue to do so for several generations to come.

four

Lara, Lolita, and Other Things that Start with *L*

But if it were given to man to gaze on beauty's very self—unsullied, unalloyed, and freed from the mortal taint that haunts the frailer loveliness of flesh and blood—if, I say, it were given to man to see the heavenly beauty face to face, would you call his, she asked me, an unenviable life, whose eyes had been opened to the vision, and who had gazed upon it in true contemplation until it had become his own forever?

—Plato, *Symposium* [1]

Love passed, the Muse appeared . . .

—Pushkin, *Eugene Onegin* [2]

L is for the way he looks at her. The grammar is not accidental. At her: she does not need to look back or even know he is looking. Of course, it can be a terrible thing, that object, predicate, subject complement, but nor is inspiration to be easily dismissed. I issue myself an orange alert to tread lightly here. Potential pitfalls abound, far too many for any one person to ever see—I am trying to be one person, let's not forget. This is the crossroads between inspiration and titillation, sacred and secular, art and manipulation. These are the stakes. I might as well set them out from the start.

To be honest, I am a little blinded by the two lights I've brought with me. They are incomparable, except perhaps with each other. That claim will probably surprise some and I'll get to it, but first things first. It is not what she looks like: I've already said the light is too bright to see clearly, and anyway wouldn't that be just too predictable of a certain aged white male, *l'homme moyen sensuel*, rounding about the middle as he looks for some accordant

buoyancy, anything more uplifting than the mere words that have hitherto
kept him afloat? I was not aware when I began this project that man in crisis
would be so central to it. Not human in crisis, man. If it turns out predictable
that I should be implicated in that discovery because of my age and gender, so
be it. It is something I'm going to live with. Perhaps that too is why it doesn't
matter what she looks like.

The crisis of male middle age is a thin veneer atop the masculinity in crisis I have in mind, the crisis inaugurated by the decline of the heroic ethic
amid the spread of the commercial one that I have been tracing in this book.
It is something more than what Deirdre McCloskey has grouped under the
title "anachronistic courage," by which she seems to mean the stiff upper lip
of British officers in World War I and the later John Wayne ethos of American popular culture.[3] That is a kind of epigonal nineteenth-century (or, if
you like, Homeric) aristocratism whose peak she identifies with the Greatest
Generation's postwar experience, the extended homecoming of the 1950s. Perhaps it isn't at all out of place in my comments that her primary example of
such an ethos in action was the Russian-born Harvard economist Alexander
Gerschenkron. In McCloskey's idiom, "Gerschenkron was, as we say, quite a
guy."[4] He was also of the same generation and class as the two Russian male
authors invoked in this chapter.

In McCloskey's contrast of taciturn masculine courage and feminine
words (223–230), surely she has neglected the distinction between words and
voice that would have been so immediately apparent to the men and women
of that generation of revolutionary upheaval. Just as surely she is correct in
asserting that the silent tough guy is a gendered cultural type often contrasted
to the empty wordiness of women, but her emphasis on this point tends to
eclipse the equally important fact that acquiring a voice, and words with it,
has a long-standing political association with power, particularly subaltern
power. Thus when Maxim Gorky's Mother comes at last to political self-consciousness at the end of his novel of that name, she starts talking, and she
talks so much that a soldier has to strangle her to shut her up.[5] In other words,
she, like so many others of her time, acquires words when she comes to political understanding, and her words are associated with revolutionary force,
not feminine blather. It would be quite a stretch to say that the man kills her
because he cannot stand the racket. Talking such that a soldier must silence
one is integral to the generational experience of men like Gerschenkron, and
I would say, Pasternak and Nabokov, too. It is a value McCloskey does not
credit enough, I think, and it is central to the something more in the search
for masculine character whose outlines I am tracing here.[6]

McCloskey wants to argue, among other things, for well-timed, phronetic efficacy in place of the kind of manly confrontationalism that makes courage an all-or-nothing necessity.[7] Like most strict dichotomies, this is only a helpful starting place. The ideal extremes she has identified make the more commonly crossed middle seem obscure by contrast. In practice it is not obscure at all. On the contrary, common ground is both very well lit and where all the most interesting work takes place. Neither battlefield nor cloister, common ground is both fantastically powerful and delicately changeable. We give it the solid name of ground because, like the vast array of symbolic value that undergirds modern life, it is not in fact solid. It is the space where words meet other words, and the life of consensual fantasy transforms and gives shape to the world in which we live. How the urge to maintain a single face inside it remains one of the most consistent and powerful cultural responses is something I hope this chapter will make clear.

McCloskey's account of the bourgeois virtues, moreover—or the virtue of being bourgeois, for these are bound up together in one and the same econo-moral argument—relies on instrumentalist presumptions so profound that they find no articulation in her work. It is not just that the account is for something else, or the various kinds of behavior described in it are presented as the means to achieving something else. The presumptions I have in mind are prior to these. They are tied to the discovery or invention of modernity; they give birth to or arise with it; they envision it as a mise-en-scene of inert materials to be acted upon, linked together or disassembled, created or destroyed in our image or some image we have devised for our purposes. The vision is secular humanist and late modern and contemporary. It characterizes, moreover, the hypermodernity of both Soviet and American cultures of the early twentieth century, the extension of instrumentality from things to persons to the earth itself, and the intensification of modern conditions that creates the necessity for now-familiar repair concepts like therapy and empathy.[8] Like the commercial metaphor inside which Tolstoy implicitly equates adulterous sex with murder in *Anna Karenina*,[9] such instrumentalist presumptions are likely to slip by without comment, indeed, without notice. They have become assimilated to the bulk of our interactions. They often blend in.

The heroic ethos stands largely in opposition to such a trend. Its historical precedence makes it difficult to call it a repair concept, but its various incarnations, and the ingenious means by which it has managed to make and remake itself, up to and including in the present day (one need only think of popular science fiction, fantasy, or video games), indicate its continuing importance, perhaps psychological, clearly artistic and cultural. The degree to which man thus envisioned—as heroic masculine character—can continue to be depicted as finding all-encompassing meaning and inspiration by Framed Woman, is indeed remarkable in an age so otherwise thoroughly imbued with the virtue of prudence. This is not to say that the tropic relationships have remained stable. As other moments in this study have shown, heroic masculine character is in flux through the nineteenth and twentieth centuries. He may still look at Her. But what he sees and what he does as a result no longer resonate within the heroic mode of old. That music has long since become largely atonal and fragmentary.

Lolita and Doctor Zhivago may, I am aware, appear an odd couple to use for illustrating this point, especially together, and from the outset I have my doubts about being able to pull it off. But my lights are here, shining bright. I hope it is no mere conceit of male middle age to think that among the paths they illuminate is one well suited to my purpose.

Two Books, Four Movies

Published within two years of each other in the mid-1950s, Lolita and Doctor Zhivago were both written by Russian authors, one in Russian, one in English, on either side of the Atlantic.[10] Both had troubled publication histories and were surrounded by scandal. Both transformed the lives of their authors.[11] And both stand as central markers of domestic and international cultural politics of the Cold War. Both in turn were adapted to the screen by major film directors, Stanley Kubrick and David Lean, respectively, in the 1960s, with smaller-budget remakes appearing in the post–Cold War 1990s and early 2000s.

Such similarities are probably not enough to throw a pedophile and a poet together. Let us leave that for later. For now it is enough to reconsider the work of their respective fictional lives. While both books begin with a portrait of the artist—ten-year-old Yury's observation of his mother's funeral, Humbert Humbert's recounting of his pivotal erotic encounter at the age of thirteen (between ten and thirteen one senses the great fulcrum)[12]—both books end with the art itself, Yury's poems, Humbert's revelation of the work we have just read as an artistic monument:

> That husband of yours, I hope, will always treat you well, because otherwise my specter shall come at him, like black smoke, like a demented giant, and pull him apart nerve by nerve. And do not pity C. Q. One had to choose between him and H. H., and one wanted H. H. to exist at least a couple

Figure 6. The Refuge of Art. *Lolita,* dir. Kubrick, 1962.

of months longer, so as to have him make you live in the minds of later generations. I am thinking of aurochs and angels, the secret of durable pigments, prophetic sonnets, the refuge of art. And this is the only immortality you and I may share, my Lolita.[13]

She is dead at this point in the story, of course, a stipulation of H. H.'s confession being made public. It was a text for others from the start, a remembrance in durable pigments. A remembrance of what exactly—love, guilt, perversity, sickness—isn't the issue, not yet. Lara too is dead when Yury's poems about her become known to the world, just as both male characters have died by then as well, of heart failure no less.

    Kubrick is most blatant in making the theme of artistic refuge central to his adaptation. In the closing moments of his film, he has Humbert Humbert fire his revolver at Claire Quilty through a painting of a woman, apparently the same portrait lying on its side at the entrance to Pavor Manor, Quilty's cavernous mansion, as H. H. makes his way through the debris of Western culture to commit his murder.[14] The bullets rip through the canvas on which the woman is represented, beginning at the bottom and making their way up the portrait to end with her face. Quilty is sprawled on the other side, his groans audible as the bullets, having passed through the painting, presumably enter his body off camera. The scene ends with a lingering full screen of the pictured woman's face and the holes through the painting that could not protect him. So much for the refuge of art.

The setting does two things well. First, it cleverly translates H. H.'s invocation of artistic refuge at the close of his literary confession by employing other, highly filmable, objects—two portraits of a woman, one leaning, the other displayed in a room full of bric-a-brac and assorted art pieces. Second, it pronounces judgment on that invocation through the room's apparent disorder and association with the moral-free aesthete Quilty, and, most effectively, by having Humbert Humbert shoot holes through the woman's face, laying waste to the art as a simple by-product of his drunken, jealous rage. It is a sweeping gesture on Kubrick's part. In effect, he offers up the refuge-of-art line and then unveils the monstrosity that such an enterprise can become, a move that accords with the basic antihumanist thrust of his darker film oeuvre, from *A Clockwork Orange* to *Full Metal Jacket* and *Eyes Wide Shut*.

In Kubrick's version, however, H. H. destroys the woman in the window a little too definitively. The proviso needs clarity: this is James B. Harris's and Stanley Kubrick's *Lolita*.[15] Nabokov's endings, to both the novel and the screenplay he created on its basis, leave room for doubt as to the murderer's intent, let alone the author's, in invoking artistic refuge, which is, of course, more in keeping with both the author and the character he has created, arch-trixters *tous les deux*. Some scholars have even argued that the entire last section of the book, in which H. H. reunites with Lolita and tracks down and murders Quilty, should be read as imaginary, a form of authorial sleight of hand, up to and including H. H.'s receipt of her letter.[16] Kubrick appears to gesture toward such an interpretation when he breaks the narrative to introduce the close-up of a typewriter in action—invention momentarily eclipsing mimesis. This move suggests something of the subtle complexity of Nabokov's depiction, but only something of it.

Plenty of readers have understood the final pages of *Lolita* as demonstrating a real change in the character of its narrator, who, at the very least, seems to lament the loss of a child's voice. That, however, is about as much as we can say when he remarks,

> Reader! What I heard was but the melody of children at play, nothing but that, and so limpid was the air that within this vapor of blended voices, majestic and minute, remote and magically near, frank and divinely enigmatic—one could hear now and then, as if released, an almost articulate spurt of vivid laughter, or the crack of a bat, or the clatter of a toy wagon,

but it was all really too far for the eye to distinguish any movement in the lightly etched streets. I stood listening to that musical vibration from my lofty slope, to those flashes of separate cries with a kind of demure murmur for background, and then I knew that the hopelessly poignant thing was not Lolita's absence from my side, but the absence of her voice from that concord. (308)

Read by Jeremy Irons, as in the Adrian Lyne film adaptation of 1997, or the more recent Random House "books on tape" version of the novel, this passage is as lyrical as can be, poignant and regretful, but also fundamentally one-sided in the most un-Nabokovian manner imaginable. What has happened in such adaptations is something akin to the inevitable choice a translator might make in the face of a pun that works in the source language but not in the target. Part is all you can manage, a narrowing occurs, and the multiplicity of readings that an audience might bring to it gets reduced to one.

Sensitivity to audience, which is present throughout the narrative but especially prominent in hortative passages like this, makes rhetorical concerns essential. This is speech intended to move. As such, a little skepticism is not at all out of place since by now we have some sense of the speaker's shifty ethos. What exactly is the sensation he describes? It could be simple nostalgia for all we know, rather than the regret, let alone remorse, we might like him to be experiencing. Perhaps he is merely sorry she's not a child anymore.[17] On the other hand, this summing up is laden enough with pathos to accommodate remorse too, especially with a narrator as aware as this one—he seems to be missing something after all. Read in this way, his account could be seen as pulling no punches with regard to his own brutality and culpability toward Delores Haze: he knows what he has done and is sorry for it. Moreover, despite Kubrick's apparent dismissal, the possibility of artistic refuge is real in Nabokov's oeuvre, even when it is perverse. Nabokov's fictional world is, moreover, undeniably muse-centered, and traces of that world are evident even in the distorted and morally ugly form that the novel *Lolita* unveils.[18]

The possibility of art as refuge in Nabokov, however, is a thin shadow of its bulk in Pasternak. The argument needs to be explicitly made in the former, while in the latter it seems self-evident.[19] Calling art mere refuge is in fact saying far too little for its role in Pasternak's life and work, in *Doctor Zhivago* above all. "Where shall I put my joy?" is the typically momentary revelation of the splendor of being alive that Pasternak believed could be raised by the artist to "a constant poetic symptom."[20] Art is a celebration of living in all its authentic mundane detail, an invitation to "wake up and see afresh."[21] It is also a response to suffering, particularly feminine suffering. This peculiar mix of symbolist impulse (art as a response to suffering) and modernist motivation (art as a way of overturning conventional perceptions of the world) is, for Pasternak, "not the name of a category, not an aspect of form, but a hidden mysterious *part of the content* [of life]."²² The content of Pasternak's envisioned world is mysteriously artistic. The manner in which it links the most disparate things provides a key to the many, often striking figurative connections in his writing. Such, in fact, are the sutures that bind together a vision of the magical, green world that Yury Zhivago constantly witnesses around him.

> All the flowers smelled at once; it was as if the earth, unconscious all day long, were now waking to their fragrance. And from the Countess's centuries-old garden, so littered with fallen branches that it was impenetrable, the dusty aroma of old linden trees coming into bloom drifted in a huge wave as tall as a house.
>
> Noises came from the street beyond the fences on the right—snatches of a song, a drunken soldier, doors banging.
>
> An enormous crimson moon rose behind the crows' nests in the Countess's garden. At first it was the color of the new brick mill in Zybushino, then it turned yellow like the water tower at Biriuchi.
>
> And just under the window, the smell of new-mown hay, as perfumed as jasmine tea, mixed with that of belladonna. Below that a cow was tethered; she had been brought from a distant village, she had walked all day, she was tired and homesick for the herd and would not yet accept food from her new mistress.
>
> "Now, now, whoa there, I'll show you how to butt," her mistress coaxed her in a whisper, but the cow crossly shook her head and craned her neck, mooing plaintively, and beyond the black barns of Melyuzeyevo the stars twinkled, and invisible threads of sympathy stretched between them and the cow as if there were cattle sheds in other worlds where she was pitied.
>
> Everything was fermenting, growing, rising with the magic yeast of life. The joy of living, like a gentle wind, swept in a broad surge indiscriminately through fields and towns, through walls and fences, through wood and flesh. Not to be overwhelmed by this tidal wave, Yury Andreyevich went out to the square to listen to the speeches. (140–41)

The lyricism of this passage, or the many others like it in the book, is not mere celebratory song. Nor is it a safe capturing of landscape for consumption by a bourgeois readership. The world around Zhivago is being obliterated in sheer marvels of senseless destruction. His observations constitute acts of creation, a countermeasure of sorts that Pasternak's character, at this moment in the narrative, mistakenly associates with the revolution. He learns better.

What he learns is already implicit in this passage, which contains a contrast between, on the one hand, the artistic observation of the ordinary as an inspired creative act, an act that gives meaning and fullness to life and, on the other, the directed political activity of revolution, which curtails such fullness. In effect, the call to create a better life, like the speeches that subdue the tidal wave of emotion building in Zhivago, are countered by unassuming life itself, often some marvelously obscure corner of it observed inopportunely, undramatically. Countless times in the book, Zhivago, whose name, it should be remembered, derives from the Russian root word for life,[23] observes the mundane and soars—so much so that his responses, by any ordinary standard, sometimes seem ill-placed. Amid the dismembered corpses of the dissecting room, he finds the human body beautiful "even in its smallest sections." He senses wonder in the continuing connection between the body of "some water nymph brutally flung onto a zinc table," a drowning victim, and "her amputated arm or hand." His observation infuses the dead space between the body and its appendage with life.

This creative act of filling the apparently empty, unifying the apparently disparate, is the most important thing Zhivago does in the book, his principal virtue. It is also likely the most difficult trait to capture cinematically, especially in the nondramatic guise Pasternak gives it. Shots of Omar Sharif's eyes or the sounds of Maurice Jarre's swelling score do not quite manage it; in fact, they have the opposite effect, turning the ordinary revelations into something too special. These are not revelations or climactic moments. Pasternak consistently deflates climaxes in his storytelling, defusing nearly every potentially explosive encounter in the book by skipping them all and informing his readers of what happened "back there" in some subsequent passage. When, for instance, at the climactic parting between Zhivago and Lara after Komarovsky has reappeared at their Varykino hideaway, readers might reasonably be expecting to witness a dramatic scene. But Pasternak provides nothing of the kind—the entire passage leading up to the parting is made up of dialogue between Zhivago and Komarovsky, with no description of any kind and no interaction between the lovers. One chapter ends on Komarovsky's words, "Would you like some? I've got enough"; and the next begins with Zhivago's lament to himself, "What have I done? What have I done?" Other important moments are similarly skipped, as when Yevgraf saves the starving Gromekos and Zhivagos by showing up at their Moscow home to provide much-needed supplies and information, or when Zhivago comes face to face with Lara at her Yuryatin apartment after his escape from the Partisans. Neither scene is

Figure 7. The "constant poetic symptom." *Doctor Zhivago,* dir. Lean, 1965.

actually shown. It might be possible to explain these moments of deflated drama as a by-product of limited third-person narration—Zhivago is unconscious during the latter two—were it not for the fact that Pasternak's book employs a variety of points of view and is not limited consistently to that of his main hero. He could have approached these momentous meetings and partings differently but chose not to. According to the convention-bound creative writing industry of contemporary letters, this is simply bad storytelling, the mark of an immature writer, someone who knows how to lead up to the set piece but shies away from delivering it.[24]

That would be a weak reading of Pasternak, whose hyper-Tolstoyan technique unfortunately makes his book appear inferiorly constructed: dramatic climax, like a story that ends with a marriage or a death, or like a plot without extraneous details and only the characters you need to remember, is always contrived, always artificial. Conventional storytelling might make for good stories, but it makes for unlikely lives. *Pace* David Lean and Paul Bowles, who provided Lean's screenplay, *Doctor Zhivago* is an experimental modernist novel, not a romance. This is why passionate observation, the hero's "constant poetic symptom"—rather than the trite courageous struggle to find love against the backdrop of war and revolution—should be seen as the hero's chief virtue. Even the apparently conscious composition of the poems he leaves behind is something he suffers rather than calls forth. They come to him, overwhelm him, and he merely directs the flow. I shall return to this theme of artistic inspiration below. Here it is worth remembering that the two films in question attempt different things, Lean by making the book of poems the central organizing feature of his work, Giacomo Campiotti, director of the more recent BBC production, by making Yury's poetry his first and most consistent defining trait, the apparent purpose of his life, with Lara a close second and his obvious muse. Both miss the point, but neither because of any limitation of medium or technique.

The problem is interpretive. The desire to see the story as being primarily about a cosmically fated love turns the novel's genre inside out, making Zhivago's life into something of a tool for the realization of romance, or perhaps for the creation of the Lara poems. If that is what one claims the story is mostly about, then who can blame contemporary readers, many of whom have been primed with reminiscences (those of their parents and grandparents usually) of a great love narrative if they see the character as a failure, or at least of questionable moral fiber? If this is about a man and a woman attempting to find happiness in the midst of war and revolution, the man may be a tragic testament to the revolution's fundamental inhumanity, but he falls short of being a worthy hero. He lacks the virtuous constancy of purpose it requires, especially in his passionate loves for different women at different times.

Women in Windows

Such constancy is not a failing of Nabokov's hero, though some readers will surely see this as an objectionable manner of characterizing Humbert Humbert's attachment and motivation. Nevertheless, Nabokov clearly suggests such a line as he too, like so many before him, invokes the recuperative trope of the woman in the window, albeit with characteristic circumspection, and filtered through several layers of narrative fog, when H. H. recounts in his diary the following:

> Dorsal view. Glimpse of shiny skin between T-shirt and white gym shorts. Bending, over a window sill, in the act of tearing off leaves from a poplar outside while engrossed in torrential talk with a newspaper boy below (Kenneth Knight, I suspect) who had just propelled the Ramsdale *Journal* with a very precise thud onto the porch. (54)

In the window she is, and H. H. is the one seeing her there. But his view is backward, skewed. As he puts it later in the same passage, "I seemed to see her through the wrong end of a telescope" (54). Lest we slip too quickly into symbolic readings, Knight, it turns out, is a classmate. He never enters the narrative again (except in the list that makes it clear he is in Lo's school). H. H. may really think he is standing down there, so the self-conscious manipulation of the trope is probably V. N.'s alone rather than his character's. More important, however, is the deformation of the heroic vision that the scene suggests: the inspiring image is uncannily distant, just as the inspiration linked to it is morally ugly. But it is still a vision rooted in the heroic: here is the woman in the window, though she is no woman and the inspired seeker is a pedophile who sees her askew and may only be imagining the boy Knight looking up at her from below. That desire transforms the vision is evident from earlier attempts to peep at her through a pane, only to find some seductive part of Her dissolve into a man's hairy forearm.

The dorsal view is a transformation of the trope akin to that performed by Dostoevsky at the end of *Crime and Punishment* and, as we shall see below, by Pasternak in *Doctor Zhivago*. But where both Dostoevsky and Pasternak appear to operate within the dichotomies of whore versus Madonna, or, as Laura Mulvey has put it, the "voyeuristic" and the "fetishistic,"[25] Nabokov's treatment questions the position of the viewer and, by extension, the reader, more fundamentally. The inspired viewer inside the book (Humbert) may very well sense that he sees the woman in the window incorrectly somehow; at least he says as much. But the fact that his is the only voice through which the viewers outside the book (us) experience the inspired gaze, the extended contemplation of the beloved object, implicates us as well. We see her, think of her, only through his depiction, his manipulation. He clothes her, makes her talk for us, act for us; he gives her expressions, gestures, emotions. There is no Lolita (as if this were her name) without the collection of graphemes he sets running along the page of his diary in this passage and everywhere else. We are implicated by our consent from the moment we begin accepting these symbols as representing something, the girl and the man who make this story so beautiful and so ugly.

Nabokov's critique of the minor reader in us is perfectly apropos. There is nothing morally objectionable about this story as long as we agree that it refers to no thing, no person. Thus when Leland de la Durantaye, in his 2007 book *Style is Matter*, laments that Lolita "is everywhere referred to, everywhere described, everywhere poetically loved, but of her *thoughts* and *feelings*, Humbert offers us scarce a glimpse," whatever specific point he may be trying to bring home (in this case, that H. H. will not see things from her point of view) must be preceded by the recognition that, technically speaking, she does not have any thoughts or feelings, not until we give them to her, not until we allow him to give them to her for us.[26] This is as true of H. H. as it is of V. N. Whatever inspiration, or, if you are a pervert too, whatever titillation, you might experience at the depiction Nabokov provides is dependent upon your willingness to see the fiction as representing something, someone.

The play upon our sensibility is palpable. When Humbert (as if that were his name) catches up with Lo on the street in Elphinstone after she appears to have given him the slip in chapter 19, he questions her closely on what she has been doing, where she has been for the past several minutes. On quickly checking her excuses, he ends up standing with her in front of a shop window where she claims to have been looking at dresses with a friend.

> It was indeed a pretty sight. A dapper young fellow was vacuum-cleaning a carpet of sorts upon which stood two figures that looked as if some blast had just worked havoc with them. One figure was stark naked, wigless and armless. Its comparatively small stature and smirking pose suggested that when clothed it had represented, and would represent when clothed again, a girl-child of Lolita's size. But in its present state it was sexless. Next to it, stood a much taller veiled bride, quite perfect and *intacta* except for the lack of one arm. On the floor, at the feet of these damsels, where the man crawled about laboriously with his cleaner, there lay a cluster of three slender arms, and a blond wig. Two of the arms happened to be twisted and seemed to suggest a clasping gesture of horror and supplication.
>
> "Look, Lo," I said quietly. "Look well. Is not that a rather good symbol of something or other?" (226)

Humbert immediately darts off to another topic, leaving Nabokov's "your symbol here!" announcement apparently undeveloped, so let us see what we can do: Sexless "girl-child," naked and formless, without protection (she has no arms) but also without animation, the ultimate in plasticity (she is plastic), waiting to be clothed and reordered by the man at her feet; second "damsel," adult woman figure, also inanimate, adorned as bride by the man at her feet; and the man at her feet, a mere shop clerk, one who dresses up the figures for others to look at—admire, be inspired by, order their lives around—through the window. And who is looking now? A broken girl-child and the parody of a father, parody of a lover, parody of a husband, at her feet, clothing and reordering her for himself and for us.

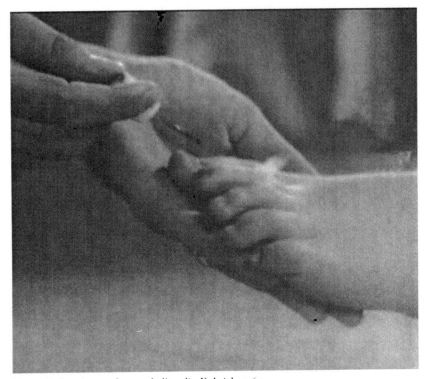

Figure 8. Dressing up figures. *Lolita*, dir. Kubrick, 1962.

Kubrick manages the iconicity of the latter relationship elegantly in his opening credits, which feature a man's hands in the act of deftly painting a young woman's, or child's, toenails: at her feet, serving her, dressing her up in private for presentation to a public.[27] Here, moreover, the trope has morphed yet again, with attendant layers of representation and, in effect, an unmasking of the objectifying gaze. If one response to the pictured woman is to lament her absence of agency, give her roundness, and convert the trope into a character, Nabokov's move here does the opposite, stripping the trope completely of its person-like veneer and clarifying as a result what we are all doing here—dressing up figures and pretending together that they are persons. The former nudges art into morality; the latter pulls the two apart. The scene's magic derives from the delicate play between the two realms, which depend on each other, and from the marvelous duplicity it encourages in readers, who can understand very well that they are referring to no one, but no matter how many times they remember this, can continue to feel compassion and remorse the moment these no ones are made to dance.

She is not such a plastic affair in Pasternak's hands, but nor is she the singularity that Nabokov insists on for his hero. Not that there aren't indications in the text that a cosmic love between Lara and Yury exists. There are. He sees Lara framed after all, or rather, he appears to sense her aura behind the casement, as he sleds across snowy Moscow, in a moment that defines him in the minds of many as the romantic poet par excellence.

> As they drove through Kamerger Street Yury noticed a dark melted slit in the icy crust of one of the windows. Through it the flame of a candle glimmered, imbuing the street almost with consciousness, as if it were watching the passing carriages and waiting for someone.
>
> "A candle burned on the table, a candle burned . . . ," he whispered to himself, the beginning of something confused, unformed; he hoped the rest would come by itself, without constraint. It did not come. (81)

Behind the window is Lara, of course, and the cosmic interpretation puts her at the tipping point of his universe without his knowing it. A facile reading has us turn to the end and feel vindicated in discovering the line used as a refrain in one of the poems in "The Poems of Yury Zhivago."

Winter Night

Snow swept the world over
from end to end.
A candle burned on a table,
a candle burned.

Like a horde of summer midges
flying to a flame,
the flakes swarmed from the yard
up to the windowpane.

The blizzard sculpted on the glass
circles and spears.
The candle burned on the table,
the candle burned.

Shadows lay
on the lighted ceiling:
crossings of arms, of legs—
crossings of destiny.

Two small boots fell
to the floor with a thud.
Wax tears from the nightstand
dripped on a dress.

And all was lost in snowy murk,
gray and white.
The candle burned on the table,
the candle burned.

A draft blew on the flame,
and the fever of temptation
lifted two angelic wings,
like a cross.

It snowed through all February,
and almost always
the candle burned on the table,
the candle burned.[28]

Now, the thrill of recognizing the moment of inspiration, not to mention the crystalline beauty of the poem itself, serves to draw plot lines together and provide closure and meaning to the story. But it is not at all clear that Zhivago wrote this poem about Lara. There is a linguistically simple concreteness in it: midges, snow, wax, a candle, a window, but no distinguishing marks, no clearly delineated actions, only shadows. For all the poem's remarkable suggestiveness, it is impossible to be certain how many characters are silhouetted by it, let alone who they might be.

Even if we assume this is a love poem and Yury and Lara are the lovers whose shadows play fatefully on the ceiling, the uniqueness of the encounter is spread across time and across the entire snowy expanse of the earth. There may be an exceptional moment assumed behind the depiction, but equally if not more important is the generalized experience it projects outward, which becomes exceptional only when singled out by the "eyes of genre," in this case those of romance, which find the magical other and are blind to everything else.[29] When we realize that Zhivago sees much of life in this manner, that such moments are peppered throughout the novel, that his vision of the world's magical connectedness has indeed been raised to a constant poetic symptom, then this apparently unique communion of star-crossed lovers becomes merely one coincidence among many—one spellbinding, miraculous, and utterly mundane coincidence among all those that make up life. Nor is there any blinding light of unmediated vision outside this cave; the poet's gift *is* a gift of vision. This is why "Winter Night," which could easily be some unique, transforming eve, is not that at all. Just as Pasternak's tragic partings and wondrous meetings are skipped, this moment is stretched and broadened, made nondramatic, general.

Romantic exclusivity also disappears. He will love Tonya, and very likely Marina (his third wife, generically expunged from the film versions—the audience's tolerance for his polygamy goes only so far), in much the same manner that he loves Lara: passionately, that is, sufferingly, as one suffers a burden, an insult, a poetic gift, a heart attack. Oh, all right, perhaps he'll love Lara just a bit more or at least express it differently, because the conditions are more tragic, and he is a younger man, and he can't do anything with himself during his time together with her except write anyway. I shall return to Zhivago's manner of loving shortly. The point here is that romance skews the picture, creates a spotlight that excludes the rest of the poet's vision, which extends in his case as far as imaginary cowsheds in other worlds.

While it is narratively simpler than Nabokov's, Pasternak's use of the trope of the woman in the window is not merely a clichéd attempt to invoke a dead heroic ethos by anchoring the man or giving his life purpose through her imagined constancy and unattainability. It is an invitation to find meaning in life itself, of which the candle is an easy, if somewhat hackneyed, symbol. He does not see her, after all, he sees only the light, and his response is the simplest statement of fact: "A candle burned on a table; a candle burned."[30]

Doubles and Heroes

The power of these images to inspire is directly proportional to their consensual fantasticality, their promise for the future, the degree to which we can imagine into them our hopes about tomorrow. Money and other symbolic values can thus stand in for the woman in the window when heroic man cedes his place to commercial man. The construction of Dostoevsky's *Double* implies such a direct relationship: the hero begins by counting his paper money and ends by staring up at Her window.[31] The fact that he is sent off to the madhouse as a result suggests something of the social reception that staring up at women's windows is likely to occasion under modern conditions. I am only half joking, for there is another half to the man: the other, the "usurper," the "upstart," takes on a modern mantle to live a modern life—in

Golyadkin's case one of salaried dependency, obsequious shapeshifting, and a rejection of the "firmness of character" that defined an older virtuous ideal. In effect, Dostoevsky's portrayal places the two masculine characters in opposition to each other, the lover and the opportunist, the conscience and the careerist. They fight it out in mock heroic fashion, a battle that Humbert and his double Quilty's slug fest appears to echo:

> Fussily, busybodily, cunningly, he had risen again while he talked. I groped under the chest trying at the same time to keep an eye on him. All of a sudden I noticed that he had noticed that I did not seem to have noticed Chum protruding from beneath the other corner of the chest. We fell to wrestling again. We rolled all over the floor, in each other's arms, like two huge helpless children. He was naked and goatish under his robe, and I felt suffocated as he rolled over me. I rolled over him. We rolled over me. They rolled over him. We rolled over us. (298–99)

Subject and object grow confused as the hero and his double grapple for the means to destroy each other. But where the relation of authentic and fraud was relatively clear in Dostoevsky's book of a hundred years before, the masculine character whom we might wish to see as hero here, the one who "really" loves, with constancy and truth and "firmness of character," is the same Humbert Humbert who has impersonated a hero throughout the book, both to the characters in it—through his "adult disguise," his "great big handsome hunk of movieland manhood" (39) looks, and the various frauds he perpetrates on adults and children alike—and to us, through his rhetorical skill and narrative posturing: he has played on trust.

If before I seemed especially insistent on the genre distinction of what is and is not romance, it is because the shaping of sensibility that romance occasions is itself insistent, culturally pervasive, seductive in its ease, and Nabokov's treatment has played on this "genre trust" of ours as well. The suggestion that romance entails, of a purpose in artistic achievement for the artist's life (he has lived knightlike in order to love and produce this work) is as pernicious as the impulse, however brief, to accept Humbert Humbert's claim of a purpose in the refuge of art (he has lived in order to love Lolita and produce this book). In his argument, she is the reason for his poetic treatment of her. In writing about her, he makes her into a means. This is the context for his claim that, contrary to Freud, "sex is the ancilla of art" (259). Both these approaches reduce the life lived to an instrumental end, discounting the life lived in the process. It should not be difficult to see that Humbert Humbert evokes Lolita as an instrument for fulfilling his own needs, as a means to such fulfillment, throughout his account, up to and including the book's final lines, which attempt to elevate that account to the level of something akin to, well, romance. The even momentary acceptance of such an emotional manipulation implicates our own habits of reading, just as the reception of *Doctor Zhivago* as primarily a story of star-crossed lovers marks us far more than it does Pasternak.

Doubles are equally formative in *Zhivago*, with Pavel Antipov (aka Strelnikov) mirroring Yury's life as angel or demon, an anti Yury as it were, and the similarities and contrasts are palpable: both support the revolution but for the "wrong" reasons; both tend toward the ascetic but also passionate excess. Strelnikov is characterized by willful action and the desire to make change happen, while Zhivago tends toward endurance, acceptance. Pasha's doubt leads to a split; from Lara's husband he becomes another man, a masked rogue Red militant, whose fall from power leads in the end to his fateful encounter with Lara's lover in the cabin in the woods. They do not roll on the floor. Nor do we ever lose track of where one character begins and the other ends. There is never any confusion between his and Yury's character, and only the slightest play on our sensibilities: Antipov seems to suggest what following the revolution might have meant for a hero of the old school, and indeed his devotion to his (one) wife and family is a defining trait. His story resonates in the romantic mode, ending in the tragic.

What Pasternak has attempted with his main character, however, is a more radical recasting. Yury does not see anyone through the wrong end of a telescope, but nor does he rush past the symbolic when it is staring him in the face, as Humbert appears to do in front of the shop window. Unlike Humbert, he is prepared to see himself in heroic guise, as a knight if need be, constant and courageous, a fact suggested by his poetic version of the legend of St. George (Georgy, Yury) and the dragon, as recounted in the poem "Fairy Tale" of the final chapter.

The immediate impulse for this call to the heroic mode, the context of its creation, is the howling of the wolves that Yury hears in chapter 9 of part 14, which gradually turn into a creative theme for him, the symbol of "a hostile power bent upon destroying him and Lara and on driving them from Varykino," which looms "like a prehistoric beast or some fabulous monster, a dragon whose tracks had been discovered in the ravine" (44). These lines suggest that the poem is little more than an allegorized projection of his fear of losing Lara at this moment, an inspiration under the constraints of their imminent danger. But the habitualized poetic vision noted earlier runs beneath the theme, making the heroic mode rather more modulation than recourse. He has been thinking these thoughts for some time now.

Traces are evident, for instance, when he is traveling with his family to the Urals and reflects on seeing a waterfall in a ravine that "it was like a living conscious creature, a local dragon or winged serpent who levied tribute and preyed upon the surrounding land" (238); or when Strelnikov remarks to him in their encounter on the train: "This is a time for angels with flaming swords and winged beasts from the abyss" (252); or when, during his captivity with the Partisans, he is transfixed by the image of a sunset in the woods.

> At such moments he felt as if he too were being pierced by shafts of light. It was as though the gift of the living spirit were streaming into his breast, piercing his being and coming out at his shoulders like a pair of wings. The archetype that is formed in every child for life and seems forever after to be his inward face, his personality, awoke in him in its full primordial strength, and compelled nature, the forest, the afterglow, and everything else visible to be transfigured into a similarly primordial and all-embracing likeness of a girl. Closing his eyes, "Lara," he whispered and thought, addressing the whole of his life, all God's earth, all the sunlit space spread out before him. (343)[32]

He speaks to a girl here, a young girl (*devochka*), not a grown woman, not the Lara waiting in Yuryatin. If his words pertain to any actual incarnation of her, it is to the "girl from another circle" whom he witnessed suffering in the novel's second chapter.[33] But even that experience has been generalized to such an extent that her physical existence is now interwoven with his life experience. In contrast to Humbert's tendency to let the symbolic pass without comment, Zhivago is willing to allow her to stand for no less than the "whole of his life" and, simultaneously, "all God's earth."[34]

Zhivago's aesthetized, anthropomorphized vision of his love for life, for the suffering girl, and for "God's earth" provides the clearest contrast to what I would claim is Humbert's instrumental orientation to his love object—I use the words advisedly—in *Lolita*. Humbert's appeals to artistry, his claims to be "lost in an artist's dream" (153), from beginning to end of his confession, function equivalently to the peasant Mikolka's claim, in Raskolnikov's nightmarish memory, that the horse he is about to kill is his "goods" (*dobro*). Mikolka's mare and Humbert's Her are equivalently instrumentalized, with Raskolnikov's old pawnbroker standing squarely between the two—the image of a person whose own internal ends are sacrificed in favor of the misguided and misunderstood ends of the protagonist.

The confusion revolves around notions of ownership, property, and authority, but these in turn are conditioned upon a conception of the figures as representing something fundamentally material and plastic. Zhivago, by contrast, lives in a different world altogether, one in which magic and symbol invite us constantly into other worlds and times and the represented materiality of persons yields to a sacramental mode where agency turns into a form of self-revelation, memory becomes anamnesis, and heroism suffers itself in all its mundane and otherworldly splendor.

DeLillo's *Cosmopolis* and the End of an Idiom

Led by dear charity, hired by sweet hope, fond fancy essays this feat; but in vain; mere dreams and ideals, they explode in your hand, leaving nothing but a burn behind.

—Hermann Melville, *The Confidence-Man*

He lives from day to day indulging the appetite of the hour. . . . His life has neither law nor order; and this distracted existence he terms joy, and bliss, and freedom.

—Plato, *Republic*[1]

The triumph of symbolic value, with its attendant liquidity of character, and the implications these hold for the move from virtue to virtuality, are especially promising in American space. These infuse the author's sense of place, his sense of home, such that he finds the prosaic, secular world of Nabokov's *Lolita* more familiar, more comfortable even, than the world of Pasternak's *Zhivago*, with its marvels and magic. It saddens me to assert this, probably because Yury's inner life appears to extend an attractive hopefulness of depth and meaning. Nor do I think it is merely the realia of daily existence or landscape that makes me feel more at home in a place where surface matters so much. The triumph of the public persona, the confident presentation of self at ease in motherless space, hovering atop the surface of the land, is a remarkable achievement of American culture and a powerful harnessing of consensual fantasy's liberating potential. This is the progressive statement, the leap to embrace the ether I noted in my introduction. It should not be surprising that an old-world aristocrat like Nabokov might side with the burrowing response: Humbert's corrosive character is aptly situated in the midst of a landscape without Mother.

One finds a sense of floating above in Russian culture, too. It is perhaps its dominant nineteenth-century mode, inaugurated most powerfully in Pushkin's *Bronze Horseman*, where the steed is Russia rushing forward but also fixed in time and space, a monument to a man and a country that, like Sobakevich's girth, may have little or nothing behind it. Perhaps inflated claims, with feet planted clearly too far apart to stand that way for long, might serve to compensate for what Andrei Sinyavsky has characterized as the general formlessness of the Russian national character,[2] which hovers in cultural space, amoeba-like, without a moral framework such that, depending on the circumstances and specifics of influence, it may become different things according to "who treats the wood."[3] It is significant that Sinyavsky feels the need to note in the same passage that he does not see this state of affairs as "necessarily bad." Why would he, writing in 1988, see such openness of character—or, as Sherry Turkle has expressed it, such fluidity, emergence, multiplicity, and flexibility—as bad, necessarily or not?[4] Both Sinyavsky's and Turkle's claims, it should go without saying, sit squarely upon traditions of thinking about character. And while in the Russian context, it is hard to find the positive figures associated with consensual fantasy, the American equivalents offer greater variety.

Russian floaters and their accompanying exclamatory marks are easy to spot, flitting across the literary landscape, from Gogol's Chichikov and Khlestakov to Turgenev's Rudin and Bazarov, Cernyshevsky's Rakhmetov, and a Dostoevskian panoply. And in the twentieth century, Andrei Bely once more picks up the flying yet constant beast and fixes it with new urgency:

> Russia, you are like a steed! Your two front hooves have leaped far off into the darkness, into the void, while your two rear hooves are firmly implanted in the granite soil.
>
> Do you too want to separate yourself from the rock that holds you, as some of your mad sons have separated themselves from the soil?[5]

This is not just about Peter driving a wedge between the intelligentsia and the people, leading an upper layer of European-educated Russians away from their native traditions, their "soil" (*pochva*). It also points to the harnessing of consensual fantasy associated with those very Western cultural practices and modes of social life embraced and promoted by Peter—modern finance and government, self-interest, and the partializing, salaried bureaucratic dependency associated with the dominance of a commercial culture, a commercial ethic. Or rather, more often in the Russian context, not the harnessing but the unleashing, with attendant fundamental questions about what terrible things might be perpetrated by those "mad sons" who, like the hooves of the great steed, have thrust themselves into the symbolic realm, rising above the earth, leaving it behind. Humbert and Raskolnikov, Chichikov, Golyadkin, Hermann, and the horseman's Yevgeny are thus variations on the theme of inspired instrumentalization, the confusion of what is "good" with what is "good *for*," once the earth's surface begins to recede below.

And yet these are all sick male characters, suffering and split by their entrance into the world of consensual fantasy. Their remedies, by contrast, have a kind of whole certainty that is earthly and rooted to the same degree that the former float: the eighteenth-century landed "virtuous man" for Chichikov, for instance; the man of singular, direct "strength of character" for Golyadkin Senior; Sonya Marmeladov's ideal man of the soil, who kisses the earth out of gratitude and shared human suffering; Konstantin Levin's peasant; Yury Zhivago's living, folk-inflected poet-creator. Masculine character suffers at the hands of consensual fantasy in this genealogy, with nary a positive figure to be found exploiting and prospering in the ethereal heights, even ambiguously, and the only healthy counterweights with their feet firmly planted.

In American depictions, by contrast, ambiguous prospering within the consensually fantastical dimension has a much richer history. It begins in the nineteenth century and carries through to present popular imaginings, to the extent that Americans even today are often seen as imbued with a kind of confidence that appears to depend on itself alone. As an Italian acquaintance once put it in an imperfect yet profound English expression, Americans have "a big hope." This trait of boundless confidence in confidence finds something of a manifesto—if a manifesto can be ambiguous—in Hermann Melville's *The Confidence-Man: His Masquerade,* an equivalent of sorts to Dostoevsky's infatuations with consensual fantasy of the 1840s to the 1860s. Melville's 1857 book, however, is not a negative portrayal of such phenomena, as Dostoevsky's clearly are; it comes closer, rather, to the dubious successes of Chichikov in part 1 of *Dead Souls.*

Indeed, the similarities between these two writers, and even more, these two works, are remarkable. I will not detail the plot of *The Confidence-Man* here for those who have not read the book because, in truth, there isn't much of one. Men and women, but mostly men, get on and off a boat headed down the Mississippi, talking with each other, mostly about business, American business, which means mostly about confidence: the lack of it, the need for it, the results of having it or not. The book begins with a beggar setting up his sign on deck and ends with an elderly man trying to authenticate a coin. The climax, if there is one, occurs in a conversation between a man with confidence and a man without it. It is a strange and rich book, perhaps a novel only in the sense in which Bakhtin treats Dostoevsky's novels, that is, as a development of Menippean satire.[6]

Melville shares with Gogol a similarly baroque prose, replete with digressions of a lyrical sort. And in much the same manner that Gogol's Chichikov flits across the landscape, Melville's heroes of *The Confidence-Man* engage one another on a steamer, floating down the Mississippi, thereby pointing to the notion of earthly value, that is, the value of the earth somewhere under one's feet, the uncertain, "unlocatable (or floating) standard" noted by Goux in regard to modern systems of symbolic value.[7] The play with identity that is central to Chichikov's character and the impossibility of self-authentication in Melville's book are thus removed from the land per se in the latter. The conditions of mutual recognition, especially those based upon property, become ever more indeterminate, as socially constructed identity floats down-current into the liquidity of character with which we are all intimately familiar, the aqueous foundations of the modern social agent. Under modern conditions, how do you know, how does one ever know, with whom one is dealing?[8] That man you're talking to who seems so affable, he could be Napoleon in disguise.

Melville's book suggests, on one level, that we must have trust, confidence in the words of our interlocutors; we must "credit" them with value, truth in short, by believing them and believing in what they say, in the same way that we trust, have faith, that government bonds or money have value, or will have value when we redeem their promise at some future time. The boat on which they (we) are all traveling is thus aptly named *Fidèle* (faithful), and the characters never rise above the level of self-presenting surfaces, coin faces, whose value they themselves constantly wonder about, like the authenticator at the end of the book.

On another level, however, *The Confidence-Man* draws into question such faith as naïve and perhaps immoral. We may all just be stupid for taking "at face value" the coin peddled to us by strangers. There may be nothing—or worse, nothing good—behind these facades, masks, personae, suits, roles, or whatever you might call them, as long as it's not real round people with living souls because they are not that. And, more broadly, perhaps this system of spreading around wealth by means of speculative self-interest and promises to pay in some unspecified future time is not the best way of caring for people, especially those who do not have the means or the minds to enter the realm of consensual fantasy with us, at least not on the same terms. The juxtaposition of charity and commerce that Melville creates—from the beggar at the start to the coin authenticator at the end—is thus an expression of conflict between two visions of social welfare. It is equivalent to Dostoevsky's placement of self-interested rational egoist reasoning in the mouth of Luzhin in *Crime and Punishment*. Dostoevsky implicitly ridicules the self-interest notion by making Luzhin's underhanded, supercilious, and ultimately selfish motives apparent, even as he allows the character to more or less correctly present the self-interest argument in the form of a brief discourse on the virtue of whole coats. Melville's treatment suggests the tension between, on one hand, the perhaps morally compromising practice of the confidence man, who is also the expression of the wealth-generating consensual fantasies of modernity, and, on the other, the righteous distribution of wealth through charity, which saves individuals yet impoverishes society.

And just as Gogol's ringing expulsion of the virtuous man from *Dead Souls* motivates an entire series of responses, so Melville's implicit questioning of the relationship of confidence to conning inaugurates a rich line of explorations of the modern notion of consensual fantasy and the presentation of self, long before Erving Goffman's calling it such. Not knowing who to trust, and anxious about being the mark in someone else's scheme for making a killing—these are symptoms of a perennial American condition, and part of its rich tradition of confidence tales, in which not only are such heroes not darkly sick or split by the conditions of modernity, they are downright infectious in their enthusiasm for such conditions, inviting the rest of us in with a wink and a nudge. For these are the conditions of the con themselves, just as they are the conditions of confidence and the real wealth and sometime well-being generated by it.

There is a kind of marvelous headiness in all this. Let us all assume together that what we're pretending is real might in fact one day be real, and, in the meantime, on that basis, let us build! A Doges' palace! Skyscrapers! A Palace of the Soviets! Well, some dreams can be realized, it seems; others not so much. I don't want to be misunderstood here: the heady flight of the con and the heady flights of confidence, the wealth that can be generated by each, as long as all the players agree—perhaps with a wink and a nudge, perhaps with the faith of true believers—these are real things, a real foundation on which to build. Those who might suggest that they are "nothing but" fantasy, idea, and so on misconstrue their absent corporeality for an absence of effect—a very old blind-spot that still prevents many from seeing tall buildings looming just over there. These promises are made good on through the accomplishments of modern societies, even small ones, like Japan or Singapore, with few natural resources of their own but grand pools of national confidence, national trust, "fictional richesses," as Montesquieu called them, on which to draw.[9] Only where he saw the principal virtue of such *richesses de fiction* as a strictly national phenomenon, one government borrowing from its own citizens, the world of the past two hundred years has increasingly been interlaced from country to country, continent to continent, with such promises, creating a vast squishy network of IOUs for us to stand upon, though with varying degrees of stability.

World City

> And a city is something bigger than an individual?
>
> —Plato, *Republic*

My use of Don DeLillo's 2003 novel *Cosmopolis* as a kind of coda to this book may disappoint some of his fans. The approach is instrumental in a manner that may also appear contradictory in light of my previous comments. But given the fact that reviewers did not think the book a success,[10] the analysis I offer, in addition to circling back to the beginnings of this book, may also, I hope, prove an example of scholarly consideration over critical shortsightedness. Others may wonder at the inclusion of DeLillo's book at all in the sequence that begins with Chichikov's and Golyadkin's passionate embrace of symbolic value and the questioning of masculine character that they mark. I promise to return to this discussion in due course.

Cosmopolis, I shall argue, presents a critique of the world of cybercapital that invokes, and is indeed framed by, the long-standing Atlantic republican contrast of virtue and corruption. By extension, it both gestures toward the global edifice of contemporary commercial culture and pokes at its precarious foundation. In part DeLillo manages this by means of a network of allusive associations of his hero and his book with previous works engaged in querying the same or similar issues—psychological integrity, social justice, trust and trickery, confidence and doubt. Like generic allusions, these hints place DeLillo's work within a context of like-minded depictions without prescribing a specific set of features by which it must be evaluated.[11] But *Cosmopolis's* most intriguing innovation occurs at the confluence of virtue and corruption themselves, categories that the book ends up drawing into question, as the physical, bodily foundations of one are ultimately subsumed by the solipsism of the other. This is partly a reformulation of familiar DeLillo themes—the "deathward logic" of plot (as in *Libra*), anxiety over the relations of bodies and signs in postmodernity (as in *Mao II*), and the resulting inward movement into a mediated mental state tenuously connected to the real (as in *White Noise*).[12] In offering up all these themes once again and all together, *Cosmopolis* may at first appear as a kind of DeLillo smorgasbord, but this view overlooks the virtue-corruption frame, which transforms the familiar material into something new. As always, corruption endangers the republic. But in the increasingly mediated and distanced reality of the contemporary *kosmou polites,* or "world citizen," the traditional weights of virtue dissolve, leaving him who might have attached himself to them without the body to do so. The woman in the window, who might have offered him a raft in some past historical moment, is now empty, not to mention broke.

The conceptual frame for this discussion has been prepared previously. It traces the vagaries of virtue from its origins in functional purity (the excellence of a table, etc.) through Greek-inspired notions of masterly corporeality—as in Machiavelli's distinctive usage of the Italian *virtuoso* primarily in the sense of effective, able, and with a masculine tinge—through its subsequent linkage to land, the body politic, and the tradition of republican thought. This is the tradition of thought whose foundations began to dissolve with the increasing spread of commercially inflected consensual fantasy. It is within this context that *Cosmopolis* finds its greatest resonance, raising it from the topical concerns of early twenty-first-century popular culture in a manner that links it to other lasting ruminations on the meaning of modernity.[13]

Body, Mind, Body

> There's nothing like a raging crap, she thought, to make mind and body one.
>
> —Don DeLillo, *The Body Artist*

Even for the most progressive minded, the veneer of solidity atop the network of late modern symbolic value, so DeLillo's depiction would imply, begins to peel away in the realm of cybercapital, where present consensual fantasies concerning things without material foundation become the basis for future consensual fantasies concerning things without material foundation. In focusing our attention on this concrete fact of modernity, DeLillo's account draws into question contemporary assumptions not only about the reality of a technologically mediated commercial life but also about the implications of modern decorporealization for psychological, social, and political health.

Eric Packer, DeLillo's cybercapitalist hero, does not need to confront such issues of our time directly, for he is a man ahead of our time. He is ahead of time in general, discerning a world that does not yet exist. This talent has made his fortune, put him at the head of the world's currency trading industry, but it has also called into question his position in time and space. This is a major theme of the work, signaled by his remedy for the insomnia that, as announced in the book's first lines, now afflicts him four or five times weekly:

> What did he do? . . . He was reading the Special Theory tonight, in English and German, but put the book aside, finally, and lay completely still, trying to summon the will to speak the single word that would turn off the lights. Nothing existed around him. There was only the noise in his head, the mind in time.
>
> When he died he would not end. The world would end. (6)

The divorce from body, the uprooting of thought and its solipsistic repercussions suggested here, is maintained and intensified as the book proceeds, the plot devolving as Packer's limo makes its way across Manhattan, until he ends up in an abandoned high-rise where a mysterious double murders him, or is about to. The rupture of sorts in the time-space dimension, as perceived by Packer, is evident in the work's closing lines: "He is dead inside the crystal of his watch but still alive in original space, waiting for the shot to sound" (209).

Packer's visionary perception of his future non-self is technologically mediated, but the technology he employs for this is dubious. The crystal of his "watch" is also a screen. He has used it in the past to "hack into corporate systems, testing their security for a fee" (123). In the course of the novel he hacks into his wife's bank accounts, impersonating her "algorithmically" and transferring her millions into his company, "where he open[s] a new account for her more or less instantaneously, by thumbnailing some numbers on the tiny keypad that was set around the bezel of the watch" (123). Any assumptions one might have retained to this point about the work's neo-realist foundations begin to give way before a variety of possible symbolic interpretations. And indeed, in the work's final pages the device turns out to be still more versatile and powerful: it is also an "electron camera . . . a device so microscopically refined it was almost pure information. It was almost metaphysics" (204). And through this almost metaphysical device he glimpses "a body . . . facedown on the floor" and wonders, "Whose body and when?" (205). Thus the nominal timepiece bridges Packer from himself now, "in original space" (209), to himself in an apparently inevitable future moment, while the split between technologically mediated mind and the physical grounding of body must be seen as fundamental to Packer's, and the book's, exploration of meaning and mortality, a recurrent theme in DeLillo's oeuvre.[14]

To state this differently, Packer lives a life of thought divorced from body. He recognizes himself in his body but sees it as a "structure . . . to dismiss in theory . . . redundant and transferable . . . convertible to wave arrays of information, the thing he [watches] on the oval screen" of his security system (48). By contrast, when he observes the rise and fall of currencies on the touchless screens in the back of his limo, the data is not a reduction of "unruly human energies" to him, not a "cold compression of . . . every sort of yearning and midnight sweat reduced to lucid units" (24). It is life itself, "realized in electronic form," the "heave of the biosphere." Packer believes he can discern the life of the planet through these "streams of numbers running in opposite directions," "the figural diagrams that [bring] organic patterns into play" (24). This is presumably the same visionary power that enables him to see bank towers looming "just beyond the avenue . . . covert structures for all their size . . . tall, sheer, abstract, with standard setbacks, and block-long, and interchangeable" (36). He likes the "empty look" of such structures "from here." Their emptiness corresponds to the emptiness of the diagrams he sees on screen, for of course, in "original space" they really are empty, of the physical at least. But their future reality exists through the hopes and fears of people, through "every sort of yearning and midnight sweat":

> They were made to be the last tall things, made empty, designed to hasten the future. They were the end of the outside world. They weren't here, exactly. They were in the future, a time beyond geography and touchable money and the people who stack and count it. (36)

Such structures are the end of the outside world because they are part of an internal, thought-generated world. And what makes these realized fantasies possible is not, in Marx's phrase, the "universal equivalent" of money, not at least in its touchable form. For this is as much of an anachronism to Packer as are the words "cash register" (71), or "phone" (88), or the "arms and legs" of a chair (164). No, they are made real by what Vija Kinski, Packer's "chief of theory" calls the "glow of cyber-capital," money "without narrative quality," property without weight or shape, all "living in the future" (78–79). They live in the future because, like all consensual fantasies, they rely on promises for their realization.

Eventually, however, people must do something with their bodies in order for these promises to be kept, and this is the source of Packer's uncertainty. He sees the future realizations of promises made today, but the corporeal is shadowy and strangely immaterial to him. He tests his body's reality throughout the work, as if in compensation somehow for a tendency to find life outside it. "There were days when he wanted to eat all the time, talk to people's faces, live in meat space," so—the conjunction is implied—"he stopped looking at computer screens and turned to the street" (64). He recognizes that the street is "an offense to the truth of the future," presumably because the future is composed of mortgaged time, but responds to its palpable throb and rhythm nonetheless. At twenty-eight, he has a medical examination every day, wherever he happens to be (44). Perhaps this enables him to abandon himself to his appetites for food and, especially, sex—physical with Didi Fancher, his art dealer (25–32); verbal with Jane Melman, his chief of finance (50–52), the latter during the discomfort of a rectal examination, apparently a daily occurrence; again physical with Kendra Hays, one of his bodyguards (111); and finally physical once more with his rather abstract wife, Elise Shifrin (177), in the boarded-off section of a city sidewalk. These all appear as rather casual encounters, like almost everything that happens in the book. The plot, too, appears rather casual—a cross-town jaunt for a haircut, during which things happen, on the street, in the limo, in Packer's head perhaps.

But what is merely probative in part 1 of the book becomes self-destructive in part 2, as he inflicts ever greater pain on himself, pain acting as an unambiguous counterweight to thought: "He sat head down, out of ideas, and felt the pain" (197). The spiral inward begins just after the sex with Kendra Hays, who appropriately dons her "ZyloFlex" body armor during their encounter. Shoveling peanuts into his mouth by the fistful as he watches her dress, Packer suddenly asks to be stunned:

> I mean it. Draw the gun and shoot. I want you to do it, Kendra. Show me what it feels like. . . . Stun me to my DNA. Come on, do it. Click the switch. Aim and fire. I want all the volts the weapon holds. Do it. Shoot it. Now. (114–15)

As instances of discomfort multiply amid the increasing violence of the work's final fifty pages, Packer feels a renewal of physical strength, which feeds on itself, necessitating, according to its own implacable logic, the elimination of all impediments to his own corporeal end. In the process, he first assaults "the pastry assassin" André Petrescu, along with the photographers who have filmed Packer being "glopped" (with a pie); then murders his staunchest bodyguard, Torval; then lies naked in the street with three hundred others (apparently being filmed) in the desire to be undifferentiated "among them, all-body, the tattooed, the hairy-assed, those who stank" (176); and then, on a sudden guilt-inspired whim, shoots himself through the hand (197). In all this he appears to be merely satisfying momentary desires, or better, impulses. He thinks of something and then does it. There are no moral or ethical impediments, only physical ones, and those are treated rather as invitations, infantile dares to be acted upon. The realization of each thought is treated as a natural extension of his mind's activity. Indeed, we might call him a postmodern Krell, destroyed by his own subconscious, were it not for the apparent underlying deliberation with which the sequence of his actions unfolds and the threat of death that draws him on. Instead, he seems more like a child, or perhaps a teenager who has played a video game for so long that he's begun to see its options and aims as he drives his car or walks down the sidewalk, with snipers or ninjas behind every bush.

Property, the Road, and the Confidence Man

> There's something secret and guilty about investing. It's the wrong use of the future.
>
> —Don DeLillo, *The Names*

As noted earlier in this study, the manner of thinking about the republic as fortified by a body of virtuous property owners has tempted Americans since well before their independence.[15] Two countertraditions, each resting on its own moral and political assumptions, have come to exist alongside it. The first, embraced by the framers of the American Constitution, aims at political stability and freedom by ensuring that no selfish group can secure absolute power for itself, the assumption being that no one group is more virtuous than any other, and none may strive toward virtue at all. The other, which is more to my point here, suggests that property owners, rather than being made substantial by their possessions, are encumbered and deformed by them, and true freedom may be found only in liberation from real estate and, more broadly, from material property in general. This second strain in American thought is akin to, and ultimately derives from, ancient Stoic injunctions against dependence upon "externals," those aspects of life that lie outside one's control, up to and including one's own bodily state. This line of thinking conditions the apotheosis of the rootless wanderer, the frontier hero in certain of its incarnations, the drifter, especially the virtuous kind. Such a liberatory image intersects with the American road narrative, providing counterexamples to the corrupt, morally compromised "townspeople" who may want to do good but are too complicit in the system to manage it. This image is fundamental in DeLillo's *Cosmopolis* as well, though in an unexpected and original manner.

DeLillo's is a road novel that never leaves the city of Manhattan, that is, a road novel in effect, a virtual road novel. Eric Packer sets out across town for a haircut,[16] shedding possessions as he goes, and comes gradually closer to himself in the process. Only once he has been stripped down to his essentials—except for the fantastical time piece, of course—is he able to engage in the crucial climactic encounter with his supposed former employee, Richard Sheets, aka Benno Levin, the man who has issued the "credible threat" on Packer's life, which invigorates the latter's existence from the final lines of part 1 to the end of the work:[17]

> The credible threat was the thing that moved and quickened him. The rain on his face was good and the sour reek was fine and right, the fug of urine maturing on the body of his car, and there was trembling pleasure to be found, and joy at all misfortune, in the swift pitch of markets down. But it was the threat of death at the brink of night that spoke to him most surely about some principle of fate he'd always known would come clear in time.
>   Now he could begin the business of living. (107)

The first order of this "business" appears to be the deliberate destruction of his company. Where before he was confident that the Japanese yen could go no higher and he would recoup his losses in a market swing, now

> the yen spree was releasing [him] from the influence of his neocortex. He felt even freer than usual, attuned to the registers of his lower brain and gaining distance from the need to take inspired action. . . . There were currencies tumbling everywhere. Bank failures were spreading. He found the humidor and lit a cigar. (115)

Part of this is merely a figurative flexing of muscle. Packer enjoys the fact that he can destroy everything, an echo of the unattributed paraphrase of Bakunin he offers to Vija Kinski: "'The urge to destroy is a creative urge'" (92).[18] But more fundamentally, the "quickening" of Packer's existence is directly associated with his losses, the business of living with the business of business destruction, and by extension, the destruction of himself, especially his public self.

Considering the prominence of the novel's commercial theme, what most prevents it from becoming merely an anticapitalist pamphlet with a plot is the organic connection between Packer's destruction of self and the kind of business that has made him who he is. Packer trades in electronic currencies, predicting their rise and fall. As the book opens he is expecting the rise of the dollar against the yen. These float against one another, in relative market freedom, depending for their value on people's hopes and fears, on people's

verbal communications, and, in the end, on the spaces between them. As Jane
Melman explains,

> There's a rumor it seems involving the [Japanese] finance minister. He's
> supposed to resign any time now. . . . Some kind of scandal about a mis-
> construed comment. He made a comment about the economy that may
> have been misconstrued. The whole country is analyzing the grammar and
> syntax of this comment. Or it wasn't even what he said. It was when he
> paused. They are trying to construe the meaning of the pause. It could be
> deeper, even, than grammar. It could be breathing. (48)

DeLillo's dark humor conveys the modern anxiety over the floating standard
of contemporary symbolic value noted above. It also helps to flesh out Packer's
otherwise rather skeletal character. The value of his wares is nothing without
people's hopes about the future. He thus trades in trust, faith, and other "fictional riches." In this, he extends the tradition of the confidence man, as a
relative of Gogol's Chichikov, the enigmatic exemplars of Melville's *The Confidence-Man,* Fitzgerald's Jay Gatsby, Fowles's *Magus,* and a host of others.[19]

Packer's business is not technically illegal, of course, which would, on
first consideration, seem to exclude him from the con-man panoply. As John
Blair has argued, "An ordinary swindler falsifies legitimate money-making
schemes. . . . A con man, on the other hand, offers his victim partnership
in an illegal scheme."[20] I think this distinction unduly excludes from consideration the anxiety-laden schemes of the market, where one can "make a
killing" with legal impunity. Even were we to remove from consideration the
explicit Marxian world the novel invokes—through the rioters' adapted quo-
tation from the *Communist Manifesto* ("a specter is haunting the world"[21])—
we could still point to the long-standing associations of psychological anxiety,
along with moral and social corruption, that have accompanied the spread
and amplification of commercial life, particularly in its credit and cybercredit
stages.[22] In this sense, what Blair calls the "compounded" guilt of the con
man may lie elsewhere than in questions of law per se; it may lie in questions
of justice. Here again, DeLillo's book demonstrates its aspirations to what
Bakhtin has called "great time," justice being one of the fundamental themes
of Western literary expression.[23]

Confidence, in any case, encompasses far more than just the con. Packer's
customers believe they are in on the game, privy to secret information. They
hope to acquire vast sums (without necessarily working for them) in the magical turn of market forces. When these "sums" appear on Packer's screens as
abstractions to which he gives life, pieces he moves around and manipulates

for gain, they seem to be part of a scheme, a con or something very close to it. When we understand them as representing and resulting from a social rapport between living, thinking subjects, then they are based upon the purest form of trust in people's interactions, their promises to make good in the future. In the first case they are tokens, in the second icons.

To the rioters who surround Packer's limo, his success depends upon a basic instrumentalization of human beings (probably the reason he has such difficulty "seeing" people throughout the book), on the objectification of their lives through labor. The rioters' exploitation of the rat—by flashing a line from the poet Zbigniew Herbert, "A rat became the unit of currency," on a giant electronic display—is an attempt to vitalize, grotesquely, Packer's commodities. The fact that the line is also the novel's sole epigraph suggests that this is the work's central intended contrast, namely, between electronic market information on the one hand, "the hellbent sprint of numbers and symbols, the fractions, decimals, stylized dollar signs, the streaming release of words, of multinational news" (80), and rats on the other, the unsavory, corporeal beings that have long accompanied human progress, particularly in its urban environment, particularly in New York City, where, so the anecdote goes, there is one for every human inhabitant.[24] The shift of perspective that sees one measure of human activity (Melman's "it could be breathing," Packer's "heave of the biosphere") replaced by the other (the earthly, fleshy, smelly, dirty rat) illustrates DeLillo's contrastive technique in this work.[25] It also makes apparent the suggestion of an underlying organic filth to Packer's business existence, both to the person he is and to the nominally abstract things he manipulates. Claims about the unsavory nature of trade have a long pedigree.[26] Apparently, the fact that Eric Packer never touches a penny taints him no less.

Doubt, the Double, and the Sick Cosmopolitan

A cosmology against the void.

—Don DeLillo, *White Noise*

There is one crucial trait that the contemporary confidence man Eric Packer appears to have lost. Didi Fancher notes it when she comments on the "element of doubt" that has entered his life: "You're beginning to think," she whispers, "that it's more interesting to doubt than to act. It takes more courage to doubt" (31–32). He must not have doubted earlier in his life, as Vija Kinski corroborates: "'Doubt. What is doubt? You don't believe in doubt. You've told me this'" (86). But the apparent entrance of doubt into Packer's thought at this point has created a paradox—a confidence man without confidence—and this has the power to bring down the system he represents from the inside. When combined with the unruffled *exterior* confidence of the confidence man, doubt makes another kind of hero possible, and this is where DeLillo takes his greatest creative risk: by invoking the well-worn theme of the double and weaving it into the fabric of his novel. False Seeming has entered the city, the world city, the cosmos.

Cosmopolis is rather schematically structured in two parts, with two chapters in each part, and two brief interludes—"The Confessions of Benno Levin"—between chapters 1 and 2 and chapters 3 and 4. The first confession is subtitled "night," the second, "morning," and they appear to be temporally reversed, with the second relating things that happen earlier and the first describing a moment after the end of the final chapter, thereby confirming that the body Eric Packer sees in the final lines is his own. The mirrorlike organization, which seems to circle in on itself, is only one of many indicators that, despite its bodily paraphernalia, what we are reading is a kind of *psychomachia,* or "battle for the mind."[27] The twin roots of DeLillo's title suggest, moreover, a Greek conceptual origin to the work that is reinforced by Vija Kinski's sudden invocation of classical thought amid the riot raging outside Packer's limo (77).[28]

With this second, internal plain in mind, we may return to the suggestion of justice, rather than legality, at the heart of Packer's culpability. The *polis,* the second of the Greek roots that make up the novel's title—the other being *kosmos,* or "world"—suggests on one level New York, the "world city," the capital of global finance, Packer's business domain. But this superficial reading ignores the significance of the Greek coinage, which ultimately invokes the Stoic notion of the *kosmou polites,* or "world citizen," and its long line of Utopian descendants in the Western tradition, from Augustine to Kant and Marx.[29] By understanding his place within the metaphorical "world city," the "world citizen" is supposed to come to see others as intrinsically valuable ends. He is supposed to respect the dignity of all no matter what the accidents of their birth. He is supposed to learn to be guided primarily by considerations of justice and human well-being. DeLillo's account creates more than merely an ironic juxtaposition when it places this "world" within Eric Packer's mind at the book's beginning (6), based on the kinds of consensual fantasies that undergird the modern world, and which are by their very nature public, not private. Such a world is quintessentially prey, in Pocock's formulation, to postcivic acquisitive humanity's fantasies, passions, and appetites, forces "known to feed on themselves and to be without moral limit."[30]

Two paths of corruption follow from this, one for the polity, the other for the person.

The first is indicated in Packer's refusal to recognize anything but a personal impediment in the president's visit to New York City. Packer hates him because he is the president and more powerful, at least politically, than he is: Packer finds it unacceptable that he was once forced to wait in the president's outer office before a visit (76). Even more telling is Packer's obvious annoyance at the fact that his cross-town jaunt will be slowed by the diversion of traffic necessitated by the president's visit. He questions Torval, "Just so I know. Which president are we talking about?" (11). In much the same way, Packer does not acknowledge the legitimacy of any nonpurchasable public goods, goods that might belong to all people. He thus echoes the peasant Mikolka's words in *Crime and Punishment*, "It's my goods, I can do what I want," by insisting to Didi Fancher that if he buys the Rothko Chapel, it will be his to do with as he pleases. In short, this *kosmou polites* recognizes neither the representative nor the fact of the *res publica*.

The person's corruption, which cannot ultimately be separated from the public's in this account, is framed by Packer's encounter with Levin/Sheets, which, as previously noted, comes by the end to look all but internal. Packer appears to be gradually clearing the way for this clash with himself by removing subsequent layers of his persona, his propertied character—his money, his clothing, his wife's money, his company, his limousine. He sheds two of his bodyguards—one goes home, the other falls behind without comment—and murders the third, Torval, who has stuck doggedly by him, and whose passing, we are told, "cleared the night for deeper confrontation" (148). Packer's journey across Manhattan has fused, it would appear, with a journey into his own psyche, or perhaps his own future psyche, as the play with time merges with his growing psychic split. The guards who had protected his public self, the people who had reflected him back to himself, the possessions that had filled out his public persona—all these fall away as his limo departs, and he is left on the street, wondering, "Where was the life he'd always led?" (186). But the indecision is momentary. After the second gunshot rings out, he hears his full name on the wind and reflects, "So it was personal then" (187). Deeply personal, it would seem, the more so considering Levin/Sheets's repeated designation as "the subject" (see, for example, 186, 187, 196).

The referent, moreover, is at times ambiguous, making it unclear which is original, or at least unclear enough to require specification: "The man fired a shot into the ceiling. It startled him. Not Eric; the other, the subject." The two figures battle as we roll over ourselves in this old narrative ploy, a favorite of Nabokov, and his teacher Dostoevsky, and his teacher Gogol before that, which invites us to attempt to see through the filter of the narrative to what lies beyond and ask, "What's really happening here?" Who is the subject? Where is the masculine character? Perhaps we've been wrong all along; perhaps Eric is really the "subject's" fantasy. Could all this be merely an extended dream? We recall the book's opening in sleeplessness. Could such a character as Eric Packer really exist after all, someone with an electron watch and an elevator that plays only Satie, and who has sex four times in the course of a cross-town drive, once with a doctor's finger up his butt? When Packer responds to Benno Levin's name by saying, "That's a phony name," why shouldn't we be tempted to say the same about his?

In a narrative where the smoke is well directed amid the mirrors, there can be no definitive answers to such questions: the text and the filter are one and the same. In other words, if DeLillo is worth his stuff as a writer, he has provided conflicting evidence, hints at more than one reality or at dream and reality simultaneously. He appears to have done just that. Levin/Sheets has no way of knowing Packer will ride his limo to the point he does or be left standing on the street where he is, where he can be shot at or called out to. He hasn't been following Packer: he has no car. Indeed, Packer appears to have been dropped right in front of the building where Levin/Sheets is squatting. All this suggests the involution of dream. On the other hand, there remain enough naturalistic details sprinkled through the end text—the passage of a bike messenger on the street, for instance, or the presence of a dead or sleeping man in the vestibule of the building where Packer and Levin/Sheets come together—to suggest a difference between the filter and the reality on the other side, inviting us to peer through. Peering leads to frustration and an interpretive impasse. More than that, the attempt to locate the boundary between truth and fantasy in such a narrative points to what Slavoj Žižek has called the fantasy of "ontological consistency,"[31] the pervasive truth of fantasy in the modern world, or, in another formulation, the "positive structuring of social reality by shared fantasy."[32] This thought leads us back once more to the notion of consensual fantasy that lies at the heart of Packer's business life and to the construction of a public persona that has provided the value base, the "standard," for the objects of his trade.

Here the theme of the double as developed by Dostoevsky in his eponymous novel provides an essential interpretive step. That work, which also begins with a conspicuous curtailment of sleep and engages questions of monetary and social worth, similarly skirts the boundary between madness and sanity, pitting an unleashed public persona against its doubtful counterpart and suggesting less a clinical exploration of growing madness than a symbolic battle for the mind of the modern everyman. Dostoevsky's Golyadkin is vanquished by his public persona, who relegates the retiring, conscience-ridden "hero" to the asylum. DeLillo, by contrast, appears to have reversed the pattern. The year-2003 everyman equivalent is not the highly successful Eric Packer, but the shadowy, introspective, doubt-ridden Levin/Sheets. It is the homeless and elder Levin/Sheets—he who, in a scene that recalls the opening pages of Dostoevsky's novel, confesses to going "from branch to branch well into the night, moving money between accounts or just checking [his] balances" (149)—who does away with his "successful" junior twin.[33]

Dostoevsky's retiring hero is obsessed by the masks of modern society and insists that he is his own person, that he "goes his own way."[34] But in the end the public self that he has unleashed into the world takes complete control. His public face becomes his face. And this is how we find Packer, whose image, we are told, "used to be accessible nearly all the time, video-streamed worldwide from the car, the plane, the office and selected sites in his apartment" (15). The public self is here the mask that supports the entire fantasy framework of worth that surrounds Packer and his enterprise. The two-dimensionality of this image of worth, like a face on a coin, suggests an absence of depth to the character, the skeletal quality noted above, an effect maintained consistently. Packer is an impulsive bastard, simple-minded, vindictive, but also completely self-absorbed, a trait highlighted by the fact that while the cameras used to show other people his face as a way of maintaining the value of his business, "because there were security issues to address . . . now the camera operated on a closed circuit" (15). Packer looks at his own mask, everywhere he goes, every hour of the day.

As suggested in chapter 1, Dostoevsky's book was not primarily about individual sanity, but about the health of the social—rather than the individual—body. By directing our attention inward, to modernity's fantastical foundations, to the fashioning of public personae, the wearing of masks, the acquisition of status, and the effects of such "progress" on the inner life of one "not handsome, but also not bad looking, neither too fat nor too thin" individual, Dostoevsky's *Double* questioned the moral health of a society, that of the rapidly modernizing Russia of the mid-1840s. *Cosmopolis,* by association, reprises this "Romantic critique of the bourgeois order," which, from Fourier and Marx to Freud and Weber, portrayed the triumph of the ideology of self-interest as an impoverishment of the "full human personality."[35] But by reversing its ultimate emphasis, focusing not on the mind of the defeated elder but on that of the supposedly successful junior partner, DeLillo manages to draw into question the most cherished ideals of the "junior partner" in European social debate, of specifically American progress—its faith in the future, its confidence in the power of ideas and in the salutary effects of market-based innovation. Just as Dostoevsky's doubtful hero ensures his own destruction by unleashing a public persona who is adept at manipulating the valuable units of modern consensual fantasy—government documents, money, people, his own public self, what have you—so DeLillo implicates the contemporary world in the foundation not only of today's society but of whatever future life it is already complicit in one day bringing into being, through its hopes and fears, its "hellbent sprint of numbers and symbols," its "streaming release of words," the "heave" of an ever more exosomatic "biosphere" (24).

In *Cosmopolis,* DeLillo resurrects the double's retiring alter ego from Dostoevsky's 1846 book in order to murder the successful public persona to which his own ambition gave birth a century and a half earlier, thereby ending the double's power on earth and bringing the consensually fantastical world of finance capital to its knees. In a telling scene, Eric Packer catches sight of his trophy wife through the window of her car but does not recognize her. She is framed like many inspirational exemplars of the past; their "carriages" come together and are unable to move temporarily, much as Gogol's Chichikov was thrust up to the window of the governor's daughter. What does masculine character do in the face of a potentially life-changing "vision"? Reevaluate where he has been and where he might be going? Examine his life choices? Write a divine comedy? Chichikov was not that kind of man. Nor is Eric Packer. Indeed, the age of the multiplicitous, commercial persona has little place for the necessarily unitary masculine character of the heroic past, the person who would find himself centered, inspired, and made meaningful by the framed face of the beloved. He may not even remember who she is.

Behind the Kitchen Door

A friend and good reader has asked, So what, then, must we do? The sense of loss in reading these works this way is indeed palpable. I could, in answer, recite a litany of ills associated with the "old" virtue ethic whose loss is not such a bad thing, from the stiff-lipped brutality of officers in World War I, or other wars besides, to the cowboy ethos of American foreign policy, and the often misplaced confrontationalism that such images seem to encourage some to adopt, even today. Not to mention the accompanying misogyny and homophobia. Moreover, when applied to national groupings, an ideal of steadfast purpose also historically went hand in glove with the extermination of minority cultures: one virtuous people was rather more square-jawed Ancient Greek or Roman than, let's say, Persian, with all its monstrous variety and color. The kind of crossing that is characteristic of us late moderns was poorly if at all envisioned by many a virtue-minded predecessor, for whom a culturally, ethnically, religiously, racially crossed person could never be anything but a bastard. This is a subject for another book, no doubt.

Here let me note simply that I do not see why the ethical goal of trying to be one person should preclude recognizing, validating, even celebrating ethnic, racial, and cultural multiplicity. The one is about persons, the other about peoples, and the desire to have all thought converge in a single point does both a disservice. In at least one case examined above, that of the character Yury Zhivago, I hope to have shown a way in which the heroic virtue ethos might be transformed rather than discarded, retaining some of its motivational force and much of its beauty in the process. Yury sees with his mind's eye the living connections between corporeal realities, celebrates them, sings their intrinsic worth, recreating them in fact through one and the same grateful, poetic breath.

Having written these words, I must step back, embodied as I am, in this here and now, not in some magical realm of my own inspiration. The confidence index is up today, or maybe it is down. Consensual fantasy follows its course with all its floating standards in tow, powerful and inscrutable. My conceit is not nine months old anymore, waving his little hand on the other side of the glass. He has accumulated years with this book, he and his little brother. Their choices may or may not be described in these pages. I rather hope that they are not. Maybe what I've written here will help them in some small way, if not in making sense of their life—these are just some thoughts about stories, after all—then at least by suggesting a way of reading (you like to read, thank goodness) and thinking about these stories that have helped me in making sense of mine.

Introduction

1. By "ornaments of the darkness," Michelstaedter refers to the rhetorical commonplaces that allow people to live without understanding, especially as aided by the "god" of
phylopsychia, or pleasure, attachment to life, *viltà,* cowardice. See Michelstaedter 2004, xvi,
xvii, 137, 139.

2. For a rich exploration of Hercules as the *vir perfectissimus,* a symbol of virtue in all
its aspects, see Galinsky 1972. On Renaissance *virtus,* see Skinner 1978: 88–94.

3. MacIntyre 1984: 131.

4. *Honestas* is the other Latin word sometimes used to translate the Greek *arete,* leading, for instance, to parallel Renaissance Italian usages, Macchiavelli's *virtù,* which is
invariably masculine, and the *onestà* of a woman: both derive from a functional or teleo-
logical presumption and implicitly invoke the concept of *arete.* On the difference between
a plural and a singular usage—the virtues as opposed to Virtue—with particular attention
to the history of Stoicism, see MacIntyre 1984: 168–70. For a defense of the singularity of
virtue, see Becker 1998: 81–137.

5. This functional usage is akin to the "effect" or "force" that survives in the English
idiom "by virtue of."

6. Exactly when this revolution of the term began is unclear, though the suggestion of
radical doubt that such a claim entails may ultimately derive from the nominalist position
of medieval Scholasticism. I am indebted to David Depew of the University of Iowa for
this suggestion, which surely deserves more extensive investigation than I am competent
to give it.

7. The notion of virtue as effect or function will be familiar to students of Machiavelli,
whose use of *virtù* emphasizes the effectiveness of a variety of behaviors as "virtuous" without reference to ethical judgment. Thus the cruelty of Hannibal was virtuous (in the sense
of being effective) for a military commander. Machiavelli's remarkable, and nuanced, use
of the term is treated extensively in Mansfield 1996: 6–52.

8. This usage likewise allows the still looser synonym with "near" in phrases like "the virtual loss of all subsequent Egyptian manuscripts" or "Cato's death made suicide into a virtual art form," where no corporeal claim is apparent and where the speaker does not wish to be taken literally.

9. Hence the frequently encountered modern contrast of virtue and corruption. On the revival of these classical republican notions in the Renaissance, see Skinner 1978: 152–89. For a discussion of the role of virtue in contemporary republican theory, see Dagger 1997: 194–201; on early American reformulations, see Pocock 1975: 506–552.

10. Pocock's work addresses a set of related problems in the history of ideas, namely, the conceptual linkage between property, military organization, and constitutional theory from Machiavelli to the founders of the American republic, the simultaneous shift from medieval to modern conceptions of time and value, and the role of centrally modern notions such as commerce, corruption, and credit in this overarching process. Pocock's is of course just one of many works amid the late twentieth-century wealth of modernity studies. Other noteworthy examples that have influenced my thought here include Taylor 1989, Gellner 1989, and Thompson 1996.

11. An example of the former is Montesquieu, who, in a not-so-veiled reference to the practice of national stock in the Bank of England, remarked that the nation in such circumstances "would have a sure credit [*un crédit sûr*] because it would borrow from its own self and pay back its own self. It might even borrow beyond its natural strength [*Il pourrait arriver qu'elle entreprendrait au-dessus de ses forces naturelles*] and make valuable [*ferait valoir*] against its enemies immense fictional riches [*d'immenses richesses de fiction*], which the confidence and nature of its government would render real" (Montesquieu 1951: 577; translation mine). On the development of the anticorrosive country ideology in England, see Pocock 1975: 401–22 and 423–61.

12. See, for instance, Turkle 1997, Sunstein 2001, and Sunstein 2007. For a trenchant survey of contemporary responses, from the utopian to the hysterical, see Rodman 2003.

13. While not a coherent movement per se, this resurgence of interest in virtue theory is often motivated by stated desires to reevaluate, and in some cases resurrect, the classical tradition of virtue as exemplified in the writings of Aristotle, the Ancient Stoics, and their descendants. Prominent examples include MacIntyre 1984; Nussbaum 1986; Sherman 1989, 1997, and 2005; Becker 1998; Peterson and Seligman 2004; McCloskey 2006 and 2010; and Sachs 2011. McCloskey's work stands out as something of an intervention. While it too draws upon classical thought, her opus on the "bourgeois virtues," two volumes of which are in print as of this writing, sets out to show how virtue and commerce go together rather than clash; in other words, by contrast to the tradition of thought which sees bourgeois values as ethically and politically pernicious, she wants to show how capitalism makes us not only richer but better.

14. Žižek 1989: 55–57, 169–72.

15. Locke uses "Fansy" and "agreement" in tandem in his *Two Treatises of Civil Government*, where he suggests that the origins of money may be found in the discovery of "some lasting thing that men might keep without spoiling, and that, *by mutual consent*, men would take in exchange for the truly useful but perishable supports of life*" (Locke 2003: 120; emphasis added). His statement that "gold, silver, and diamonds are things that fancy or agreement hath put the value on" must be modified only slightly to accord with my suggestion: not "fancy or agreement" but "fancy *and* agreement" should be the operative term, for only together can the two effect the real change I have in mind. We might specify

still further that it is only in agreeing *about* fancy that gold, silver, and diamonds might be taken "in exchange for the truly useful," that the fiction might be agreed upon as the real, capable of transforming things as they are into things as they might be, as if those objects of exchange really were valuable in the way that we are pretending they are.

16. In late eighteenth-century American social thought, the position represented by Jefferson's classical republicanism, where virtue guarantees the uncorrupt foundation of the republic, is tempered by Madisonian federalism, as expressed, for instance, in the *Federalist* No. 10, which maintains the need for a balance of powers and suggests thereby that either virtue will never be pervasive enough to prevent corruption or virtue alone is not enough to do so.

17. Pipes 2000: 286. Pipes's account implicitly contrasts Anglo-American and Russian conceptions of private property (it explicitly contrasts English and Russian practice). In this sense, it is unique among discussions of the relationship between property and social personality, which generally focus on Western Europe and North America. For a substantive critique of Pipes's reading of his sources, see Ryan 1999.

18. Pocock 1975: 532–45.

19. Of particular interest is Lindberg 1982.

20. Sunstein 2001 goes so far as to make government policy recommendations that might counteract the socially fragmentary effects of the Internet. His is essentially a variation on the "unleashing" version of the power of consensual fantasy noted above. Turkle's (1997, 2012) approach is more descriptive and empirical, while her suggestions about the fluidity of current identity formation among young people are less easily contextualized within the extremes of virtue conceptualization noted here.

21. Things are concrete, existent individuals that lack rationality and, as such, have often been opposed to persons, a distinction that appears to have originated with medieval Scholasticism (the *suppositum* and the *persona*). See Halfman 2002: vol. 14, 4–5.

22. Pocock 1985: 109.

23. Rees 1996; Pohl and Tooley 2007; Kaufmann 1879.

24. Schama 1995: 478–90.

25. Pocock 1975: 535.

26. Schama 1995: 574. Schama shows that Thoreau did not actually maintain this stance in practice, attesting frequently to the manner in which landscape made sense to him through the images and practices of life in other times and places, despite his apparent desire to see it as a historical *tabula rasa*.

27. For detail and a thorough reading in the context of virtue as a moral concept, see Cafaro 2000.

28. One can find hints and scratches of such notions in the works of Mikhail Shcherbatov and Alexander Radishchev in the late eighteenth century and Nikolai Turgenev in the early nineteenth. The republican impulse in most other cases turned, as with Marx, toward revolutionary and tactical thought, as with Alexander Herzen and Mikhail Bakunin.

29. See, for instance, Poe 2003, which is very good on the historical sources but dates the rise of messianic notions too late, in my opinion; for a comparative turn, see Rowley 1999; what is missing for the Russian case is an equivalent to what Tuveson 1968 accomplished for the American one, that is, tracing the ideas, not just the documents.

30. At least as striking is how thoroughly such parallels were later eclipsed by the apparently opposing approaches to modernization adopted by the United States and USSR in the twentieth century and by the contrasts that the Cold War made most apparent.

31. See his historical survey in Pipes 2000: 159–208.

32. Gimbutas 1971; Ivanits 1992; Hubbs 1988. The connections between Russian Orthodox worship of the holy "Mother Earth" and Slavic paganism are discussed by Fedotov 1966: 135–48.

33. Frost 1969: 348.

34. Cf. Pocock 1975: 526–45.

35. For general discussion of the concept of *pochvennichestvo* in Dostoevsky's life and work, see Frank 1986: 34–48 and Dowler 1982. I use the term *modern* here and elsewhere with care. New Age, eco-friendly conceptions of landed connection are a more recent phenomenon, if not "postmodern," then at the very least marginal to mainstream social and political thought in the United States for its first hundred fifty years of existence.

36. Rock 2007 offers an intriguing take on the mixing of pagan and Christian beliefs in Russia.

37. It is equivalent to the moment of confusion between Bassanio and Shylock in Act I, Scene 3 of *The Merchant of Venice*, where Shylock says that Antonio is a "good man" and Bassanio asks whether there has been any imputation to the contrary. Shylock clarifies at length, and with apparent irony, that he merely means his credit is good, that is, he is good *for* it. For a fine reading of the "political body" of Shylock, see Bassi 2007.

38. A phrase from Dostoevsky's notebook entry of April 16, 1864, quoted by Mochulsky 1967: 261.

39. For a more detailed reading of this aspect of *Crime and Punishment*, see chapter 3.

40. For a more detailed reading of this aspect of *Anna Karenina*, see the second half of chapter 3.

41. This topic is explored in Valentino 2001: 60–65.

42. The richest exploration of the virtue vocabulary associated with the modern European and the modern North American political personality is found in Pocock 1975.

43. The word is thought to have been borrowed from Old Slavic, as *dobraia* (good) and *detel'* (action, deed), which were combined in order to render the Greek concept of *arete*, or excellence. It is attested in the early eighteenth century and became a commonplace in the writings of Fonvizin, Sumarokov, and Kheraskov. Its usage in contemporary standard Russian is marked as bookish and archaic. See, for instance, Shanskii 1973: 146.

44. Hippisley 1989: 44, plate no. 172. Such books feature multiple small depictions of famous historical scenes on each page with aphorismic captions most often in Latin, English, French, and German. Maksimovich-Amvodik's book enjoyed popularity through the middle of the nineteenth century. It is noted, for instance, as an object of play for young Fedia Lavretsky in chapter 11 of Ivan Turgenev's *Nest of the Gentry* (1858). Lavretsky is, of course, highly influenced by the republican ideas of his Anglophile father.

45. There are two possible candidates suggested in the book: *tsel'nost'*, which means "wholeness" or "integrity," is noted by Stiva Oblonsky at the start of the novel; *sila zhizni*, or "strength of life," is a quality that Levin muses about when talking with his brother Sergei. Both appear to translate portions of virtue in a combination of its moral-ethical and civic republican guises, though Levin is clearly not reducible to a representative of either strain of thought. A different possibility, *muzhestvto*, which usually translates as "courage," lingers in the background with its root association with manliness but is not explicitly offered up in the book.

46. Gogol 2009, vol. 7, part 1: 210–11. Subsequent citations from this work are indicated parenthetically in the text. All translations, unless otherwise noted, are my own.

47. E.g., Fanger 1979: 192–225; Maguire 1994: 318–41.

Chapter One

1. Yerushalmi 2005: 114–15.
2. In a letter of December 21, 1817, see Wu 2005: 1351.
3. Turkle 1997: 263–64.
4. Ibid.: 261–62.
5. Most trenchant are the remarks in MacIntyre 1984: 115–17, which place Goffman's views in a series proceeding from Nietzsche to Weber to our own day. There are other reflections of Goffman's thought current in contemporary therapy circles, most prominently the notion of the self as performed in a variety of contexts. See, for instance, the work of Newman and the East Side Institute for Group and Short Term Psychotherapy (http://www.eastsideinstitute.org). This line of thought parallels the development of American Pragmatism from William James through George Herbert Mead, finding clear elaborations in the sociology of Parsons 1937 and Merton 1951, among others. I am grateful to Professor David Depew of the University of Iowa for helping me understand this genealogy more clearly.
6. Gunsalus 2006: 43.
7. Becker 1998: 3; on the manner in which evaluative and factual statements parted ways in philosophy, see MacIntyre 1984: 77–87.
8. MacIntyre 1984: 73. His example was imitated more recently by McCloskey, who gives us four instead of three—warrior, cultivator, merchant, and priest. McCloskey 2006: 347.
9. The merging becomes especially noteworthy in translations from the above languages into English, where the associations with "character" grow richer with increased polyvalence. For instance, Roland Barthes's precise distinction between *personnage* and *figure* in his *S/Z* becomes in English "character" and "figure," suggesting a variety of possible ethical connotations that may or may not be in the French. See Barthes 1970: 74–5.
10. The central locus is Mead 1934.
11. Her suggestion that we "have access—broader and broader access in the modern world—to multiple characters at different times" (McCloskey 2006: 347) restates in a different manner the prevailing postmodern view of the discredited unitary subject noted above.
12. Taylor 1989: 3–24.
13. Dostoevsky 1972: 139. Unless otherwise indicated, translations from this text are my own.
14. On *Le parfait négoçiant* see chapter 2. "Miserable details" is how Clerval characterizes the business of his family in Mary Shelley's *Frankenstein* (Shelley 2003: 30).
15. Golyadkin, states Dostoevsky, "goes mad out of *ambition*, while at the same time fully despising ambition and even suffering from the fact that he happens to suffer from such nonsense as ambition" (Frank 1986: 300).
16. Frank 1986: 299–300.
17. Agreeing, in effect, with Charles Davenant's earlier assessment: "Trade, without doubt, is in its nature a pernicious thing; it brings in that wealth which introduces luxury; it gives rise to fraud and avarice, and extinguishes virtue and simplicity of manners; it depraves a people, and makes way for that corruption which never fails to end in slavery, foreign or domestic." Davenant 1771: 275.
18. Frank 1986: 307.

19. Sleuths are referred to chapter 2. *Dead Souls* carries on where Pushkin left off in "A Queen of Spades," presenting a politically conservative response to a perceived destabilization of social value as the result of commercial culture's spread in post-Napoleonic Russian society. But Gogol's depiction leaves out the psychological implications—evident in the madness of Hermann—that such a transformation of social and political personality represented for Pushkin. *The Double* recreates the psychological dimension Gogol omitted but accompanies it with a characteristically Dostoevskian emphasis on morality and aesthetics.

20. See Mulcaire 1999 for an articulate formulation of the role of public credit, especially in early eighteenth-century England.

21. Likewise, his concerns about Petrushka appear as fears of being "sold out" (*prodan*) (Dostoevsky 1972: 111, 188).

22. See also chapter 3.

23. The causal connection is shrouded in the mists of nineteenth-century medical understanding. The boy dies of tuberculosis, but the wound he received in the chest by a rock thrown by one of his classmates is suggested to have brought on the final crisis and, indeed, his death.

24. Pocock 1985: 109.

25. For these forms of property, "the appropriate term in the republican lexicon was corruption." Pocock 1975: 464.

26. Hirschman 1977: 132–33.

27. Dostoevsky 1972: 223–24.

28. Bakhtin 1963: 291–92; Vinogradov 1929: 261–67; and Terras 1969: 206–12.

29. Hirschman 1977: 9–12.

30. Retarded commercial culture in Russia and its artificial freezing by the Soviets meant in practice a preservation and canonization of certain aristocratic attitudes toward commercial enterprise—Gogol's narrator refers to this as what "the world dubs as *not quite clean.*" In the socialization of school-age Russians one finds even today a suspicion of self-interested motives and a tendency to denigrate the individual who puts Ya (I) at the front of the alphabet, instead of at the end, where it belongs. Such suspicion may have been institutionalized in the Soviet period, when the works of "great" Russian authors were canonized, but its roots in Russian culture run far deeper.

31. Gogol 2009, vol. 7, part 1: 9.

32. Bakhtin 1981: 13–20.

33. Lynch 1998: 2–3, 9–10, 15–17, 118–19, 123–28.

34. Fusso 1993: 20–51.

35. The turning point comes in chapter 8, when he meets the governor's daughter again and, dumbstruck, earns the wrath of the ladies through his inattention, fueling the train of speculation and rumor stoked by Nozdryov, which transform him into "Napoleon in disguise" (Gogol 2009, vol. 7, part 1: 156–60).

36. My analysis here converges in some respects with that of Roland Barthes in *S/Z*, where he discusses the replacement of the old indexical order of landed wealth by the arbitrary signifier of Parisien gold as the reigning model of unbacked representation. See "L'indice, le signe, et l'argent" (Barthes 1970: 46–7). Indeed, the aspiring bourgeois artist's attempt to characterize and "frame" the ideal woman, only to discover that she is not a woman at all, puts the Sarassine narrative in an odd sort of parallel with those under dis-

cussion. I am indebted to Garrett Stewart of the University of Iowa for pointing out this convergence of method and theme.

37. Canto 11. Sincere thanks to Ed Folsom of the University of Iowa for the reference.

38. Dostoevsky 1972: 212–21.

39. Schiller 1943: 368–70; Zhukovsy 1959: 137–39. A distinction between Golyadkin's disparaging attitude of the poem and Dostoevsky's lifelong adoration of the poet is in order. For a fine extended treatment of the importance of Schiller in Dostoevsky's oeuvre, see Vil'mont 1984.

40. Dostoevsky 1972: 221–22.

41. Lotman 1995: 434–44.

42. Dostoevsky 1972: 185.

43. *Bezobrazie*, according to its linguistic roots, "without form," also carries connotations of abomination. It is alternately translated as "ugliness," "hideousness," "outrage." At its root lie the words for form, face, and holy icon. For a full discussion see Jackson 1966.

44. Golyadkin Senior prides himself on this in his letter to Vakhrameev. Dostoevsky 1972: 183.

Chapter Two

1. Gogol 2009, vol. 7, part 1: 194.
2. See Leighton 1977.
3. Pushkin 1936: 250, 252.
4. Bayley 1971: 316.
5. Lotman 1978: 476–77.
6. The translation cited is by James Falen. See Pushkin 1990: 41 (chapter 2, stanza XIV).
7. Thus are fate and chance intimately linked in the depiction of Hermann, whose attempt to control chance is similar to Chichikov's attempt to control his chance encounters—with Korobochka, Nozdryov, and the governor's daughter—those which in the end prove to be his undoing. On the pattern of planned versus unplanned encounters in *Dead Souls*, see Fusso 1993: 20–51.
8. Part 1 of the book is often thought of as a "gallery of portraits," with little or no organic unity besides, perhaps, the road itself. See, for instance, Fanger 1979: 164–91; Gippius 1989: 119; and Shevyrev 1978: 282–90. The approach I take here presupposes that the landowners are neither "completely unconnected with one another" (Tamarchenko 1959: 18–19), nor occurring "without logical order" (Freeborn 1973: 91). Gogol's own statement to the effect that his sequence is based on an increasing degree of *poshlost'* (Gogol 1937: vol. 8, 293), while suggestive, is secondary to the evidence of the text itself. In any case, there is little reason to exclude the possibility of an equivalency of sorts, in Gogol's estimation, of *poshlost'* and the gradually increasing spiritual commodification I am suggesting.
9. Cf. Frank Friederberg Seeley's suggestion that "the new world of *Dead Souls* is a new psychological world reflecting the transformation of society in the sixty years spanned by [Pushkin's *Captain's Daughter*, Lermontov's *Hero of Our Time*, and Gogol's *Dead Souls*]; the new age is that of incipient capitalism." While my suggestion of a commercial sequence in Gogol's landowners is, to my knowledge, original, my analysis occasionally converges with Seeley's, especially in his suggestion that "from his school-days onward [Chichikov] has

used his fellow-humans; his life has been organised in terms not of personal feelings but of the cash nexus" (Seeley 1968: 42). I am indebted to Emeritus Professor Ray Parrott of the University of Iowa for bringing Seeley's article to my attention.

10. On the importance of the concept of soul in the book, see also Fanger 1979: 168–9, 178–81.

11. The term comes from Daly and Cobb 1989: 33–34.

12. As Pushkin makes clear in chapter 1, stanza 7 of *Eugene Onegin*, his hero is a "profound economist" (*glubokii ekonom*) and reader of Adam Smith.

13. Following Napoleon's invasion, the government was forced to issue large amounts of paper money; the assignat was made legal tender for all transactions, and taxes were thenceforth set and collected in assignats only, measures that effectively created two currencies—paper and metal—with fluctuating relative values, making currency problems the most widely discussed economic issue of Nicholas's reign and leading eventually to the reforms of 1839–40. See Pintner 1967: 5, 184–85.

14. I am indebted to an anonymous *Slavic Review* reader for this succinct phrasing.

15. Heroes from Nikolai Karamzin's "Poor Liza" (1792) and "Yuliya" (1801), respectively. Robert Maguire suggests these Gogolian names "serve the double purpose of mocking the recent vogue for things classical and establishing a decidedly non-Russian presence in this estate." See Maguire 1994: 30. Such a vogue was characteristic of Russian culture from the age of Catherine II into the nineteenth century.

16. Gogol's narrator relates that Chichikov "added that the treasury will even benefit, for it will receive legal duties," but he does not specify from whom or on what (35). There is additional irony here in the fact that the soul-tax or *podushnaia podat'*, upon which Chichikov's transactions rely, was instituted, under Peter I, precisely as a means of generating much-needed revenue for the state. See, for instance, Lewitter 1987: 103–6. The issue of the soul tax is treated at length by Ivan Pososhkov, whose 1724 *Kniga o skudosti i bogatsve* (Book of Poverty and Wealth) was first printed only in 1842, the same year as Gogol's *Dead Souls*. It was brought to light and published by Mikhail Pogodin, professor of history at Moscow State University and Gogol's friend and correspondent of many years. I am indebted to Professor David Herman of the University of Virginia for bringing this important text to my attention.

17. "The Moral End of Business." See Dewey 1901: 252.

18. From his "Six Ways to Make People Like You," widely used by salespeople as a basic technique for increasing effective selling.

19. Hirschman 1977: 61.

20. Fusso 1993: 45–47 discusses Nozdryov's lying as a spontaneous and creative phenomenon, linked to the health and vitality of his character and contrasted to the carefully planned fabrications of Chichikov.

21. Cf. Sobakevich's consistency in assigning a labor function to each of the serf-names he is preparing to sell, noted by Zeldin 1978: 100.

22. Mavrokordato (1791–1835), Kolokotronis (1770–1843), Miaoulis (1768–1835), and Kanaris (1790–1877) were all participants in the Greek struggle for independence from Ottoman Turkey.

23. Laskarina Bouboulina (1771–1825), Greek heroine of Greece's independence movement, known to Russians of Gogol's day especially because of her family's support of Russia in the Russo-Turkish wars of the early nineteenth century, and because after her murder in 1825, she was awarded the rank of admiral by the Russian navy.

24. Cf. Gavriel Shapiro's discussion of the accuracy of Gogol's portraits vis-à-vis luboks of the time in Shapiro 1993: 71–73. Michael Holquist proposes an interpretation of "Diary of a Madman" along similar lines to that which I have suggested here: Peter I's willful changing of the calendar (from the Orthodox to the Julian) in order to bring it into keeping with European temporality is seen as analogous to the madman's arbitrary diary datings, not to mention his delusions of grandeur. See Holquist 1977: 3–27.

25. Bagration died in the battle of Borodino, which slowed but did not halt Napoleon's advance on Moscow.

26. See, for instance, Hirschman 1977: 9–12; Pocock 1975: 133–35.

27. For a contrasting reading of the conception of value in *Dead Souls*, especially as relates to questions of meaning and interpretation, see Morson 1992: 206–15.

28. This line, "*Pravo, u vas dusha chelovecheskaia vsë ravno, chto parenaia repa,*" has been rendered as "Your soul is like a boiled turnip" in the translations of Garnett, Magarshak, and Reavey, who adds the word "human" before "soul." There is ambiguity in the Russian sentence because of the peculiar combination of *u vas* (*chez vous*), which suggests the personal, and *chelovecheskaia* (human), which suggests the general. The immediately following phrase, "Give me at least three rubles each," creates two possibilities: if Sobakevich's comment is directed at Chichikov's person, it implies the latter is too cheap to offer a fair price; if it is directed at Chichikov's notions of the world (as in *pravo, u vas liudi—drian'*; "in truth, you think people are garbage"), the comment accords with Sobakevich's attempts to increase the market value of his wares and might be paraphrased as "Do you really think the human soul is worth so little?" The latter appears to me more accurate; or, as Bernard Guerney's translation has it: "Really, you hold a human soul at the same value as a boiled turnip."

29. See Fusso's fascinating speculation on Nozdryov's "figurative androgyny," the sexual connotations of his name, and its apparent connection to the vulgar woman's synechdoche *nozdria*, in Fusso 1993: 160–61 n.; the original suggestion, that of an early listener to Gogol's text, was partly corroborated by Gogol himself, who responded, "If such an idea occurred to one person, that means it could occur to many. It must be corrected." See Annenkov 1952: 244.

30. It is significant that the last object noted on Plyushkin's table is the completely yellowed toothbrush, with which "the master, perhaps, picked his teeth back *before the French invasion of Moscow*" (108; emphasis added). This is the only item located historically in all Plyushkin's collection.

31. On the importance of the word as Romantic medium in Gogol's oeuvre see Maguire 1994: part 3.

32. Cf. also Fanger 1979: 188–89.

33. For a discussion of the distinctive disintegration of Plyushkin see, for instance, Woodward 1978: chapter 5.

34. The term is suggested by Morson 1992: 210.

35. The runaways are a marginal case, neither strictly dead nor provably living. Their place between living and dead may be part of a general tendency in the novel for the qualities of the serfs being purchased to become more lifelike while the landowners more and more resemble death—for example, the absence of soul in Sobakevich, the death imagery surrounding Plyushkin. Thus, Chichikov is struck by several of the names and nicknames among the peasants he acquires at Korobochka's; Sobakevich then insists on the living nature of the serfs he is selling, on their very real qualities and works; finally, Chichikov

assigns not only qualities but also dialogue to his serf purchases when reviewing the lists in his hotel room. What were before merely names and, in Chichikov's words, "but a dream," become very real indeed, as Chichikov portrays them to himself in imagined living situations.

36. As noted above, an equivalent subjection of the sacred or divine to a commercial relation is evident in "The Portrait," where moneylending begins the chain of worldly evil. In this connection, it is important to realize that, in the absence of a regularized and widely accessible system of credit, Chichikov is, in effect, in pursuit of a loan.

37. The phrase, which is introduced by the conjunction "but," suggests it indeed marks the turning point, but no further reason for Plyushkin's transformation is offered, except perhaps the suggestion in the next line that, "like all widows, Plyushkin became more suspicious and stingier."

38. By the middle of the nineteenth century, the state held *in mortgage* two-thirds of all serfs. Riasanovsky 1984: 341.

39. See the earlier treatment of Montesquieu's usage in my introduction and n. 11. It is tempting to think of Chichikov's dead serfs as something like the "*immenses richesses de fiction*" that the Russian state counted on to support its military and economic system.

40. "*C'est presque une règle générale, que partout où il y a des moeurs douces, il y a du commerce; et que partout où il y a du commerce, il y a des moeurs douces.*"

41. For definitions and for examples of Gogol's use, see Shapiro 1993: 194–99. Asyndeton usually refers to parts of a sentence, not to sequences of scenes or chapters.

42. Skillful as the interpretation suggested in Morson 1992 may be, I disagree with its starting point. Arguably, no amount of historicization will explain all aspects of Gogol's idiosyncratic book. But raising Gogolian senselessness to heuristic heights risks blocking the exploration of the myriad ways the book may in fact make sense, leaving it in an ahistorical limbo of sorts, far from its literary, cultural, and historical roots.

43. Hirschman makes the notion of *reconstruction* explicit when he writes, "By drawing on a wide range of sources I have attempted to show that the [interests-versus-passions] thesis was part of what Michael Polanyi has called the 'tacit dimension,' that is, propositions and opinions shared by a group and so obvious to it that they are never fully or systematically articulated." Hirschman: 1977: 69. The overview provided here draws on the treatments provided in Pocock 1975; Pocock 1985; Hirschman 1977; Holmes 1995: 42–68; and, more broadly, Skinner 1978.

44. Hirschman 1977: 33.

45. Ibid.: 39–40.

46. Ibid.: 41 (emphasis in original).

47. Holmes 1995: 61 so designates the entry under "self-interest" in Diderot's *Encyclopédie*.

48. Ibid.: 60–62.

49. Hirschman 1977: 42.

50. Holmes 1995: 54.

51. The words are those of the lady Pekuah relating the story of her captivity at the hands of the Arab, chapter 39. Johnson 2009: 328.

52. Hume 1760: 125.

53. Holmes 1995: 54.

54. Boswell 1933: vol. 1, 567.

55. Savary 1713: 1. Quoted with emphasis in Hirschman 1977: 59–60.

56. Hirschman 1977: 62.

57. Montesquieu 1951: vol. 2, 585. For a brief summary of Montesquieu's views of commerce, see Shklar 1987: 107–8; for a discussion of the civic humanist roots of Montesquieu's assertion, see Pocock 1975: 491–93.

58. Hirschman 1977: 62.

59. Gogol's well-known secrecy about his reading habits has prompted speculation ever since his creative years. Fanger has addressed what he calls the "vexed question of [Gogol's] literary filiations," noting that "he is no Flaubert with respect to the articulations of his reading, knowledge, tastes, or even specific awareness of literature in the forms he himself cultivated." Fanger 1979: 12–13; see also Chudakov 1908 and Annenkov 1928.

60. Goux 1999: 115.

61. The classic statement is that of John Locke in his *Second Treatise on Civil Government*. For a suggestive reading of Chichikov's scheme as akin to a contemporary hedge fund, see Crossen 2008.

62. On Chichikov as catalyst, and for a series of insightful character readings, some of which touch on my own, see Zeldin 1978: 95–104.

63. Pletnev 1885: 491.

64. Pocock 1975: 464.

Chapter Three

1. Dostoevsky 1973: 5. Subsequent citations from this work are indicated parenthetically in the text. Unless otherwise indicated, translations from the Russian are my own.

2. The words are those of the student that Raskolnikov overhears by chance on Hay Market Square, but the thoughts, as the narrator makes clear on the following page, are also Raskolnikov's.

3. See Jackson 1966.

4. Raskolnikov lays out his theory to Porfiry Petrovich in chapter 5 of part 3 (199–204). The suggestion that he might think of himself as a new Napoleon is made explicit by Zametov, who remarks, "Wasn't it some kind of new Napoleon who bumped off our Alyona Ivanovich with an axe last week?" (204).

5. The treatment of Dunya and especially Sonya as commercial commodities is, of course, obvious throughout the work. Svidrigailov alludes to such a treatment when, upon introducing himself to Raskolnikov in the opening lines of part 4, he states, "I'm dreaming [*mechtaiu*] that you perhaps will not afford me assistance in a certain undertaking [*predpriiatie*] directly concerning the interest [*interes*] of your little sister" (214). Here as in Raskolnikov's opening thoughts, the combined lexicon of fantasy and enterprise is striking.

6. On the distinction between literary signification and symbolic or sacramental signification, see Lewis 1958. On this distinction in Dostoevsky, see Valentino 2001: 112–18.

7. See chapter 1, pp. 30–32.

8. See chapter 1, pp. 37–38.

9. Dickens 1967: 328.

10. Tocqueville 2000: 403.

11. McCloskey 2006.

12. Frank dismisses the passage and the reference as providing "a touch of grotesquerie to Svidrigailov's sinister end" (Frank 2002: 302). In a more recent work (Fleishman, Safran,

and Wachtel 2005: 440–41), he is still less interested in unraveling the scene. But in both cases, he appears to be reacting to those who have found an explicit and rather simple anti-Semitic symbolism in the scene. Goldstein, by contrast, calls the symbolism "unquestionable but inscrutable" (1981: 14–15). Rice treats it similarly but within the context of Freud's interaction with Russian literature and thought (1993: 138). These and other sources explain that the crested helmet of Russian firemen in the nineteenth century was thought to resemble, and to be derived from, the helmet worn by Ancient Greek warriors. None of these sources comments on whether the service of a Jew as fireman would have been an unusual occurrence; nor does the academic edition's extensive commentary, from which I assume that it would not have been.

   13. Arnold 1949: 559–60.

   14. On Arnold and his context, see DeLaura 1969. Arendt explains Greek greatness versus the "teachings of the Hebrews" regarding the sanctity of human life in Arendt 1993: 52–54.

   15. I hesitate to state that the juxtaposition of categories that Dostoevsky highlights in his character was a commonplace of European representation and thought because I have not explored the sources thoroughly enough to be certain. But Arnold is suggestive when he notes that "the two [notions] very often are confronted" in his references to a sermon on Hellenism by Frederick Robertson, and to Heinrich Heine "and other writers of his sort" who engage in similar confrontations (Arnold 1949: 559). Dostoevsky may have been anti-Semitic, of course. Others have done far more research into the question, which is really tangential to this study. But this scene does not provide evidence one way or the other about Dostoevsky's personal beliefs or attitudes. See, for instance, Goldstein 1981, Morson 1983, Dreizin 1990, Rice 1993.

   16. See chapter 2, p. 48.

   17. Aristotle 2003: 101. He quotes an unknown source.

   18. Tolstoy, vol. 8: 291. Subsequent references to this work are provided parenthetically in the text. Unless otherwise noted, translations are my own.

   19. Levin is not alone in facing the question of public versus private good as a problem in the novel. The proper public display of private life is central to the depiction of the Karenin household, suggesting at least a genre distinction (the boundaries of the society novel) and perhaps a gender distinction as well, as the depictions of women in social space assume greater importance with modernization. The question is clearly related to changing notions of the categories of public and private themselves and deserves a fuller treatment than I am able to provide here. For background on the notion of "the public" in much the sense that Tolstoy appears to be operating with in *Anna Karenina*, see Auerbach 1984; on changes in the depiction of the individual in public space, see Sennett 1974.

   20. See in particular Hirschman 1977: 33–41.

   21. Borovoi 1958: 98–101, 136–55, 244–47, 258–74.

   22. Pocock 1985: 103–123.

   23. Ibid. 115.

   24. Ibid. 110.

   25. I have two instances in mind: his diatribe on the impoverishment of the nobility (vol 8: 202) and his criticism of the up-start Vronsky-like families of the upper class (vol 8: 204).

   26. The rational egoism preached in the Chernyshevskian self-interest camp is evident in the instruction of Mr. Nosovich, the high school literature teacher of the narrator-hero in *Gnilye bolota* (*Putrid Swamps*), Aleksandr Sheller-Mikhailov's 1864 novel serialized in

The Contemporary: "Egoism is the main motor of all that is accomplished on the earth. . . . [One must cultivate] love of one's *I* [and] always and in all cases strictly observe one's actions with the necessities of one's self-interest, one's personal well-being. . . . The rational egoist [*blagorazumnyi egoist*], acting in his own interest, always acts also in the interests of all" (Sheller-Mikhailov 1904: 171).

27. "[Tolstoy] was considered the representative and even the ideologue of 'the nobility, the Russian estate-owning nobility, inscribed in the genealogical registers by guberniya.' He is the heir of that old, waning, oppositionist nobility that long before (even as early as the reign of Alexander I) had withdrawn from state service and settled on the land. He is an aristocrat-agrarian rejecting urban civilization and despising the serving nobility and the liberal bourgeois nobility of the zemstvo." Eikhenbaum 1982: 32.

28. Pocock 1985: 41.

29. Pocock 1975: 37. See also Semmel 1984: 6–8. On the literary historical front, my analysis here and elsewhere parallels that of McKeon 1987, especially in his overall claim that the novel as a genre arises in the dialectic between worth and birth, value and inherited wealth. I am indebted to Garrett Stewart of the University of Iowa for pointing out how well Pocock's distinction between virtue and fortune maps onto McKeon's argument.

30. Anna critiques Lydia Ivanovna's character: "Indeed it was funny: her goal was virtue [*dobrodetel'*], she was a Christian, but she was always angry, she had enemies everywhere, and they were all enemies for the sake of virtue and Christianity" (vol 8: 131); Madame Stahl is depicted through Kitty's eyes: "Some said Madame Stahl had created for herself the position of a virtuous, highly religious woman" (vol. 8: 259).

31. Kitty subsequently repeats her idea of Varenka as a "whole" or "perfection" (*sovershenstvo*) about which she could only dream (vol 8: 265), and later says to her friend, partly trying to soothe her feelings after implying that all such virtuousness amounts to pretense, "You are perfection; yes, yes, you are perfection" (278).

32. On such linkages see Stenbock-Fermor 1975.

33. Gustafson 1986 notes the spiritual force (*sila*) within Levin (142) and the "force of life" (*sila zhizni*) Pierre Bezukhov comes to learn from the example of Platon Karataev (79), suggesting a uniquely Tolstoyan approach to self-interested behavior as "what shuts off the living water of divine life within us" (178). While taking nothing from Gustafson's achievement, I am interested in the broader European discursive context within which Tolstoy's thought resonates.

34. For a contemporary take, see Mansfield 2006.

35. See especially Morson's discussion of Dolly's attention to prosaic detail in Morson 2007: 33–54.

36. See chapters 1–3 of part 3.

37. For a recent alternative that contrasts the forms of illumination surrounding and penetrating Levin and Anna, see Kaufman 2011.

Chapter Four

1. Plato 1952: 562–63.

2. Pushkin 1990: 48–49.

3. As indicated earlier in this study, I understand McCloskey's body of work within the resurgence of virtue talk of the past several decades. For a brief characterization and context, see note 13 of the introduction.

4. McCloskey 2006: 243–44. Study has perhaps worn my skin thin here, but surely, in her scathing profile of Gerschenkron's masculine heroism, McCloskey does not want to claim he was not really learned or eloquent or any of the rest. Indeed, his neo-aristocratism, myth or not, was likely a fundamental source of his strength as a person and scholar. An aristocratic self-mythos might look a lot like an anachronism, indeed might be one, and she does ridicule it as such (a circular argument, and actually not an argument), but it can also be one of the more motivating self-mythoi behind the accomplishments of men and women both.

5. Gorky is a counter example to what McCloskey advances as an early twentieth-century rule. Literary man of action par excellence, Maxim Gorky was one of the leading public intellectuals of his day on both sides of the Atlantic. His *Mother,* moreover, was first published in English in New York in 1906. The Russian work would not be published until 1918.

6. To be fair, McCloskey states, "There is a time for aristocratic courage. Courage, not prudence or love or faith, is sometimes what is called for" (2006: 211). But it is difficult to reconcile such a concession with her claim that "the old tales of Western courage . . . that throng our Western culture are phony from the start" (212).

7. See, for instance, McCloskey 2006: 253–62.

8. Depew 2005; Valentino 2005.

9. See chapter 3, pp. 81–82.

10. Nabokov reportedly did not like Pasternak's novel. For a review of *Zhivago*'s reception by English-language critics, see Bayley 1991; Johnson 1985. To my knowledge, Pasternak never commented on *Lolita.*

11. *Lolita*'s *succès de scandale* propelled Nabokov to international notoriety and gave him the financial independence to resign his teaching position at Cornell and move back to Europe. *Zhivago* made the retiring poet into an international cause célèbre, endangering his longtime mistress and the model for *Zhivago*'s Lara, Olga Ivinskaya. Pasternak won the 1958 Nobel Prize for literature largely on the basis of the novel, but he was pressured to refuse the award by the Soviet authorities. For examples of their tactics, see the appendices to Conquest 1961: 131–89. Ivinskaya and her daughter were arrested six weeks after the author's death. They were tried and sentenced to prison terms in Siberia of eight and three years, respectively.

12. The sexlessness of Yura's trauma is reinforced by the setting of the subsequent scene: the dark cell of a monastery on the eve of the Feast of the Intercession of the Virgin.

13. Nabokov 1970: 309. Subsequent references to this work are included in the text with page references indicated parenthetically.

14. The setting is not in Nabokov's screenplay, which stipulates "a photograph of Duk-Duk ranch which Lolita had visited." Nabokov 1974: 2.

15. The film announces Harris and Kubrick first, then moves to Nabokov's novel and screenplay. On Nabokov's judgment that he might have easily been removed from the credits based on the amount of material from his screenplay included in the film, see his foreword to Nabokov 1974: xii–xiii.

16. Humbert notes on the final page that he started writing fifty-six days earlier. He died, according to Ray's foreword, on November 16, 1952, fifty-six days before which was September 22, the day he received Lolita's letter. Boyd 1995 has argued against such a reading, suggesting instead that the inconsistency was a mistake of the author. For arguments in favor of it, see Bruss 1976: 145–45; Tekiner 1979: 463–69; Toker 1989: 198–227; Dolinin 1995: 3–40

(esp. n. 1); and Connolly 1995: 41–61. It is hard to resist the thought that Nabokov would have savored creating such a "controversy" among his most careful readers.

17. I have heard the passage quoted as an example of empathy, as fine an instance of wishful reading as ever there was.

18. Its implicit reliance on Pushkin, especially his quintessentially sublime Tatiana, from *Eugene Onegin*, is treated by Meyer 1984. It is also worth recalling that Nabokov dedicated every book he ever published "To Vera."

19. "It has often been remarked that all Pasternak's own work can be read as being in some sense about the way art originates, especially the way it originates in the course of something very ordinary and day-to-day." Livingstone 1985: 13–14.

20. "Where shall I put my joy?" is a line from the poem "*Nasha groza*" (Our storm), in Pasternak 1961: 26. The artist who raises intense awareness to "a constant poetic symptom" is characterized by "*Povest'*" (A Tale), in Pasternak 1982.

21. "*Liubit' inykh tiazhelyi krest*" (The Heavy Cross of Loving Others), in Pasternak 1961: 337.

22. From an entry in Zhivago's diary (Pasternak 1958: 281). Other references to this work are provided parenthetically in the text.

23. More precisely, the name is the genitive case of the Church Slavonic adjective *zhivyi*, which may be translated as "alive" or "living." As I. A. Esaulov has indicated, the name has a Biblical source in Luke 24:5—"Why seek ye the living among the dead?" where "the living" of the Slavonic and Greek texts is genitive singular and male: in other words, "Why do you seek one living man among the (many) dead?" Zhivago may thus indicate a name for Jesus Christ (Esaulov 2006: 67). Susanna Witt has also made a case for Zhivago as a translation (to Church Slavonic) of the Greek *zosimos*, or "living," thereby connecting Pasternak's hero to the Elder Zosima in Dostoevsky's *Brothers Karamazov*. See Witt 2000: 80.

24. For the conventional wisdom on how to construct a plot, see, for instance, Dibell 1999. Some naïve readers have assumed that Pasternak must have thought such triteness was effective storytelling. This is a poor reading that does not accord with his intellectual milieu, his poetic oeuvre, and his other, highly sophisticated and complex prose fiction.

25. Mulvey 1975.

26. de la Durantaye 2007: 91.

27. There may also be a distant reference here to Pushkin's ode to the female instep in *Eugene Onegin*, chapter 1. See, for instance, Nabokov's discussion of what he refers to as the "pedal digression" in Pushkin 1964: vol. 2, 115–17.

28. The translation from the Russian is my own.

29. The term is Bakhtin's, in Morson and Emerson's English. Morson and Emerson 1990: 275–277.

30. The disembodied and nearly abstract quality of the afterimage is inherent in the conception of inspiration itself. The image of the beloved reflected upon afterward for the poet is akin to the "glowing coal" from Shelley's defense of poetry, with which both Pasternak and Nabokov agreed. Cf. Nabokov's commentary on Pushkin's line (used in my epigraph) "Love passed, the Muse appeared," which specifies four stages of artistic inspiration: "(1) Direct perception of a 'dear object' or event. (2) The hot, silent shock of irrational rapture accompanying the evocation of that impression in one's fancies or actual dreams. (3) The preservation of the image. (4) The later, cooler touch of creative art, as identified with rationally controlled inspiration, verbal transmutation, and a new harmony." See Pushkin 1964: vol. 2, 211.

31. See chapter 1.

32. For a compelling comparative treatment of the manner in which memory is imbedded in the images of sunsets in *Doctor Zhivago* and Dostoevsky's *Brothers Karamazov*, see Witt 2000: 72–94. Witt refrains from placing these scenes in their proper intellectual historical context, namely, the Platonic doctrine of recollection or *anamnesis*, as developed in the dialogues *Meno* and *Phaedo*; in this context, the Eucharistic themes in each of the two books resonate more fully.

33. *Devochka iz drugogo kruga* (A Girl from Another Circle) is the title of part 2.

34. He is no less willing to allow himself to assume the symbolic value. The basically Platonic conception of character that Pasternak accords his main figures is suggested in the "nearly Platonic dialogues" that Yury and Lara engage in during their time at Varykino (Pasternak 1958: 395).

Conclusion

1. Plato 1952: 411.

2. Sinyavsky 1990: 259.

3. He is quoting Ivan Bunin's journal from the period when he was composing *Well of Days* (1933). Sinyavsky 1990: 259. Joseph Conrad implicitly agrees with such an assessment when he depicts the only European character apparently unaffected by the raw savagery of the jungle in *Heart of Darkness* as a Russian.

4. Turkle 1997: 263–64. See also my earlier treatment in chapter 1.

5. Bely 1978: 64.

6. The reconstruction of the ancient Menippean satire as a form-shaping impulse in modern fiction is laid out in Bakhtin 1984: 114–18. For additional discussion of the ways that menippea may combine with other textual constituents (e.g., polyphony, carnivalesque laughter) in order to question ethical grounds and facilitate the exploration of ultimate questions, see Morson and Emerson 1990: 465–69, 490–91.

7. Goux 1999: 99.

8. For a treatment of confidence men (and painted ladies) as an aspect of American middle-class culture of the latter half of the nineteenth and early part of the twentieth centuries, see Halttunen 1982.

9. See also the earlier discussion of Montesquieu's usage in my introduction.

10. Franscell 2003 compares *Cosmopolis*, unfavorably, with *Ulysses*, and expresses hope that "DeLillo wrote it as a comedy, too" (par. 8); Kakutani 2003 refers to it as "a major dud, as lugubrious and heavy-handed as a bad Wim Wenders film, as dated as an old issue of Interview magazine" (par. 2); Kipen 2003 offers a more positive assessment, calling the work an "odd, bottomless book" that "refuses to go away" (par. 12).

11. I have in mind the approach to generic allusion and family resemblance in Fowler 1982. On generic allusion, see pp. 88–92; on family resemblance, see pp. 40–44 and 58.

12. I am indebted to an anonymous reader of *Modern Fiction Studies* for this succinct overview of constructional and thematic patterns in DeLillo's opus. Win Everett ruminates on the "deathward logic of . . . plot" in *Libra* (221). Jack Gladney repeats the notion almost verbatim in *White Noise* when he declares, "All plots tend to move deathward" (26). The "knotted twine" linking characters and concerns in these passages is unraveled in Cowart 2002: 75. There is a considerable body of literature exploring DeLillo's complex treatment

of signs and mediation throughout his opus, particularly in the context of the postmodern theoretical frameworks of Jean Beaudrillard and Jean-Francois Lyotard. Cowart 2002: 1–13 provides a most helpful overview and excellent starting point.

13. For the suggestion that virtue might be a central concern in DeLillo's work, I am indebted to a presentation by Mark Osteen of Loyola College, at the May 7–8, 2004, *Critical Exchanges* conference at Northwestern University. For a coherent vision of DeLillo's pre-*Cosmopolis* opus through *Underground*, see Osteen 2000, which shares several points of contact with the trajectory I follow in these pages, in particular DeLillo's intense intertextuality.

14. Fear of death is a central theme in nearly all DeLillo's works. The acceleration of time that allows Packer's mind to race ahead of his body is prepared earlier in the book: 52, 93–94.

15. Ryan 1987: 27.

16. As Walker 2003 makes clear, a "haircut" is also a slang term for losing a lot of money in an investment.

17. The encounter eerily recapitulates the end of DeLillo's 1985 *White Noise*, a subject that must be left to another study. The fact that a credible threat is a threat likely to make good on its promise of being a threat is just one of the many darkly humorous word games DeLillo plays in the book.

18. Bakunin's phrase in context: "Let us put our trust in the eternal spirit which destroys and annihilates only because it is the unsearchable and eternally creative source of all life. The urge to destroy is also a creative urge." In "Reaction in Germany—A Fragment by a Frenchman," published under the pseudonym of Jules Elysard in Arnold Ruge's *Deutsche Jahrbücher für Wissenschaft und Kunst* (1842).

19. John G. Blair excludes Chichikov, erroneously it seems to me, from his list (Blair 1979: 13). Lindberg 1982 offers an expansive interpretation of the type, and the phenomenon, in American literature and culture since Ben Franklin. Joanne Gass treats another echo of Gatsby, *Underworld's* Nick Shay, also from the perspective of an American mythos, which she calls that of the American Adam. See Gass 2002.

20. Blair 1979: 12.

21. DeLillo 2003: 74, 89, and 96.

22. The threat of social corruption is extensively treated by Pocock. For a discussion of the rise of self-interested acquisition and the attendant "decline of glory," see Hirschman 1977: 9–12.

23. Bakhtin 1986: 4–7.

24. Cf. Sullivan 2004.

25. The Herbert line is from "Report from the Besieged City": "Monday: empty storehouses a rat became the unit of currency" (Herbert 2001: 76). DeLillo performed a public reading of the poem at the New York City Town Hall event October 11, 2001. For an earlier intimation of the relationship of rats and humans in DeLillo's thought, see DeLillo 1985: 124–25.

26. E.g., Aristotle's *Politics*, book I, chapter 9, which focuses on the "limitless" and "unnatural" character of trading in exchange value (as opposed to "use value"). It should be noted that Kinski's predicted cure for the contemporary pandemonium is to "bring nature back to normal, more or less" (79): an Aristotelian cure?

27. "Psychomachia" is the title of Prudentius's fifth-century allegory that pits the Christian virtues against the pagan vices in a battle for the *psyche* of man.

28. She echoes Pocock when she maintains that "property is no longer about power, personality and command. It's not about vulgar display or tasteful display. Because it no longer has weight or shape" (78).

29. "The idea of the world citizen . . . requires us to place justice above political expediency, and to understand that we form part of a universal community of humanity whose ends are the moral ends of justice and human well-being." Nussbaum 1997: 58. This, indeed, is the argument of the Cosmopolitan, the central character of Melville's *The Confidence-Man*.

30. Pocock 1985: 112.

31. Žižek 1989: 68.

32. Mulcaire 1999: 1039.

33. See chapter 1 for an analysis of Golyadkin's attempt to manipulate the icons of consensual fantasy in his creation of a public persona. For speculations on another set of DeLillo doppelgangers, the multiple Edgars of *Underworld*, see Dewey, Kellman, and Malin 2002.

34. Dostoevsky 1972: 116.

35. See chapter 1. The quote is from Hirschman 1977: 132–33.

bibliography and filmography

Annenkov, P. V. 1928. *Literaturnye vospominaniia*. Leningrad: Akademia.

———. 1952. "N. V. Gogol' v Rime letom 1841 goda." *Gogol' v vospominaniiakh sovremennikov*. N. L. Brodskii, ed. Moscow: Gosudarstvennoe izdatel'stvo khudozhestvennoi literatury.

Arendt, Hannah. 1993. *Between Past and Future: Eight Exercises in Political Thought*. New York: Penguin.

Aristotle. 1952. "Politics." *The Works of Aristotle*. Vol. 2. Benjamin Jowett, trans. 445–584. Chicago: University of Chicago Press.

———. 2003. *Nichomachean Ethics*. J. A. K. Thompson, trans. New York: Penguin.

Arnold, Matthew. 1949. *The Portable Matthew Arnold*. Lionel Trilling, ed. New York: Viking.

Auerbach, Erich. 1984. *Scenes from the Drama of European Literature*. Minneapolis: University of Minnesota Press.

Augustine, Saint. 1963. *Confessions*. New York: Penguin.

Badalich, I. 1963. "Iurii Krizhanich, predshestvennik I. T. Pososhkova." *Trudy Otdela Drevnerusskoi literatury* (Institut Russkoi Literatury A. N. SSSR) 16: 390–403.

Bakhtin, Mikhail. 1963. *Problemy Poetiki Dostoevskogo*. 2nd ed. Moscow: Sovetskii pisatel'.

———. 1981. *The Dialogic Imagination: Four Essays*. Michael Holquist, ed. Michael Holquist and Caryl Emerson, trans. Austin: University of Texas Press.

———. 1984. *Problems of Dostoevsky's Poetics*. Caryl Emerson, trans. Minneapolis: University of Minnesota Press.

———. 1986. "Response to a Question from Novyi Mir." Vern W. McGee, trans. *Speech Genres & Other Late Essays*. Caryl Emerson and Michael Holquist, eds. 1–9. Austin: University of Texas Press.

Barthes, Roland. 1970. *S/Z*. Paris: Editions du Seuil.

Bassi, S. 2007. "Il corpo politico di Shylock." *Sul Corpo: Culture/Politiche/Estetiche*. Nicoletta Vallorani, Simona Bertacco, eds. 101–14. Milano: Cisalpino.

Baucom, Ian. 2005. *Spectres of the Atlantic: Finance Capital, Slavery, and the Philosophy of History*. Durham, NC: Duke University Press.

Bayley, John. 1971. *Pushkin: A Comparative Commentary.* Cambridge: Cambridge University Press.

———. 1991. "Pasternak's Great Fairy Tale." *New York Review of Books,* March 7. http://www.nybooks.com/articles/archives/1991/mar/07/pasternaks-great-fairy-tale/.

Becker, Lawrence C. 1998. *A New Stoicism.* Princeton, NJ: Princeton University Press.

Belknap, Robert. 1997. "Survey of Russian Journals 1840–1880." *Literary Journals in Imperial Russia.* Deborah A. Martinsen, ed. 91–116. Cambridge, MA: Harvard University Press.

Bely, Andrey. 1978. *Petersburg.* Robert Maguire and John Malmsted, trans. Bloomington, IN: Indiana University Press.

Benson, Sumner. 1974. "The Role of Western Political Thought in Petrine Russia." *Canadian-American Slavic Studies* 8: 257–73.

Blair, John G. 1979. *The Confidence Man in Modern Fiction: A Rogue's Gallery with Six Portraits.* New York: Barnes and Noble Books.

Bloomfield, Morton W. 1954. *The Seven Deadly Sins; an Introduction to a Religious Concept with Special Reference to Medieval English Literature.* East Lansing, MI: Michigan State College Press.

Borovoi, S. Ia. 1958. *Kredit i banki Rossii (seredina XVII v.–1861 g.)* Moscow: Gosfinizdat.

———. 1960. "Gosudarstvennyi dolg kak istochnik pervonachal'nogo nakopleniia v Rossii." *Voprosy genezisa capitalizma v Rossii. Sbornik statei.* Mavrodin, V. V., ed. 217–228. Leningrad: Leningradskii gosudarstvennyi universitet imeni A. A. Zhdanova.

Boswell, James. 1933. *Boswell's Life of Johnson.* New York: Oxford University Press.

Boyd, Brian. 1995. "'Even Homais Nods': Nabokov's Fallibility, or, How to Revise *Lolita.*" *Nabokov Studies* 2: 62–86.

Brauleke, Heinz-Joachim. 1978. *Leben und Werk des Kameralisten Philipp Wilhelm von Hörnigk.* Frankfurt: Peter Lang.

Bruss, Elizabeth W. 1976. *Autobiographical Acts: The Changing Situation of a Literary Genre.* Baltimore: Johns Hopkins University Press.

Butler, Bishop. 1896. *Analogy of Religion* in *Works.* Vol. 1. Oxford: Oxford University Press.

Cafaro, Philip. 2000. "Thoreau's Virtue Ethics in *Walden.*" *Concord Saunterer* 8: 23–47.

Cameron, Rondo, et al. 1972. *Banking in the Early Stages of Industrialization.* Oxford: Oxford University Press.

Campiotti, Giacomo, dir. 2002. *Doctor Zhivago.* Epsilon TV Productions.

Christa, Boris. 2002. "Dostoevskii and Money." *The Cambridge Companion to Dostoevskii.* W. J. Leatherbarrow, ed. 93–110. Cambridge, MA: Harvard University Press.

Christoff, Peter. 1970. *The Third Heart: Some Intellectual Currents and Cross-Currents in Russia 1800–1830.* The Hague: Walter de Gruyter.

Chudakov, G. I. 1908. *Otnoshenie tvorchestva Gogolia k zapadno-evropeiskim literaturam.* Kiev: Tip. Imperatorskago Universiteta Sv. Vladimīra Akīsion.

Clark, Katerina. 1981. *The Soviet Novel: History as Ritual.* Chicago: University of Chicago Press.

Coleman, D. C., ed. 1969. *Revisions in Mercantilism.* London: Methuen Young Books.

Connolly, Julian W. 1995. "'Nature's Reality' or Humbert's 'Fancy'?: Scenes of Reunion and Murder in *Lolita.*" *Nabokov Studies* 2: 41–61.

Conquest. 1961. *Courage of Genius: The Pasternak Affair.* London: Collins and Harvill Press.

Conrad, Joseph. 2006. *Heart of Darkness.* New York: W. W. Norton.

Cowart, David. 2002. *Don DeLillo: The Physics of Language*. Athens, GA: University of Georgia Press.

Crossen, Cynthia. 2008. "Underbelly of Russian Provincials." *The Wall Street Journal*, June 12. http://online.wsj.com/article/SB121313454742762171.html.

Dagger, Richard. 1997. *Civic Virtues: Rights, Citizenship, and Republican Liberalism*. New York: Oxford University Press.

Daly, Herman E., and John B. Cobb Jr. 1989. *For the Common Good: Redirecting the Economy Toward Community, the Environment, and a Sustainable Future*. Boston: Beacon Press.

Davenant, Charles. 1771. *The Political and Commercial Works of That Celebrated Writer Charles D'Avenant: Relating to the Trade and Revenue of England, the Plantation Trade, the East-India Trade and African Trade*. London: Printed for R. Horsfield; T. Becket; P. A. de Hondt; T. Cadell; and T. Evans.

de la Durantaye, Leland. 2007. *Style Is Matter: The Moral Art of Vladimir Nabokov*. Ithaca, NY: Cornell University Press.

DeLaura, David J. 1969. *Hebrew and Hellene in Victorian England: Newman, Arnold, and Pater*. Austin: University of Texas Press.

DeLillo, Don. 1982. *The Names*. New York: Knopf.

———. 1985. *White Noise*. New York: Viking.

———. 1991. *Mao II*. New York: Viking.

———. 1997. *Underworld*. New York: Scribner.

———. 2002. *The Body Artist*. New York: Scribner.

———. 2003. *Cosmopolis*. New York: Scribner.

De Madariaga, Isabel. 1984. "Portrait of an Eighteenth-Century Russian Statesman: Prince D. M. Golitsyn." *Slavic and East European Review* 62: 36–60.

Depew, David. 2005. "Empathy, Psychology, and Aesthetics: Reflections on a Repair Concept." *Poroi: A Journal of Rhetorical Invention* 4(1): article 6. http://ir.uiowa.edu/poroi/vol4/iss1/6/.

Dewey, Joseph, Steven. G. Kellman, and Irving Malin, eds. 2002. *Underwords: Perspectives on Don DeLillo's Underworld*. Newark, NJ: University of Delaware Press.

Dewey, Orville. 1901. *The Works of Orville Dewey. D. D.* Boston: American Unitarian Association.

Dibell, Ansen. 1999. *Elements of Writing Fiction—Plot*. New York: Writer's Digest Books.

Dickens, Charles. 1965. *A Tale of Two Cities*. New York: Harper and Row.

Dittrich, Ehrhard. 1974. *Die deutschen und österreichischen Kameralisten*. Darmstadt: Wissenschaftliche Buchgesellschaft.

Dolinin, Alexander. 1995. "Nabokov's Time Doubling: From *The Gift* to *Lolita*." *Nabokov Studies* 2: 3–40.

Donnelley, Strachan. 1983. "The Philosopher's Poet: Boris Pasternak, *Dr. Zhivago*, and Whitehead's Cosmological Vision." *Process Studies* 13(1): 45–58.

Dostoevsky, F. M. 1972. *Polnoe Sobranie Sochinenii v tridtsati tomakh*. Vol. I. Leningrad: "Nauka".

———. 1973. *Polnoe sobranie sochinenii v tridtsati tomakh*. Vol. VI. Leningrad: Izdatel'stvo "Nauka."

Dowler, Wayne. 1982. *Dostoevsky, Grigor'ev, and Native-Soil Conservatism*. Toronto: University of Toronto Press.

Dreiser, Theodore. 1981. *Sister Carrie*. Philadelphia: University of Pennsylvania Press.

Dreizin, F. 1990. *The Russian Soul and the Jew: Essays in Literary Ethno-Criticism*. Lanham, MD: University Press of America.

Eikhenbaum, Boris. 1982. *Tolstoi in the Seventies*. Albert Kaspin, trans. Ann Arbor, MI: University of Michigan Press.

Epictetus. 1925. *Discourses*. Books I–II. W. A. Oldfather, trans. Cambridge, MA: Harvard University Press.

Esaulov, I. A. 2006. "The Paschal Archetype of Russian Literature and the Structure of Boris Pasternak's *Doctor Zhivago*." Margaret Tejerizo, trans. *Literature & Theology* 20(1): 63–78.

Fanger, Donald. 1979. *The Creation of Nikolai Gogol*. Cambridge, MA: Harvard University Press.

Fedotov, G. P. 1946. *The Russian Religious Mind*. Cambridge, MA: Harvard University Press.

———. 1966. *The Russian Religious Mind*. Vol 2. John Meyendorff, ed. Cambridge, MA: Harvard University Press.

Fitzgerald, F. Scott. 1999. *The Great Gatsby*. New York: Columbia University Press.

Fleishman, Lazar, Gabriella Safran, and Michael Wachtel, eds. 2005. *Word, Music, History: A Festschrift for Caryl Emerson*. Stanford: Stanford University Press.

Fowler, Alasdair. 1982. *Kinds of Literature: An Introduction to the Theory of Genres and Modes*. Cambridge, MA: Harvard University Press.

Fowles, John. 1965. *The Magus*. Boston: Little, Brown, and Company.

Frank, Joseph. 1986. *Dostoevsky: The Stir of Liberation: 1800–1860*. Princeton, NJ: Princeton University Press.

———. 2002. *Dostoevsky: The Mantle of the Prophet: 1871–1881*. Princeton, NJ: Princeton University Press.

Franscell, Ron. 2003. "Ode to Joyce." *Chicago Sun Times*, March 23. http://suntimes.com/output/books/sho-sunday-delillo23.html.

Freeborn, Richard. 1973. *The Rise of the Russian Novel: Studies in the Russian Novel From Eugene Onegin to War and Peace*. Cambridge: Cambridge University Press.

———. 1985. *The Russian Revolutionary Novel: Turgenev to Pasternak*. Cambridge: Cambridge University Press.

Frost, Robert. 1969. *The Poetry of Robert Frost*. Edward Connery Lathem, ed. New York: Henry Holt and Company.

Fusso, Susanne. 1993. *Designing Dead Souls*. Stanford: Stanford University Press.

Fusso, Susanne, and Priscilla Meyer, eds. 1994. *Essays on Gogol: Logos and the Russian Word*. Evanston, IL: Northwestern University Press.

Galinsky, Karl. 1972. *The Herakles Theme: The Adaptations of the Hero in Literature from Homer to the Twentieth Century*. Totowa, NJ: Rowman.

Gass, Joanne. 2002. "In the Nick of Time: DeLillo's Nick Shay, Fitzgerald's Nick Carraway, and the Myth of the American Adam." Joseph Dewey, Steven G. Kellman, and Irving Malin, eds. 114–29. Newark, DE: University of Delaware Press.

Gellner, Ernest. 1989. *Plough, Sword and Book: The Structure of Human History*. Chicago: University of Chicago Press.

Gerschenkron, Alexander. 1962. *Economic Backwardness in Historical Perspective*. Cambridge, MA: Belknap Press.

Gimbutas, Marija. 1971. *The Slavs*. New York: Thames and Hudson, Ltd.

Gindin, I. 1960. *Gosudarstvennyi bank i ekonomicheskaia politika tsarskogo pravitel'stva*. Moscow: Gosfinizdat.

Gippius, V. V. 1989. *Gogol'*. Robert A. Maguire, ed. and trans. Durham, NC: Duke University Press.

Goffman, Erving. 1959. *The Presentation of Self in Everyday Life*. Garden City, NY: Anchor Books.

Gogol, N. M. 1937. *Polnoe sobranie sochinenii*. Moscow: Izdatel'stvo Akademii Nauk SSSR.

————. 2009. *Polnoe sobranie sochinenii i pisem v dvadtsati trekh tomakh*. Moscow: Nauka.

Goldstein, David. 1981. *Dostoevsky and the Jews*. Austin: University of Texas Press.

Goux, Jean-Joseph. 1999. "Cash, Check, or Charge." *The New Economic Criticism: Studies at the Intersection of Literature and Economics*. Martha Woodmansee and Mark Osteen, eds. 98–110. New York: Routledge.

Gregory, Paul. 1974. "Some Empirical Comments on the Theory of Relative Backwardness: The Russian Case." *Economic Development and Cultural Change* 22(4): 654–65.

Groys, Boris. 1992. *The Total Art of Stalinism: Avant-Garde, Aesthetic Dictatorship, and Beyond*. Charles Rougle, trans. Princeton, NJ: Princeton University Press.

Gunsalus, C. K. 2006. *The College Administrator's Survival Guide*. Cambridge, MA: Harvard University Press.

Gustafson, Richard F. 1986. *Leo Tolstoy, Resident and Stranger: A Study in Fiction and Theology*. Princeton, NJ: Princeton University Press.

Halfman, Janet, ed. 2002. *New Catholic Encyclopedia*. 2nd ed. New York: Gale Publishing.

Halttunen, Karen. 1982. *Confidence Men and Painted Women: A Study of Middle-Class Culture in America, 1830–1870*. New Haven, CT: Yale University Press.

Hardy, Deborah. 1977. *Peter Tkachev, the Critic as Jacobin*. Seattle: University of Washington Press.

Hayek, F. A. 1952. *The Counter-Revolution of Science: Studies on the Abuse of Reason*. Indianapolis: Liberty Press.

Heckscher, E. F. 1955. *Mercantilism*. Rev. ed. by E. F. Söderlund. 2 vols. London: Allen and Unwin.

Herbert, Zbigniew. 1985. *Report from a Besieged City & Other Poems*. John Carpenter and Bogdana Carpenter, trans. New York: Ecco Press.

————. 2001. *The Collected Poems: 1956–1998*. Alissa Visson, ed. Czeslaw Milosz, Peter Dale Scott, and Alissa Visson, trans. New York: Ecco Press.

Hippisley, Anthony, ed. and trans. 1989. N. M. Maksimovich-Ambodik, *Emvlemy i simvoly (1788) The First Russian Emblem Book*. Leiden: Brill Academic Publishing.

Hirschman, Albert O. 1977. *The Passions and the Interests: Arguments for Capitalism before Its Triumph*. Princeton, NJ: Princeton University Press.

Hoch, Steven L. 1991. "The Banking Crisis, Peasant Reform, and Economic Development in Russia, 1857–61." *The American Historical Review* 96(3): 795–820.

Hoffman, E. T. A. 2000. *The Golden Pot and Other Tales*. Ritchie Robertson, trans. Oxford: Oxford University Press.

Holland, Agnieszka, dir. 1992. *Olivier, Olivier*. Oliane Productions.

Holmes, Stephen. 1995. *Passions and Constraint: On the Theory of Liberal Democracy*. Chicago: University of Chicago Press.

Holquist, Michael. 1977. *Dostoevsky and the Novel*. Princeton, NJ: Princeton University Press.

Hubbs, Joanna. 1988. *Mother Russia: The Feminine Myth in Russian Culture*. Bloomington, IN: Indiana University Press.

Hume, David. 1760. *Essays and Treatises on Several Subjects*. Vol. 1. London: Printed for A. Millar.

———. 1889. *Essays: Moral, Political, and Literary.* T. H. Green and T. H. Grose, eds. London: Longmans.

Ivanits, Linda. 1992. *Russian Folk Belief.* Armonk, NY: M. E. Sharpe.

Jackson, Robert Louis. 1966. *Dostoevsky's Quest for Form: A Study of His Philosophy of Art.* New Haven, CT: Yale University Press.

James, Henry. 1981 [1877]. *The American.* New York: Penguin.

Johnson, D. Barton. 1985. "Pasternak's *Zhivago* and Nabokov's *Lolita.*" *The Nabokovian* 14: 20–23.

Johnson, Samuel. 2009. *Selected Writings.* Peter Martin, ed. Cambridge, MA: Belknap Press.

Kafengauz, B. B., ed. 1951. *I. T. Pososhkov, Kniga o skudosti i bogatstve i drugie sochineniia.* Moscow: Izdatel'stvo Akademii Nauk SSSR.

Kakutani, Michiko. 2003. "Books of the Times; Headed Toward a Crash, Of Sorts, in a Stretch Limo." *New York Times,* March 24, late ed., E: 10.

Karamzin, Nikolai. 1984. *Sochineniia v dvukh tomakh.* Leningrad: Khudozhestvennaia literatura.

Kaufman, Andrew D. 2011. *Understanding Tolstoy.* Columbus, OH: The Ohio State University Press.

Kaufmann, Moritz. 1879. *Utopias: or, Schemes of Social Improvement. From Sir Thomas More to Karl Marx.* London: C. K. Paul and Co.

Kipen, David. 2003. "DeLillo's High-Style on Cruise Control." *San Francisco Chronicle,* March 30. http://www.sfgate.com/books/article/DeLillo-s-high-style-on-cruise-control-2659316.php.

Kozmin, B. P. 1922. *P. N. Tkachev i revoliutsionnoe dvizhenie 1860–kh godov.* Moscow: Novyi mir.

Kubrick, Stanley, dir. 1962. *Lolita.* MGM.

———. 1971. *A Clockwork Orange.* Warner Brothers.

———. 1987. *Full Metal Jacket.* Warner Brothers.

———. 1999. *Eyes Wide Shut.* Warner Brothers.

Lamanskii, E. 1859. "Gosudarstvennye chetyrekhprotsentnye nepreryvno-dokhodnye bilety." *Ukazatel' politiko-ekonomicheskii* 14: 317–24.

Lang, Fritz, dir. 1944. *The Woman in the Window.* United Artists.

———. 1945. *Scarlet Street.* Universal Pictures.

Lean, David, dir. 1965. *Doctor Zhivago.* MGM.

Leighton, Lauren G. 1977. "Numbers and Numerology in 'The Queen of Spades.'" *Canadian Slavonic Papers* 19(4): 417–43.

Lemke, M. 1907. "K biografii P. N. Tkacheva (Po neizdannym istochnikam)." *Byloe* 8: 156–72.

Lewis, C. S. 1958. *The Allegory of Love: A Study in Medieval Tradition.* New York: Oxford University Press.

Lewitter, L. R. 1987. *Ivan Pososhkov: The Book of Poverty and Wealth.* A. P. Vlasto and L. R. Lewitter, eds. and trans. London: The Athlone Press.

Lindberg. Gary. 1982. *The Confidence Man in American Literature.* New York: Oxford University Press.

Livingstone, Angela, ed. 1985. *Pasternak on Art and Creativity.* Cambridge: Cambridge University Press.

Locke, John. 2003. *Two Treatises of Government and a Letter Concerning Toleration.* Ian Shapiro, ed. New Haven. CT: Yale University Press.

Lotman, Jurij M. 1978. "Theme and Plot: The Theme of Cards and the Card Game in Russian Literature of the Nineteenth Century." *PTL* 3: 476–77.

———. 1995. *Besedy o russkoi kul'ture.* Vol. 1. St. Petersburg: Iskusstvo.

Lynch, Deirdre Shauna. 1998. *The Economy of Character: Novels, Market Culture, and the Business of Inner Meaning*. Chicago: University of Chicago Press.

Lyne, Adrian, dir., 1989. *Lolita*. Showtime.

Macchiavelli, Niccolo. 1984. *The Prince*. Daniel Donno, trans. New York: Bantam.

MacIntyre, Alasdair. 1984. *After Virtue*. Notre Dame, IN: University of Notre Dame Press.

Madison, James. 1961. "*Federalist* No. 10." *The Federalist: By Alexander Hamilton, James Madison, and John Jay*. Benjamin Fletcher Wright, ed. 129–136. Cambridge, MA: Belknap Press.

Maguire, Robert A. 1994. *Exploring Gogol*. Stanford: Stanford University Press.

Mansfield, Harvey. 1996. *Machiavelli's Virtue*. Chicago: University of Chicago Press.

———. 2006. *Manliness*. New Haven, CT: Yale University Press.

Matthewson, Rufus W. 1958. *The Positive Hero in Russian Literature*. New York: Columbia University Press.

McCloskey, Deirdre. 2006. *The Bourgeois Virtues: Ethics for an Age of Commerce*. Chicago: University of Chicago Press.

———. 2010. *Bourgeois Dignity: Why Economics Can't Explain the Modern World*. Chicago: University of Chicago Press.

McKeon, Michael. 1987. *The Origins of the English Novel, 1600–1740*. Baltimore: Johns Hopkins University Press.

McReynolds, Susan. 2008. *Redemption and the Merchant God: Dostoevsky's Economy of Salvation and Antisemitism*. Evanston, IL: Northwestern University Press.

Mead, George Herbert. 1934. *Mind, Self, and Society*. C. W. Morris, ed. Chicago: University of Chicago Press.

Meinecke, Freidrich. 1957. *Machiavellism: The Docrine of Raison d'Etat and its Place in Modern History*. Douglas Scott, trans. London: Routledge.

Melville, Hermann. 1989. *The Confidence-Man: His Masquerade*. New York: Oxford University Press.

Merton, Thomas. 1951. *The Ascent to Truth*. New York: Harcourt Brace.

Meyer, Priscilla. 1984. "Nabokov's Lolita and Pushkin's Onegin—McAdam, McEve and McFate." *The Achievements of Vladimir Nabokov: Essays, Studies, Reminiscences, and Stories*. George Gibian and Stephen Parker, eds. 179–211. Ithaca, NY: Center for International Studies.

Michelstaedter, Carlo. 2004. *Persuasion and Rhetoric*. Russell Scott Valentino, Cinzia Sartini Blum, and David J. Depew, ed and trans. New Haven, CT: Yale University Press.

Mikhalkov, Nikita, dir. 1989. *Oblomov*. Mosfilm.

Mochulsky, Konstantin. 1967. *Dostoevsky: His Life and Work*. Michael A. Minihan, trans. Princeton, NJ: Princeton University Press.

Montesquieu. 1951. *De l'esprit des lois*, in *Oeuvres complètes*. Vol. 2. Paris: Nagel.

Mordukhovich, L. M. 1976. "Juraj Krizanic, W. Petty and Ivan Pososhkov." *Juraj Krizanic 1618–1683: Russophile and Ecumenic Visionary*. T. Eekman, ed. 223–24. The Hague: Walter de Gruyter.

Morson, Gary Saul. 1983. "Dostoevskij's Anti-Semitism and the Critics: A Review Article." *SEEJ* 27(3): 302–17.

———. 1992. "Gogol's Parables of Explanation: Nonsense and Prosaics." *Essays on Gogol': Logos and the Russian Word*. Susanne Fusso and Priscilla Meyer, eds. 200–39. Evanston, IL: Northwestern University Press.

———. 2007. *Anna Karenina in Our Own Time: Seeing More Wisely*. New Haven, CT: Yale University Press.

Morson, Gary Saul, and Caryl Emerson. 1990. *Mikhail Bakhtin: Creation of a Prosaics*. Stanford: Stanford University Press.

Moser, Charles A. 1964. *Antinihilism in the Russian Novel of the 1860s*. The Hague: Mouton.

———. 1989. *Esthetics as Nightmare: Russian Literary Theory, 1855–70*. Princeton, NJ: Princeton University Press.

Mulcaire, Terry. 1999. "Public Credit; or, The Feminization of Virtue in the Marketplace." *PMLA* 114(5): 1029–42.

Mulvey, Laura. 1975. "Visual Pleasure and Narrative Cinema." *Screen* 16(3): 6–18.

Nabokov, Vladimir. 1970. *The Annotated Lolita*. Alfred Appel, ed. New York: Vintage.

———. 1974. *Lolita: A Screenplay*. New York: Knopf.

Novikov, N. 1951. *Izbrannye sochineniia*, t. 1. Moscow: Gosudarstvennoe izdatel'stvo khudozhestvennoi literatury.

Nussbaum, Martha. 1986. *The Fragility of Goodness: Luck and Ethics in Greek Tragedy and Philosophy*. Cambridge: Cambridge University Press.

———. 1997. *Cultivating Humanity: A Classical Defense of Reform in Liberal Education*. Cambridge, MA: Harvard University Press.

Okenfuss, Max J. 1995. *The Rise and Fall of Latin Humanism in Early-Modern Russia: Pagan Authors, Ukrainians, and the Resiliency of Muscovy*. Leiden: Brill Academic Publishers.

O'Meara, Patrick. 2004. *The Decembrist Pavel Pestel: Russia's First Republican*. New York: Palgrave MacMillan.

Osteen, Mark. 2000. *American Magic and Dread: Don DeLillo's Dialogue with Culture*. Philadelphia: University of Pennsylvania Press.

———. 2004. *Keynote Address. Critical Exchanges: Economy and Culture in the Literature of Russia Conference*. Northwestern University, Chicago, May 8.

Parsons, Talcott. 1937. *The Structure of Social Action: A Study in Social Theory with Special Reference to a Group of Recent European Writers*. New York: The Free Press.

Pasternak, Boris. 1958. *Doctor Zhivago*. Max Hayward and Manya Harari, trans. New York: Pantheon Books.

———. 1961. *Sochineniia*, Vol. 1. G. P. Struve and B. A. Filippov, eds. Ann Arbor, MI: Ardis.

———. 1982. *Vozdushnye puti: proza raznykh let*. Moscow: Sovetskii pisatel'.

Peterson, Christopher, and Martin Seligman. 2004. *Character Strengths and Virtues: A Handbook and Classification*. New York: Oxford University Press.

Peterson, Claes. 1979. *Peter the Great's Administrative and Judicial Reforms: Swedish Antecedents and the Process of Reception*. Stockholm: Nordiska Bokhandeln.

Petishkina, S. N. 1993. *Gosudarstvennyi bank dorevoliutsionnoi Rossii*. Moscow.

Pintner, Walter McKenzie. 1967. *Russian Economic Policy Under Nicholas I*. Ithaca, NY: Cornell University Press.

Pipes, Richard. 2000. *Property and Freedom*. New York: Vintage.

Plato. 1952. *The Republic. The Dialogues of Plato*. Benjamin Jowett, trans. Chicago: University of Chicago Press.

Pletnev. P. A. 1885. *Sochineniia i perepiska P. A. Pletneva*. St. Petersburg: Tip. Imperatorskoĭ akademii nauk.

Pocock, J. G. A. 1975. *The Machiavellian Moment: Florentine Political Thought and the Atlantic Republican Tradition*. Princeton, NJ: Princeton University Press.

——. 1985. *Virtue, Commerce, and History: Essays on Political Thought and History, Chiefly in the Eighteenth Century*. Cambridge: Cambridge University Press.

Poe, Marshal. 2003. *The Russian Moment in World History*. Princeton, NJ: Princeton University Press.

Pohl, Nicole, and Brenda Tooley. 2007. *Gender and Utopia in the Eighteenth Century: Essays in English and French Utopian Writing*. Aldershot, UK: Ashgate Publishing Company.

Polanyi, Michael. 1966. *The Tacit Dimension*. Garden City, NY: Anchor Books.

Pososhkov, Ivan. 1987. *The Book of Poverty and Wealth*. A. P. Vlasto and L. R. Lewitter, eds. and trans. London: The Athlone Press.

Pushkin, Alexander. 1936. *The Captain's Daughter and Other Stories*. T. Keane, trans. New York: Vintage.

——. 1964. *Eugene Onegin: A Novel in Verse by Aleksandr Pushkin*. Vladimir Nabokov, trans. Princeton, NJ: Princeton University Press.

——. 1990. *Eugene Onegin*. James E. Falen, trans. New York: Oxford University Press.

Rees. 1996. *Utopian Imagination and Eighteenth-Century Fiction*. New York: Longman Publishing Group.

Riasanovsky, Nicholas. 1984. *A History of Russia*. 4th ed. New York: Oxford University Press.

Rice, James L. 1993. *Freud's Russia: National Identity and the Evolution of Psychoanalysis*. New Brunswick, NJ: Transaction Publishers.

Rock, Stella. 2007. *Popular Religion in Russia: "Double Belief" and the Making of an Academic Myth*. London: Routledge.

Rodman, Gilbert B. 2003. "The Net Effect: The Public's Fears and the Public Sphere." *Virtual Publics: Policy and Community in an Electronic Age*. Beth E. Kolko, ed. 9–48. New York: Columbia University Press.

Rowley, David G. 1999. "'Redeemer Empire': Russian Millenarianism." *American Historical Review* 104(5): 1582–1602.

Ryan, Alan. 1987. *Property*. Minneapolis: University of Minnesota Press.

——. 1999. "Please Fence Me In." *NYRB*, September 13. http://www.nybooks.com/articles/archives/1999/sep/23/please-fence-me-in/.

Sachs, Jeffrey. 2011. *The Price of Civilization: Reawakening American Virtue and Prosperity* New York: Random House.

Savary, Jaques. 1721. *Le parfait négoçiant, ou Instruction générale de tout ce qui regarde le commerce*. Paris: C. Robustel.

Schama, Simon. 1995. *Landscape and Memory*. New York: Knopf.

Schiller, Friedrich. 1943 [1798]. "Ritter Toggenburg." *Schillers Werke*. Vol. 1. Julius Petersen and Gerhard Fricke, eds. Weimar: Böhlau.

Seeley, Frank Friederberg. 1968. "Gogol's *Dead Souls*." *Forum For Modern Language Studies* 4(1): 33–44.

Semmel, Bernard. 1984. *John Stuart Mill and the Pursuit of Virtue*. New Haven, CT: Yale University Press.

Sennett, Richard. 1974. *The Fall of Public Man*. New York: Norton.

Shakespeare, William. 1974. *The Merchant of Venice*. *The Riverside Shakespeare*. Boston: Houghton Mifflin.

——. 1974. *The Tempest*. *The Riverside Shakespeare*. Boston: Houghton Mifflin.

Shanskii, N. M., ed. 1973. *Etimologicheskii slovar' russkogo iazyka.* Tom I, Vypusk 5. Moscow: Izdatel'stvo Moskovskogo Universiteta.

Shapiro, Gavriel. 1993. *Nikolai Gogol' and the Baroque Cultural Heritage.* University Park, PA: University of Pennsylvania Press.

Sheller-Mikhailov, A. K. 1904. *Polnoe sobranie sochinenii.* Izdanie vtoroe. St. Petersburg: Izdatel'stvo A. F. Marksa.

Shelley, Mary. 2003. *Frankenstein.* New York: Bantam.

Sherman, Nancy. 1989. *The Fabric of Character: Aristotle's Theory of Virtue.* New York: Oxford University Press.

———. 1997. *Making a Necessity of Virtue: Aristotle and Kant on Virtue.* Cambridge: Cambridge University Press.

———. 2005. *Stoic Warriors: The Ancient Philosophy Behind the Military Mind.* New York: Oxford University Press.

Shevyrev, Stepan. 1978. "Gallereiia portretov v *Mertvykh dushakh.*" *Nikolai Vasil'evich Gogol'. Ego zhizn' i sochineniia. Sbornik istoriko-literaturnykh statei.* Izd. 4, V. Pokrovskii, ed. 282–90. Reprint of the 1915 edition. Oxford: Willem A. Meeuws.

Shklar, Judith N. 1987. *Montesquieu.* New York: Oxford University Press.

Sinyavsky, Andrey. 1990. *Soviet Civilization.* Stanford: Stanford University Press.

Skinner, Quentin. 1978. *The Foundations of Modern Political Thought.* Vol. 1: *The Renaissance.* Cambridge: Cambridge University Press.

Small, Albion W. 1909. *The Cameralists: The Pioneers of German Social Policy.* Chicago: University of Chicago Press.

Stenbock-Fermor, Elisabeth. 1975. *The Architecture of Anna Karenina: A History of Its Writing, Structure, and Message.* Lisse: B. R. Grüner Publishing Company.

Sullivan, Robert. 2004. *Rats: Observations on the History and Habitat of the City's Most Unwanted Inhabitants.* New York: Bloomsbury USA.

Sunstein, Cass. 2001. *republic.com.* Princeton, NJ: Princeton University Press.

———. 2007. *republic.com 2.0.* Princeton, NJ: Princeton University Press.

Tamarchenko, D. 1959. "*Mertvye dushi* N. V. Gogol'ia." *Russkaia Literatura* 2: 18–27.

Taylor, Charles. 1989. *Sources of the Self: The Making of the Modern Identity.* Cambridge, MA: Harvard University Press.

Tekiner, Christina. 1979. "Time in *Lolita.*" *Modern Fiction Studies* 25: 463–69.

Terras, Victor. 1969. *The Young Dostoevskii 1846–1849: A Critical Study.* The Hague: Mouton.

Terts, Abram (Andrei Sinyavsky). 1995. *Strolls with Pushkin.* Catharine Theimer Nepomnyashchy and Slava I. Yastremski, trans. New Haven, CT: Yale University Press.

Thompson, James. 1996. *Models of Value: Eighteenth-Century Political Economy and the Novel.* Durham, NC: Duke University Press.

Thompson, John M. 2013. *Russia and the Soviet Union: A Historical Introduction from the Kievan State to the Present.* 7th ed. Boulder, CO: Westview.

Tkachev, Pyotr. 1873. "Tendentioznyi roman. (Stat'ia pervaia). Sobranie sochinenii A. Mikhailova." *Delo* 2: 1-29.

Tocqueville, Alexis de. 2000. *Democracy in America.* J. P. Mayer, ed.; George Lawrence, trans. New York: Perennial Classics.

Toker, Leona. 1989. *Nabokov: The Mystery of Literary Structures.* Ithaca, NY: Cornell University Press.

Tolstoy, Lev. 1960. *Sobranie sochinenii v dvadtsati tomakh.* Moscow: Gosudarstvennoe izdatel'stvo khudozhestvennoi literatury.

Tornatore, Giuseppe, dir. 1988. *Cinema Paradiso.* Les Films Ariane.

Turgenev, I. S. 1978. *Polnoe sobranie sochinenii i pisem v tridtsati tomakh.* Moscow: Izdatel'stvo "Nauka."

Turgenev, N. 1937. *Opyt teorii nalogov.* Moscow: Gosudarstvennoe sots-ekonomicheskoe izdatel'stvo.

Turkle, Sherry. 1997. *Life on the Screen: Identity in the Age of the Internet.* New York: Simon and Schuster.

———. 2012. *Alone Together: Why We Expect More from Technology and Less from Each Other.* New York: Basic Books

Turner, Brian. 2002. "Cosmopolitan Virtue, Globalization, and Patriotism." *Theory, Culture & Society* 19(1–2): 45–63.

Tuveson, Ernest Lee. 1968. *Redeemer Nation: The Idea of America's Millenial Role.* Chicago: University of Chicago Press.

Valentino, Russell Scott. 2001. *Vicissitudes of Genre in the Russian Nineteenth-Century Novel* Turgenev's *Fathers and Sons,* Chernyshevsky's *What is to be Done?,* Dostoevsky's *Demons,* Gorky's *Mother.* New York: Peter Lang.

———. 2005. "The Oxymoron of Empathic Criticism: Readerly Empathy, Critical Explication, and the Translator's Creative Understanding." *Poroi: A Journal of Rhetorical Invention* 4(1): article 7. http://ir.uiowa.edu/poroi/vol4/iss1/7/.

Vil'mont, N. 1984. *Dostoevskii i Shiller: Zametki russkogo germanista.* Moscow: Sovetskii pisatel'.

Vinogradov, V. V. 1929. *Evoliutsiia russkogo naturalizma: Gogl' i Dostoevskii.* Leningrad: Akademiia.

Vinokur, Val. 2008. *The Trace of Judaism: Dostoevsky, Babel, Mandelstam, Levinas.* Evanston, IL: Northwestern University Press.

Walker, Rob. 2003. "Cutting in Close." Review of *Cosmopolis,* by Don DeLillo. *Washington Post,* April 27. http://www.highbeam.com/doc/1P2-261772.html.

Weeks, Albert L. 1968. *The First Bolshevik: A Political Biography of Peter Tkachev.* New York: New York University Press.

Wilcox, Fred M, dir. 1956. *The Forbidden Planet.* MGM.

Witt, Susanna. 2000. *Creating Creation: Readings of Pasternak's Doktor Zivago.* Stockholm: Almquiest & Wiksell International.

Woodmansee, Martha, and Mark Osteen, eds. 1999. *The New Economic Criticism: Studies at the Interface of Literature and Economics.* London: Routledge.

Woodward, James B. 1978. *Gogol's Dead Souls.* Princeton, NJ: Princeton University Press.

Wu, Duncan, ed. 2005. *Romanticism: An Anthology.* 3rd ed. Hoboken, NJ: Blackwell.

Yerushalmi, Yosef Hayim. 2005. *Zakhor: Jewish History and Jewish Memory* (The Samuel and Althea Stroum Lectures in Jewish Studies). Seattle: University of Washington Press.

Zeldin, Jesse. 1978. *Nikolai Gogol's Quest for Beauty: An Exploration into His Works.* Lawrence: Regents Press of Kansas.

Zhukovsky, V. A. 1959. "Rytsar' Toggengurg" [1818], *Sobranie sochinenii v chetyrekh tomakh.* Vol. 2. Moscow: Gosudarstvennoe izdatel'stvo Khudozhestvennoi literatury.

Žižek, Slavoj. 1989. *The Sublime Object of Ideology.* New York: Verso.

———. 1997. *The Plague of Fantasies.* New York: Verso.

index

Achilles, 74–75

Addison, Joseph, 11, 76

Alexander I, Tsar, 143n

Alexander II, Tsar, 13

Amad, Paula, xi

ambition, 26–27, 37, 56, 79, 128, 135n

America, *see* United States

American, The (James), 36, 154

Anna Karenina (Tolstoy), 15–17, 36, 76–88, 91, 142n, 155, 158

Annenkov, P. V., 139n, 141n

anti-Semitism in *Crime and Punishment*, 74–75, 141–42nn

Arendt, Hannah, 75, 142n

arete, 3, 131n, 134n

Arnold, Matthew, 74–75, 142nn, 149

Aristotle, 76, 132n, 142n, 147n, 149, 158

asyndeton, 54, 140n

assignat, 29, 138n. *See also* money

Auerbach, Erich, 142n, 149

Augustine, 20, 22, 56, 124, 149

avarice, 27, 54–65, 135n. *See also* self-interest

Bagration, 47–51, 63, 139n

Bakhtin, Mikhail, 33, 113, 122, 136nn, 145n, 146n, 147n, 149, 155

Bakunin, Mikhail, 16, 121, 133n, 147n

Balzac, Honoré de, 31

Barker, Anna, xi

Barthes, Roland, 135n, 136–37n, 149

Bassi, Shaul, xi, 134n

Bazarov, Evgeny, 111

Bayley, John, 137n, 144n, 150

Beaudrillard, Jean, 147n

Beier, Stephen, xi

Belknap, Robert, xi

Bely, Andrei, x, 111, 146n, 150

bezobrazie (formlessness, hideousness, abomination), 39, 68–69, 111, 137n, 141n

birth control, 82

Blair, John, 122, 147nn, 150

Bloom, Harold, 75

Body Artist, The (DeLillo), 116, 151

Bolkonsky, Andrei, 84–85. See also *War and Peace*

Book of Poverty and Wealth, The (Pososh-kov), 138n, 154, 157

Bonapartism, 41, 51

Borenstein, Eliot, xi

Borovoi, S. Ya., 142n, 150

Bouboulina, 48, 51, 138n. See also *Dead Souls*

Bourgeois Virtues, The (McCloskey), 5, 73, 90–91, 155

Boyd, Brian, 144n, 150
Bowers, Katherine Ann, xi
Bowles, Paul, 98
Bronze Horseman, The (Pushkin), 112–13
Brothers Karamazov, The (Dostoevsky), 14, 30, 145n, 146n
Bruss, Elizabeth, 144n, 150
Bunin, Ivan, 146n,
buying and selling, 16, 43, 45, 80, 81–82, 138n, 139n. *See also* price; exchange relations

calendar, Julian, Orthodox, 139n
Campiotti, Giacomo, 99, 150. See also *Doctor Zhivago*
capitalism, 31, 132n, 137n
Captain's Daughter, The (Pushkin), 137n, 157
Carillo Rowe, Aimee, xi
Carnegie, Dale, 43
Carlyle, Thomas, 76
Carton, Sidney, 36, 73
Catherine II, the "Great," Tsar, 138n
character, xii, 3, 14, 16–19, 20–25: amorphous nature of Russian, 111, 146n; as written symbol, 23; liquidity, multiplicity of, 23–24, 110, 113; masculine heroic, 24, 32, 34, 36, 73–75, 83, 85, 88, 90–92, 100, 105, 107, 128, 129; Polonial, 24; Romantic, 21, 25. *See also* self
charity, 69–70, 110, 113, 114
Chernyshevsky, Nikolai, 16, 66, 77, 159
Christ, Christianity, 17, 56, 63, 71, 75, 134n, 143n, 145n, 147n
Chichikov, 28–29, 33, 34–35, 40–55, 59–65. See also *Dead Souls*
Choe, Steve, xi
Chudakov, G. I., 141n, 150
Cinema Paradiso, 36, 37 fig. 4
citizen, 76–77, 78, 115, 116, 124, 148n. *See also* land, property, virtue
Claire Quilty, 93, 94, 106. See also *Lolita*
Clockwork Orange, A (Kubrick), 94, 154
Cobb, John B., 42, 138n, 151
Cold War, 92, 133n
Collins, Daniel, xi

commerce, vi, 19, 27–28, 43–48, 54, 57–58, 65, 74, 113, 132nn, 140n, 141; and decline of glory, 32, 33, 48, 55, 85, 147n; "miserable details of," 27. *See also* virtue
Communist Manifesto, The (Marx), 122
Connolly, Julian, 145
Contemporary, The, 142–43n
confidence, 6, 12, 27, 112, 114–15, 122, 127, 129, 132n
confidence man (con-man), 8, 27–28, 31, 33–34, 51, 110, 112–13, 114, 120, 123–24, 146n, 153, 154
Confidence-Man: His Masquerade, The (Melville), 112–13, 114, 120, 146n, 155
Congress of Vienna, 40
Conquest, Robert, 144n, 150
Conrad, Joseph, 146n, 150
consensual fantasy, iii, 7 fig. 1, 2, 4–6, 6–12, 28–30, 53, 64–71, 82, 91, 105, 110–14, 116, 118, 124, 126, 128–29, 133n
"constant poetic symptom" in *Doctor Zhivago*, 95, 98 fig. 7, 104, 145n
cosmopolitan, cosmopolitanism, 123, 148n
Court versus Country, 11
Cowart, David, 146n, 147n, 151
credit, 4, 5, 21, 30, 31, 42, 62, 64–65, 67, 76, 90, 113, 132nn, 134n, 136n, 140n, 144n. *See also* money, *assignat*
Creekmur, Corey, xi
Crime and Punishment (Dostoevsky), 1, 14, 72, 100, 114, 125, 134n
Crossen, Cynthia, 141n, 151

Daly, Herman E., 138 n., 151
Davenant, Charles, 135n, 151
Dead Souls (Gogol), xii, 17, 27–29, 40–65, 84, 112, 114, 136n, 137–41nn, 152, 157, 159; portraits in 44, 47–48, 50–51, 75, 137n, 139n
debt, indebtedness, 4, 53, 67, 70, 75, 76
decorporialization, 5, 8, 116
Defoe, Daniel, 76
de la Durantaye, Leland, 100, 145n, 151
DeLaura, David J., 142n, 151

CPSIA information can be obtained
at www.ICGtesting.com
Printed in the USA
FFOW02n0819071116
29082FF